Deleuze and Queer Theory

Deleuze Connections

'It is not the elements or the sets which define the multiplicity. What defines it is the AND, as something which has its place between the elements or between the sets. AND, AND, AND – stammering.'

Gilles Deleuze and Claire Parnet, *Dialogues*

General Editor
Ian Buchanan

Editorial Advisory Board
Keith Ansell-Pearson
Rosi Braidotti
Claire Colebrook
Tom Conley
Gregg Lambert
Adrian Parr
Paul Patton
Patricia Pisters

Titles Available in the Series
Ian Buchanan and Claire Colebrook (eds), *Deleuze and Feminist Theory*
Ian Buchanan and John Marks (eds), *Deleuze and Literature*
Mark Bonta and John Protevi (eds), *Deleuze and Geophilosophy*
Ian Buchanan and Marcel Swiboda (eds), *Deleuze and Music*
Ian Buchanan and Gregg Lambert (eds), *Deleuze and Space*
Martin Fuglsang and Bent Meier Sørensen (eds), *Deleuze and the Social*
Ian Buchanan and Adrian Parr (eds), *Deleuze and the Contemporary World*
Constantin V. Boundas (ed.), *Deleuze and Philosophy*
Ian Buchanan and Nicholas Thoburn (eds), *Deleuze and Politics*
Chrysanthi Nigianni and Merl Storr (eds), *Deleuze and Queer Theory*
Jeffrey A. Bell and Claire Colebrook (eds), *Deleuze and History*

Forthcoming Titles in the Series
Mark Poster and David Savat (eds), *Deleuze and New Technology*
Laura Cull (ed.), *Deleuze and Performance*
Ian Buchanan and Laura Guillaume (eds), *Deleuze and the Body*
Stephen Zepke and Simon O'Sullivan (eds), *Deleuze and Contemporary Art*
Paul Patton and Simone Bignall (eds), *Deleuze and the Postcolonial*

Deleuze and Queer Theory

Edited by Chrysanthi Nigianni
and Merl Storr

Edinburgh University Press

Edinburgh University Press Ltd
22 George Square, Edinburgh

Typeset in 10.5/13 Sabon
by Servis Filmsetting Ltd, Stockport, Cheshire, and
printed by the MPG Books Group
in the UK

A CIP record for this book is available from the British Library

ISBN 978 0 7486 3404 0 (hardback)
ISBN 978 0 7486 3405 7 (paperback)

Contents

... so as to know 'us' better
Deleuze and Queer Theory:
two theories, one concept – one book,
many authors ...

You ask me: why bring all these texts together in this book? Why 'Deleuze *and* Queer Theory'? What does this *and* mean? You wonder whether it might be the expression of an opposition that will lead to a battle, a combat; a war that will announce winners and dark horses, will declare the past dead and will celebrate a new future. Or maybe, it is a hope for juxtaposition and collaboration based on resonances, or differences. An attempt for reconciliation through the annihilation of the differential parties perhaps?

And as the middle space, the borderline that separates but also brings together; *and* as the transit word, a force of transition towards something other that always entails a coming back: the becoming-DeleuzoGuattarian of Queer Theory, the becoming-queer of Deleuze's and Guattari's theory. *And* as the invisible in-between, the mystery gap, the topos of hidden erotic connections, of contagious exchange, of unnatural encounters based on imperceptible micro-attractions and incompatibilities; *and* as the experiment to think as two, to rethink through a two-fold process that amplifies what goes on in one's thinking, that expands one single concept (queer), transforming it from a materialising signifier to an intrinsic quality of non-representational thinking.

Thus, this project is primarily creative and not critical, and it is critical precisely by being creative. Rather than dismissing queer (theory), this collective work reaffirms the seductive power of the concept 'queer', and its continuing force to inspire thinking nowadays. Moving beyond, or along, lines of queer theory (in its institutionalised Anglo-American form) constitutes a living proof of the vital force of the concept of queerness: the force to affect and effect changes in the way one theorises, its capacity to produce deviant lines along established thinking and disciplines, its ability to queer the queer, that is, to undermine the self, to resist any normalisation. Hence, this collection emerges out of the queer's fear of being trapped in iteration, immobility, its loathing for reproduction, for repetition of sameness. Rather than starting from negation (which would be to diminish the tremendous intellectual accomplishments set in motion by *Gender Trouble* and the theory of performativity), it is born out of the positive and affirmative thinking that departs from the belief that one paradigm cannot carry an entire field, if that field is going to survive and thrive.

Moreover, by putting side by side the English term 'queer' (nontranslatable in other languages and credited as an American invention) with a French thinking (Deleuze's and Guattari's thinking), it attempts to remind us of the often neglected intervention on the part of French thinking(s) after '68, in relation to non-normative sexualities and the notion of a destabilised self (for example, Foucault's homosexual subject, Cixous's bisexuality, Lacan's *homosexuelle*, Hocquenghem's homosexual desire). Despite the significant contribution of French philosophy, psychoanalysis and feminism to the exploration and enhancement of polymorphous, 'perverse' sexualities and of the notion of a de-normalised self, we nevertheless believe that 'it is especially in the writings of Gilles Deleuze and Félix Guattari that the question of homosexuality as queering, that is, as becoming and as an ongoing differing of difference, is raised' (Conley, this volume).

You thus wonder what this volume brings that is new in relation to queer theory, how its contribution differs from other theories of (sexual) difference (for example, psychoanalysis), and even more, how it queers queer theory in a positive and affirmative way that escapes the traditional strategy of negation (queer as the non-, anti-, contra-) and while I am listening to you talking, another question enters my mind: 'Is queer theory a reflection on what it means to be queer, or does the concept of queerness change the ways in which we theorise?' (Colebrook, this volume). Whereas the first question presupposes a 'being' that is queer, and hence that theory is a mere reflection, mirroring, moulding, a grasping of what already exists as given or produced: the queer performative 'being' as a culturally given way of being queer, or better, a way of doing queer that constructs a supposed preceding being – 'the doer', which has nevertheless always been the deed[1] – the latter on the other hand signifies a rupture in the established ways of thinking, suggesting an intrinsic queerness in thinking and in theorising that breaks away from a representational thought, with the latter confusing what exists with what can be known (a conflation of ontology with epistemology). Where the Butlerian theory of performativity fits into the first definition, the DeleuzoGuattarian thinking is inherently queer by distancing itself from a representational conception of thinking; hence, a thinking, which far from being reproductive (by representing, recognising) is primarily productive mainly by being expressive of non/extra-linguistic forces.

Hence, what strikes and troubles one in the field known as 'Queer Theory' is primarily an insistence on performativity as the only adequate way to perceive the social world and the real and the consequent refusal to 'see' a positive (rather than a constitutive[2]) outside, a 'beyond' of the signifier, discourse, language: a short-sightedness in relation to body and materiality. I wonder if this is due to a passion for realism and pragmatism, or rather to a fear of accepting anything that goes beyond us, the subject, the world as the lived cultural horizon. Is after all the heterosexual matrix of imposed naturalised performances the only reality we can imagine? Is language the only air we can breathe? Is text the only land we can inhabit? Is parody the only resistance we can imagine?

> The transvestite is a mish-mash hybrid, teeming with symbols belonging to one or another, but not ambiguous enough to be constructed through the spaces between the symbols. The male-as-female or female-as-male is an established alliance at war, rather than an unnatural alliance. (MacCormack, this volume)

Yes, you are certainly right to remind me that this is not one's choice. How compulsory and involuntary it is for the subject to play with the rules and perform a gendered body and a gendered subjectivity in order to be an 'I'. I can't see though why this should lead to a rigid and restricting belief that *what exists is what can be known*, that who we are is limited to the culturally known and the interpretable acted-upon; to an obsession with the textualisation of everything and the deletion of anything that resists the latter; to a refusal to think outside the cause-effect relation and a consequent inability to imagine nondependent relations and non-unifying connections. Have you ever asked yourself 'why are we so hesitant to acknowledge powers that have force and precede the act, but which cannot be known, recognised and reduced to the act?' (Colebrook 2004: 215). Is after all the reductive mechanism of interpretation that takes us back to the Subject the only way to be in the world? And yet, why does an act always have to refer back to a constructed subject? Why, instead of being in (constructed by) the world, can we not become with the world away from the image of the subject? Has subjection always been the case?

> Whereas Foucault turned back to ancient thought to insist that one need not posit a subject and sexuality behind action, Butler argues that we cannot avoid subjection. All we can do is work critically with the systems that produce us as subjects. (Colebrook 2004: 212)

On the other hand, I can understand pretty well your fear of the a-subjective. One's celebration of the a-subjective, the imperceptible constitutes for an all-too Subjective thinking and culture a risky act, a dangerous black hole, since the latter assumes that without the linguistic organisation of the Subject, there is no-thing, no-body, no history, and that the only body that can exist is that which is created and assumed by a human and rational culture.[3] However, one's experience of this as a risk makes quite obvious that for the theory of performativity 'it is the subject – the subject of language, sexuality and consciousness or culture – who is the ground and origin of all distinction and difference' (Colebrook 2004: 207). Thus, contrary to its claims, such a thinking remains a prisoner of the 'episteme of Man',[4] a (neo-) Cartesian-like mind of a differentiating nature in opposition to a matter that lacks any intrinsic differentiating properties.

Within this framework, difference can only be conceived of as a deviation from one, single model: a hierarchical differentiation starting and descending from the dominant signifier (the white (hu)man Face, the majoritarian, white, hetero, able bodied male) (Shildrick, this volume) that leads to a prolific production of minoritarian others always in response to the established norms. It thus fails to conceive of difference beyond the level of the signifier, outside the Law; so that 'our' claim for a positive difference that precedes signification and pre-exists constitution is simply unimaginable, unintelligible within a linguistic framework. It seems for you, difference can only bear the majoritarian definition of minoritarian others, since it is doomed to remain the product of an either/or process: an exclusionary, traumatising difference working through negation, identification and melancholy that produces different-others always stuck in inferior positions.

Accordingly, queer is always already in response to a dominant heterosexual matrix: a solely reactive force of re-signification, mockery, disrespect to the dominance of heterosexuality, to the power of the norms; 'a force [that] denies all that it is not and makes this negation its own essence and the principle of its existence' (Deleuze 2005: 9). Queer then is conceived of as solely a transformation from within, as the parody of the two genders without which, however, we fail to be/do queer.

> However, one may ask to what extent such transformation is not already prescribed by the discourses, the structures and the ideologies that produce it. (Parisi, this volume)

Yes I know, 'we' may sound to you more abstract than the usual study of the social, linguistic, semiological, cultural structures that undergo identity and subjectivity, in the sense of considering oppression, dominance and subjectification in 'their ontological determinations and representative functions' (Olkowski 1999: 2). However, you don't seem to notice how much more particular the focus and perception is now: a departure from one's thinking about constructed wholes and identities, which in turn produces another discussion about (queer) subjectivities/identities, so that one instead shifts the focus to the micro, the molecular: singular acts and practices of a non-referential nature, organs and body-parts in their unnatural, anarchic connection, micro-sexualities bubbling underneath the organism, qualitative multiplicities consisting of micro-singularities, pre-constituted differences of a non-linguistic character, 'an entire world of unconscious micropercepts, unconscious affects' (Deleuze and Guattari 2003: 213). You see, I believe that the refusal to see the dilemma of 'universality versus difference' that has long underpinned feminist and queer debates, as the only political way to think and act, opens up the notion of the political to redefinitions: not an attempt to change the rules of the game (of language and signification) then, but an attempt to challenge the game itself, by abstracting thinking and narrowing down the focus to the micro, the molecular, the singular, the imperceptible.

'Identity involves a narrowing down of the internal complexities of a subject for the sake of social convention' (Braidotti 2006). The book departs from this position, and no call for a supposed political realism and pragmatism should make one overlook it (after all, the capitalist system very often deliberately conflates pragmatism with utilitarianism!). I am not just against this or that particular identity as not being politically useful, but against the very concept of identity and the thinking it engenders: a thinking that works through comparison, resemblance, analogy. However, by refusing to work with identities one is no less pragmatic or realist – on the contrary, the lines of this book constitute a 'trip through "more reality"' (Deleuze 2006: 27). Contrary to what you might assume about abstractness and a technophilic obsession with 'machines', I am here to welcome the return of 'real' bodies and 'real' matter. A body whose forces and potentialities cannot be reduced to its cultural representations and the norms of gender; a matter that is no longer seen as static and passive, a blank slate written by language and culture, but as energy and movement in variation, as modulation (and not as mould) that produces singularities.

Far from beginning with the generic idea of an undifferentiated humanity that gets differentiated through a (re-)productive performativity, I conceive of life forces and materiality as being in principle more sexual, desiring and differential than our impoverished human, gendered sexuality, as the latter is trapped within anthropomorphic sex binaries, and subjectifying gender roles.

> Sexual liberation is a mystification . . . liberation will occur when sexuality becomes desire, and desire is the freedom to be sexual, that is, to be something else at the same time. (Guattari 1996: 56)

At odds with you, for me sex comes back to sexuality in a twofold sense: as the radically and singularly differentiating body-machines (a thousand tiny sexes), as well as in the sense of raw (a-signified) materiality and directness in connecting and relating.

Please be quiet . . . one needs silence . . . so as to hear the sound of what is coming; a rather abstract feeling that the (in)coming event/thinking/ book echoes a new motto: 'intensive sexes and not sexual identities, larval sexes and not agents of sex, rhythmic sexes and not repetitive sex' (Parisi, this volume). Bringing sex back to an a-sexual gendered world of a reproduced sameness would thus mean bringing materiality back to a linguistic landscape[5] so that language ceases to make any (common) sense. Moreover, it would signal the opening up of myriad possibilities for the different bodies to relate to the world differently: 'desire as sexuality *and* "everything else" ' (MacCormack, this volume), 'differentiating (as) making connections and commitments' (Olkowski, this volume) . . .

No longer an issue of sexual orientation, object-choices, lacking desires and gender combinations, one dares to think body and (homo)sexuality essentially: that is, by defining their being through their capacity for becoming, in terms of a productive desire ('to become gay has to do first and foremost not with identity but with desire' (Conley, this volume)) and in relation to their 'powers or potentials, (their) capacities for striving and becoming, that are not yet realised in knowledge, and that can have a force to disrupt or produce knowledges' (Colebrook 2004: 236). Contrary to a definition of essence as being a monolithic and a static force of being-the-same, reproduced by established power-relations, another essence (Colebrook 2004: 236) is imagined as the force of a 'could have been otherwise', the principal force that keeps the future unpredictable and thus opens up the capacity of the body to become-other through its encounters with other body-forces, through its involvement in a multiplicity of connections that changes qualitatively with every new connection added to it – a qualitative transformation that occurs both in the act of relating as such, as well as in the relating parts.

So, yes you might not be able to find any recognisable political agency in this collection of texts. How could you do it in any case, since any being (lesbian, gay, queer, subject) has been replaced by a becoming (-lesbian, -animal, -queer, -vampire, -brittlestar)? 'To fix gay *identity*, is to try to stabilise what has to be radically destabilised' (Conley, this volume); it is to congeal becoming into being. A becoming that from a humanistic perspective constitutes a high risk, since it can be read as participating in the 'othering' of lesbians and gays in the negative sense. Nevertheless, 'we must learn to live and to embrace the destruction and re-articulation of the human in the name of a more capacious and, finally, less violent world, not knowing in advance what precise form our humanness does and will take' (Butler 2004: 35). Hence, what you conceive of as immoral – the non-humanistic connections – constitutes for anOther the exit from an unethical, all-absorbing humanism, with the latter being established and developed upon binaristic others. An exit achieved not by imitation or transition from one state to the other (from the man-order to that of animals, vegetables, and so on) – a becoming does not have an object, nor a subject – but through a symbiotic model that expresses the interconnectedness of all life elements; an interconnection that a humanistic perception is blind to, so as to establish itself as the dominant discourse.

I can very well understand, even sympathise with, the great difficulty of escaping the image of the subject as the centre of life, as the centre of all events, of abandoning the long historical obsession with the *about-ness* that precedes the subject (everything is *about* the subject after all!). However, it is precisely on the non/post-human level that real interaction begins with all those minoritarian others, excluded by an all-powerful humanistic discourse. The risk ceases to be that real anymore and becomes even less universal, since it appears to threaten only one particular thinking – the ego-thinking – that trembles before anything that might dethrone the subject from its transcendent-linguistic position and feels dizzy at the possibility of giving up the strategy of 'being' and taking the risk to experiment instead with non-human becomings that operate on the same level with all organic and non-organic elements.

Unlike you, I do believe that it is worthwhile for us to take the risk and lose the Face, so as to imagine, form and actualise new forms of political agency: instead of communities of an identitarian logic, machinic assemblages,[6] instead of the individual, a 'crowd' (Olkowski, this volume); instead of identities, singularities; instead of representations, expressions; instead of interpretations, codings[7] through mappings; instead of signifiers, signs 'which flash across the interval of a difference' (Deleuze 2004: 281). Perhaps this is what 'we' hope for this book: to produce a collective enunciation, a heterogeneous voice that will put some activism into thinking. And the very moment this 'we' is articulated I can hear its stuttering effects: a *'discordant harmony'* (Olkowski, this volume), variation notes, a becoming-in-musicality that produces an endlessly improvised, indefinite 'we'.

As you may have already noted, my discourse moves in-between a 'we', a 'one' and an 'I', all used interchangeably, when referring to this collection; an undecidability that aims at making clear that it is not the editor's intention to talk on behalf of the contributors or to present one single, personal discourse (the editorial voice) that pulls together all the different ideas and styles of writing that follow. On the contrary, it constitutes an attempt to make room for what follows: not one, single, coherent theory on sexuality and difference, but an assemblage of texts, of multiple voices, of writings-in-variation; a thinking together that presupposes a thinking in solitude, the sharing of a territory in difference.

Far from constituting then a 'root-book' (that is, a coherent, organic narrative with rationally ordered ideas), this collection works as an 'assemblage-book',[8] consisting of different plateaus that create a smooth space of thought, where thinking becomes nomadic, and the 'arborescent'[9] structure gives way to the assembling model of a qualitative multiplicity. Therefore, the 'lack' of coherence in structure – what I call a multiplicity of voices – is part of the experimental character of the book. Very often experimentation requires the 'sacrifice' of established (epistemological) values like 'coherence', as well as the occasional adoption of a more playful writing, which should not be seen as signifying the lack of seriousness in argumentation. Besides, what is more serious than taking the risk to experiment and expose the self outside the established lines?

You even seem puzzled and express anxiety at the 'lack' of discipline in thinking, and the mobility of the terms used in this collection (their becoming-in-meaning). Moreover, you claim to feel estranged by the adoption of a new, foreign vocabulary. Yet, we believe that resistance and wilful political action begin with the realisation of 'the need for a queer methodology for the production of a new vocabulary' (Halberstam 2004), the production of a new language, since 'queer is the pure indeterminate [. . .] of the unspeakable and unrepresentable, not because queer is aberrant but because within majoritarian language there are no words' (MacCormack, this volume). Thus, we suggest a new queer methodology (or methodologies?), which draw(s) on the DeleuzoGuattarian philosophy of positive forces and affirmative actions: the affirmation of an ontology of becoming, in the sense of 'rhizomatic relatedness' (Tuhkanen, this volume), as well as of an open futurity, in terms of virtualities and not mere possibilities.

Probably your general discomfort derives from my queerness and the resulting desire to always want to practise and experience 'the consequences not only of taking an author from behind, but also of being taken from behind by an author' (Kemp, this volume). I wonder, what is more queer than being taken from behind by thinking?

. . . And yes you are right. I may fall short of 'seriousness' from time to time, but the significance of parodying the proper, the expected, and the serious enough, as the ultimate queer act, seems to be far too internalised . . . Hence, my rhetorical articulations, or what you call euphoric neologism or dithyrambs of linguistic construction, are not in any case purposefully pursued. I think they are probably due to the 'discomfort I always suffered from: the uneasiness of being a subject torn between two languages, one expressive, the other critical; and at the heart of this critical language, between several discourses, those of sociology, of semiology, and of psychoanalysis – but that, by ultimate dissatisfaction with all of them, I was bearing witness to the only sure thing that was in me (however naïve it might be): a desperate resistance to any reductive system . . .

. . . (and) I began to speak differently'.

(Barthes 1993: 8)

I hope you can hear me now
and join the 'flight' with us.

Chrysanthi Nigianni

References

Barthes, M. (1993), *Camera Lucida*, London: Vintage.
Braidotti, R. (2006), 'Affirming the Affirmative: On Nomadic Affectivity', *Rhizomes* 11/12, http://www.rhizomes.net/issue11/braidotti.html [Retrieved 9 January 2007].
Butler, J. (1993), *Bodies that Matter*, New York and London: Routledge.
Butler, J. (1999), *Gender Trouble*, New York and London: Routledge.
Butler, J. (2004), *Undoing Gender*, New York and London: Routledge.
Colebrook, C. (2002), *Gilles Deleuze*, London and New York: Routledge.
Colebrook, C. (2004), *Gender*, Basingstoke: Palgrave Macmillan.
Deleuze, G. and Guattari, F. (2003), *A Thousand Plateaus*, London and New York: Continuum.
Deleuze, G. and Guattari, F. (2004), *Anti-Oedipus*, London and New York: Continuum.
Deleuze, G. (2004), *Difference and Repetition*, London and New York: Continuum.
Deleuze, G. (2005), *Nietzsche and Philosophy*, London and New York: Continuum.
Deleuze, G. (2006), *Two Regimes of Madness*, ed. David Lapoujade, New York: Semiotext(e).
Guattari, F. (1996), *Soft Subversions*, trans. David L. Sweet and Chet Wiener, New York: Semiotext(e).
Halberstam, J. (2004), keynote speaker of the 'Queer Matters' Conference at KCL, London.

Olkowski, D. (1999), *Gilles Deleuze and the Ruins of Representation*, Berkeley: University of California Press.

Rachman, J. (1999), 'Diagram and Diagnosis', in *Becomings: Explorations in Time Memory and Futures*, ed. E. Grosz, Ithaca: Cornell University Press.

Notes

1. '. . . gender proves to be performative – that is, constituting the identity it is purported to be. In this sense, gender is always a doing, though not a doing by a subject who might be said to preexist the deed' (Butler 1999: 33).
2. 'To posit by way of language a materiality outside of language is still to posit that materiality, and the materiality so posited will retain that positing as its constitutive condition' (Butler 1993: 30).
3. 'The body posited as prior the sign, is always *posited* or *signified* as *prior*. This signification produces as an *effect* of its own procedure the very body that it nevertheless and simultaneously claims to discover as that which *precedes* its own action' (Butler 1993: 30).
4. 'Because of their anthropocentrism, constructivist philosophies remain prisoners of what Foucault called the "episteme of man", while Deleuze plunges ahead into a posthumanist future, in which the world has been enriched by a multiplicity of nonhuman agencies . . .' (Rachman 1999: 41).
5. 'If language is to be used to represent the material body, then it must confront those aspects of the body deemed "unfit" for discursive representation, such as sexuality, or scatology' (Kemp, this volume).
6. 'A *mechanism* is a closed machine with a specific function. A *machine*, however, is nothing more than its connections; it is not made by anything, is not for anything and has no closed identity' (Colebrook 2002: 56).
7. 'The code resembles not so much a language as a jargon, an open-ended, polyvocal formation' (Deleuze and Guattari 2004: 41).
8. A detailed discussion of the 'root-book' and the assemblage book is found in Deleuze and Guattari's work, *A Thousand Plateaus*, in the chapter 'Introduction: Rhizome'.
9. 'What constitutes arborescence is the submission of the line to the point' (Deleuze and Guattari 2003: 293).

Chapter 1

On the Very Possibility of Queer Theory

Claire Colebrook

Is queer theory a reflection on what it means to be queer, or does the concept of queerness change the ways in which we theorise? On the one hand the concept of theory appears to be inextricably intertwined with the concept of the human: man is that rational animal possessed of a soul capable of intuiting the essential, or what truly is (Irwin 1988). On the other hand, the possibility of a true theory – a thinking without a normative image of thought – seems to be opened only after the death of God and the death of 'man' (Deleuze 1994: 109). For Deleuze, true thought and true theory – a real break with the normative image of 'man' – must include *both* the intuition of the ground from which sense, truth and problems emerge, *and* must fulfil the promise of transcendental inquiry, which has all too often fallen back upon a self or subject who subtends theory. Contrary to a popular idea of a simple anti-humanism Deleuze does not simply reject the intuition of essences, the eternal, genesis and grounds; on the contrary, his work is best understood as an argument in favour of a true or superior transcendentalism which would think beyond the residual humanism maintained both by forms of Kantian critique and by popular notions of community and interrogation (Deleuze 1994: 197).

While abandoning the idea of a metaphysical outside or 'beyond' which might ground metaphysics, post-Kantian thought has nevertheless maintained the possibility of renovating thought from within (O'Neill 1989). If, in modernity, we have abandoned the idea of *theoria* as an intuition of essences, we can nevertheless sustain some commitment to critique: an interrogation of our situation from within (Habermas 1992). From such a commitment to interrogation from within, or resignation to an ironic attitude, it might seem that the values of queer theory would be the values of the postmodern, post-human, post-metaphysical attitude in general. If our situatedness is, by definition, that which also counts as normal and normative, then theory *as such* might be intrinsically queer, as an attempt to deviate from, or pervert, that which appears self-evident, unquestionable and foundational. Accepting such a definition of queer theory would render the enterprise both parasitic and relative; queer theory would always be a solicitation of the normal, and if homosexuality and bisexuality were to become legitimate social models, then the queer would not have withered away, but merely shifted terrain: interrogating any supposed normality or normativity, having no intrinsic power. What I would like to consider in this paper is a less negative formulation of queer theory, one concerned more with the intuition of essences than with the critical distance from the natural attitude.

There are two ways to think about the theoretical point of view in modernity. The first is critical. After Kant's 'Copernican turn' we recognise that there can be no view from nowhere. To experience or live a world we must be related to that world through knowledge or perception; there cannot, therefore, be any intuition of that which exists outside the relations through which it is received (Langton 1998). All our concepts are concepts *of* some intuited world, and all our intuitions are formed as conceptually meaningful and ordered. Kant therefore defines theoretical knowledge as given through the forming power of concepts and the receptive power of intuition. There can be no theoretical knowledge of any supposed foundation or law that would lie beyond experience: to know is to relate to, and conceptualise, what is other than oneself. There cannot be a theory of that which underpins experience; theory is, by definition, always situated, relational and grounded. Theory can, however, reflect on the conditions of our situation, and this would yield practical rather than knowable outcomes. If there can be no law intuitable beyond experience, then we are compelled to give a law to ourselves (O'Neill 1989). We cannot appeal to a foundation or ground, for we are always already grounded. Theory can only tell us that we exist within mediation and experience.

Practically, though, this recognition of our location within experience allows for a radical anti-foundationalism. In the absence of any law or ground we must give a law to ourselves, and because this law is ungrounded – because there is no point of position beyond experience – no point of view can claim to speak for the law. One must give a law to oneself. As a consequence liberalism remains a primarily critical and reflective ethic. Even though one is always located, one must strive to imagine a law that could *in principle* be agreed to be any subject whatsoever; one must neither make an exception of oneself – say, by not acting in a manner that would be universalisable on the grounds that one knows better – nor can one attribute one's located preferences to others. One can only will, ethically, that which could be willed as such (Kant 1990). Such a critical recognition of locatedness has served feminism and radical politics well. No one can be excluded from the practice of self-determination; there can be no exclusion from the public sphere of reason on the basis of spurious empirical claims. Thus, Mary Wollstonecraft (1975) argued that there was no way of knowing whether women were less capable than men at the art of reason; there could be no exclusion of women from education and argument, for if there is such a faculty as reason then it behoves us all to extend that faculty to its highest power. It is precisely the absence of foundations and the impossibility of basing theory on anything other than our situatedness that releases the subject from 'imposed tutelage' and issues in the central value of autonomy, of giving a law to oneself (Kant 1990).

In addition to Kantian liberal anti-foundationalism the other possibility for modern political theory lies in communitarianism. On this model there can be no view from nowhere, but the liberal appeal to the rational self-constituting individual cannot function as a legitimate point of departure. Selves, including the modern ideal of the autonomous self-critical subject, are constituted through others. One is a self only through relations; to be a self requires that one establish oneself as recognisable through time, as having this or that character. Such recognition requires others, both so that one might be recognised as who one is now, and also so that there will be a context of norms, traditions, expectations and narratives through which one understands what it is to be human. On this communitarian model, theory does not take the form of abstracting from one's particularity to produce a purely formal procedure. Theory is not the regulation of those who would seek to exempt themselves from the claims of a universal unfounded reason. Theory is reflection on constituted norms, and is often enabled not by limiting contradiction and particularity, but by paying acute attention to those cultural moments when the conflict of founding (but irreconcilable) values are brought to the fore. If autonomy – relying on no law other than the law one can give oneself – is the key value of liberal anti-foundationalism, recognition is the key value of communitarianism. Both values follow from an acknowledgement of the theoretical predicament: that to live or be a self is to have a law, but no such law can be known or intuited. Autonomy asks how one must regulate oneself in the absence of a founding shared law; recognition looks at the ways in which such shared laws are founded communally, historically and culturally.

Judith Butler's work, from its very beginning, has maintained the force of both these founding values of modern theory. On the one hand, the self is not given as a knowable substance but must be performed or given to itself through action. On the other hand, such self-giving or performing is only possible through others and recognition. It is for this reason that Butler's work is not so much a mobilisation of twentieth-century theory for queer politics, but a theory in which the queer body becomes exemplary. For it is the queer body that exposes the essential tension of autonomy and recognition. One must both be recognised as a subject who subtends various performances, but there must also be a self who is not reducible to performances, such that actions can be posited intelligibly as issuing from this or that coherent self-fashioning subject. To be a self requires that one take on a norm; one must be recognisable *as* this or that subject. The condition of being a self – that one remain the same through time – requires a certain iterability: what one is must be repeatable or maintained. The various performances or actions that the self undergoes must be recognisable *as* repetitions *of* some style or mode of being. Gender is one of the ways in which various differing performances can be recognised as differences *of* this or that sexual subject; if one's actions do not bear this iterability then one cannot be recognised as a subject. At the same time as the self exists only in performing itself as a self to be recognised, one must not be reducible to one's performances alone. If performances are normative, intelligible or readable then one can be recognised as a sexual subject who exists above and beyond any of her recognised actions. The self who asks to be recognised is, in the very claim for recognition, never reducible to the norm or system through which she speaks and performs. Without a difference or deviation in the repetitions of the norm one could not be a subject who subtends or performs that norm. Theory, then, maintains the necessary and essential tension between subjection (to the norm) and activation: the norm has its being only through the various performances which also introduce differences and instabilities.

In many respects we might consider Butler's work to be both exemplary of the precarious model of the self that is presupposed in cultural studies, as well as being critical of the premises of identity politics. On the one hand, one can be a self only through some recognisable identity; on the other hand, the performance of that identity is also the condition for its destabilisation and possible (but not necessarily enabling) undoing. Such a theory at once provides a way to think through the classic problems of representation in cultural studies. How do we judge images of political identity? On the one hand we might argue that stereotypical representations of certain groups in the media reinforce rigid norms, preclude self-constitution and do not allow for subjects outside those norms to be recognised. On the other hand, there can be no creation of oneself *ex nihilo*. Butler's answer to the politics of representation is not to judge between good and bad representations, dividing the authentic from the imposed. Rather, the conditions of representation themselves will yield a politics in which one can be a self only through the repetition of a norm, at the same time as that very repetition is essentially queer. For the queer is not radically outside or beyond recognition and selfhood; it is that which makes a claim to be heard as human – within the norms of speech, gender, the polity and the symbolic – at the same time as it perverts the normative matrix. Perhaps too much has already been said about Butler's early championing of parody and drag (Bersani 1995), but her work is dominated by the claim that it is the necessary repetition of a norm that both allows a self to be recognised, at the same time as the repetition is also the self's undoing. To perform *as queer* is to maintain and demand recognition for that which has, hitherto, exceeded the bounds of cultural recognition. Thus, the queer is that which both partakes in the norm – one can be recognised *as* male or female – and destabilises that norm, for this male or female will not take on the desires of the heterosexual matrix.

Butler's theory therefore allows for the (albeit problematic) maintenance of identity politics; for the assertion of oneself as this or that subject demanding recognition is both necessary for the social system at the same time as it introduces a necessary dynamism of the system. At the same time, identity politics must be recognised as queer: one is not asserting one's difference *from* some already recognised other. One is asserting difference as such: that one is a self only insofar as one, through repetition, also creates and performs differently. The condition for identity is difference, but for Butler this is iterative difference. There is not a substance or subject who then goes through time and difference; it is the repetition of this differing act from which one posits a subject. Theory is the recognition of the conditions of performative difference, and through this recognition one enables a recognition of the supposedly stable and conditioning norm as itself conditioned.

Against the model of iterative difference which allows for the critical maintenance of identity politics, Gilles Deleuze offers a theory of positive difference. Crucial to the understanding of the distinction between the post-Hegelian iterative model of difference and Deleuze's understanding of difference is the status of relations. In her early work on Hegel, Butler explains Hegel's critique of internal relations: if relations were internal, then the way in which any being related to the world would be determined in advance, so that its encounters, journeys and interactions would merely unfold what that being already is (Butler 1987: 35). Against this, Hegel argues that something *is* only in its relations; it is not that there are beings – or even a Being – that then encounter difference. Rather, there is difference or relationality *from which* points of stability and recognition emerge. Absolute consciousness is just this differing – or *not* being the self-same – recognising itself. It is a relation to relationality, a consciousness aware that it is nothing other than its distance and difference from itself. We might say, then, that we have abandoned internal relations, for it is not as though any being determines its world or gives a world to itself. Rather, there is the unfolding of relations which allows any particular relation or difference between terms; consciousness is just this coming to recognition of oneself as nothing more than relationality. The essence of what something is – that which makes it what it *is* – is its existence, its actualisation, or the way in which it has established itself as this or that complex of relations.

Butler remains committed to the idea that relations are produced through a process of difference and repetition. Something *is* identifiable *as* something only if it is repeated through time, but each repetition also introduces a certain difference or *not* being at one; the self in remaining itself is always subjected to, or negated by, that which is not. Deleuze also insists that relations are external to terms. However, Deleuze does not allow a system or form of differentiation to exhaust the real or the potentiality of being. Rather, while relations do not follow from self-sufficient terms, Deleuze posits a positive virtual plane, or 'pure past', which is actualised in each encounter to produce both the term which is repeated, and the difference established in each term. Deleuze seeks to find syntheses of difference and repetition which are asymmetrical, positive and pre-individual. In *Difference and Repetition* Deleuze makes two key points with regard to the establishment of an active synthesising subject. First, the self *who repeats* and from whom relations to the world are established is grounded upon passive, pre-individual syntheses: the individual who acts is composed of a thousand tiny egos, each effected from an encounter. Thus, it is not the self who must receive sensation and organise a world, for sensations are already the effect of intensive encounters or syntheses. And intensity's synthesis is not the repetition through time of the equal – not the maintenance of this spatial being, or this quality – but is an asymmetrical synthesis in which intensity 'is' at each moment of its repetition different from itself. Before there is the 'I' of the self who repeats itself actively, there is the 'eye' which is already the establishment of a qualitative relation or the unfolding of an intensity. The 'eye' is the result of a passive synthesis that has organised the problem of light, and light – as intensity – is that which might also have unfolded or been explicated in other relations or other qualities: so that each of our organs, according to Deleuze, is a contemplative soul, not receiving so much determining data, but giving a quality to the intensities of all it encounters:

> The passive self is not defined simply by receptivity – that is, by means of the capacity to experience sensations – but by virtue of the contractile contemplation which constitutes the organism itself before it constitutes the sensations. [. . .] There is a self wherever a furtive contemplation has been established, wherever a contracting machine capable of drawing a difference from repetition functions somewhere. The self does not undergo modifications, it is itself a modification – this term designating precisely the difference drawn. Finally, one is only what one *has*: here, being is formed or the passive self *is*, by having. Every contraction is a presumption, a claim – that is to say, it gives right to an expectation or a right in regard to that which it contracts, and comes undone once its object escapes. (Deleuze 1994: 100)

Second, while the self is nothing other than repeated modifications, what is repeated is not the actual, existing, material or bare present – and does not happen *to* an individual – but is the pure past. Each event is the actualisation of a pure potentiality, a power *to be* which each present repeats. All the objects that constitute an individual's reality are haunted by another series of virtual objects that are never fully present; these are not psychic, wished for or imagined. A virtual object opens any material objective individual series to a contemplation beyond the self, a pure intensity that is beyond the habitual time of the body, and the remembered time of the psyche. The beyond of pleasure – or the individual's definition through a series of desired objects – is not an indeterminate negativity or undifferentiated 'beyond'. Deleuze objects to psychoanalysis' grounding of the 'beyond' of pleasure on an opposition between death and life, between the self and its return to a state of inanimate matter. Instead, Deleuze insists on the pure past as a virtual, eternal, intense, pre-individual and positive series which each actualised present repeats. If the individual appears as so many organised, actual and life-serving objectifications – what I take to be other than myself, and towards which I am directed – this is because the individual is grounded upon a series of virtual objects. These virtual objects are pure fragments, or shreds of the past: a past that was never present and does not exist, but is always absent from itself and *insists* (Deleuze 1994: 124–5).

To give this concrete form, we can note that any actualised, existing, acting, repeating subject – a self who defines itself against (autonomy) and through others (recognition) – has as its prior condition pre-personal series. The aim of Deleuze's ethics and politics is to analyse, affirm and open these series. Most importantly, in terms of theory and the *life* and humanity of theory, Deleuze insists on the importance of the ground or dark precursor. Any two series of resonating differences – such as the differences of a language and the differences of our bodily identity – resonate with each other and can experience forced movement only through a 'dark precursor' or ground. So, in order for the self who says 'I' and speaks the language of man to be co-ordinated with the bodily movements of the self-interested, active and organised human organism there has to be some silent, unstated, undecided, passive ground or sense that itself cannot be simply stated. Much of *Difference and Repetition* is concerned with trying to think those silent presuppositions of representation and identity which tie the series of philosophical concepts – of the self, the 'I', truth, identity and recognition – with the body of man oriented toward maintaining a state of equilibrium.

For Deleuze, thinking *beyond* the human requires some forced movement which he introduces in *Difference and Repetition* as the 'beyond' of a life and pleasure of self-maintenance: this beyond would be 'death', but not a death opposed to life and Eros. Thanatos, he argues, is Eros carried to his 'nth' power: desexualised, or rendered purely virtual and inhuman. Only here would we encounter pure intensity. The self or 'I' who loves another self (erotically) is already the effect of a whole series of virtual and intersubjective objects. The phallus, for example, is such a virtual object; it organises desires and bodies before their actual and individual encounters. Deleuze also refers here, and in *The Logic of Sense*, to the aleatory object which allows series to resonate. So, before 'I' can love or recognise 'you', our perceptions have already been synthesised in advance by the *sense* of our encounter: the sense or orientation of what counts as human, what counts as love, what counts as a recognisable body. For Deleuze this virtual plane is precisely not linguistic, for language as such can only organise bodies after those bodies have been intensively and affectively organised or synthesised. The true aim of thinking or theory would be to go back to those singular points from which relations and affects have been determined:

> Underneath the large noisy events lie the small events of silence, just as underneath the natural light there are little glimmers of the Idea. Singularity

is beyond particular propositions no less than universality is beyond general propositions. Problematic Ideas are not simple essences, but multiplicities or complexes of relations and corresponding singularities. (Deleuze 1994: 203)

How does each individual or the self who says 'I' repeat and modify a virtual series of affections, encounters and intensities that are not its own and that might also be repeated otherwise? Against iterative difference – which is a repetition *of* a being that has no existence outside its seriality, or that produces that which repeats only through a maintaining of the same through time – Deleuze insists on the positive insistence of the virtual in all its intensity.

If we were to draw an example from genetics we might say that iterative difference gives us the idea of an organism that would undergo change and modification through repeating itself; each generation or copy introducing more and more instability and alterity. Deleuze's positive difference shows how each modification of an individual is preceded by micro-perceptions or encounters: before the self repeats itself there are repetitions of intensities or pure qualities. A virus might be repeated in my body creating not a different organism but a different potentiality – a new virus or the modification of an organ, which might then effect my body's motility – not the ways in which I act but the ways in which I am acted upon. Difference is not the reiteration of some quality but occurs through the eternal return of the power to create relations, to produce connections. Concretely, this idea of difference does not yield an organism being modified through selection, but an individuation and selection which disregards the organism, creating connections among bodies that is the undoing of any organised body:

> For the I and the Self are perhaps no more than indices of the species: of humanity as a species with divisions. [. . .] The I is therefore not a species; rather – since it implicitly contains what the species and kinds explicitly develop, in particular the represented becoming of the form – they have a common fate, *Eudoxus* and *Epistemon*. Individuation, by contrast, has nothing to do with even the continued process of determining species but, as we shall see, it precedes and renders the latter possible. It involves fields of fluid intensive factors which no more take the form of an I than of a Self. Individuation as such, as it operates beneath all forms, is inseparable from a pure ground that it brings to the surface and trails with it. (Deleuze 1994: 190)

In political terms we can also distinguish iterative and positive repetition. For Butler, an individual does not exist *ex nihilo* but can be a self only through an other which it repeats and modifies. So, for example, claiming

to be a queer *subject* might involve laying claim to certain normative practices – such as marriage and gender – which would have the effect both of
normalising the self by subjection to convention and recognition. To a
certain extent all politics is queer politics or the negotiation between the
degrees of repetition to which the self submits and the amount of deviation or difference from normativity the self can effect. The queer is negative, defined as the difference *from* those conditions of recognition and
normativity which both enable and preclude autonomy. Deleuze offers a
quite different ontology and ethics of non-being. We are mistaken if we
think of non-existence as the failure, deviation or difference from the
present and actual. We need to think of non-being as positive, real and
affirmative. Each existing, actualised individual is therefore the actualisation of a non-being, which is better defined as '?-being' or as a series
of problems. The queer self might be better thought of as a counter-
actualisation of the material repetitions that make up 'man'. We could see
marriage in its current bourgeois normative and heterosexual form as the
solution to a certain problem or question: how the self forms its gender,
manages its desires and property, and organises its child-rearing. But the
queer self would repeat the problems that compose the self: counter-
actualising the present by drawing on the pure past of the questions from
which we have emerged. How might a self desire, what might count as an
object of one's desire, what relations or events might the couplings of
bodies produce and enable?

Thus, whereas Butler's model of theory is to begin with the subject and
then interrogate its conditions of possibility in the tension between recognition and autonomy, Deleuze's theory is one of positive intuition. Here,
we go beyond composed selves and problems to the affects and intensities from which they are organised. For Butler a queer theory is one in
which the conditions of being a subject are essentially queer – one must
claim to speak as a self, but can do so only through an other who is *not*
oneself. At the same time, the condition for being queer is being a subject:
one must be recognised as having a claim to speak, be and exist. For
Deleuze, the conditions of theory require a going 'beyond' of the self and
the organism. As long as we are concerned with identity, with the repetition *of* who we are, we remain within constituted matter and lived time.
To think transcendentally we need to think the pure form of time and difference, the pure intensities which each present repeats and actualises
both in the present and for all time. For Deleuze, then, the conditions of
the queer and the conditions of the new are the same: to counter-actualise
the present, to repeat the intensities and encounters that have composed
us, but not as they are *for* us.

In quite specific terms this requires a radical and distinct break from identity politics. As long as ethics is defined as the maintenance of individuals as they are we restrict the potentiality of life to one of its constituted forms. Only by thinking intensities beyond the human can we begin to live ethically. Thus queer politics would involve neither recognition of the self, nor a refusal of normativity, but the affirmation of the pre-personal. Rather than assessing political problems according to their meaning and convention – or the relations that organise certain affects and desires – we need to think desires according to virtual series, all the encounters that are potential or not yet actualised.

Such a queer politics has two direct consequences. First, practically, once we abandon conditions of recognition we can interrogate a practice according to the potentiality of its encounters. Rather than seeing gay marriage, trans-gendering or gay parenting as compromised manoeuvres in which the queer self repeats and distorts given norms, we need to look at the positivity of each encounter. How do bodies establish relations in each case, and what powers are opened (or closed) to further encounters and modifications? Second, aesthetically, against an art of parody or drag that would repeat the norm in order to de-stabilise it from within, positive repetition and difference make a claim for thinking time in its pure state, those powers to differ which are pure fragments. Art would not be the representation or formation of identities but the attempt to present pure intensities in matter, allowing matter to stand alone or be liberated from its habitual and human series of recognition. The sensations presented in art are not those of the lived subject but are powers to be lived for all time, allowing us to think the power of perception beyond the selves we already are.

This aesthetics would, in turn, give us a new distinct model of reading. On the critical identity-based model of queer theory, where the queer self is the de-stabilising repetition of an enabling normativity, we look at the ways in which works of art introduce a difference or dissimulation in the image of the human. One reading of Shakespeare's *A Midsummer Night's Dream*, for example, might focus on the ways in which the final image of normative heterosexual desire has to go through a certain detour or deviation in order to arrive at is supposed destined end. Queer reading would attend to all those moments in the text in which the normal is achieved, produced, effected and also, therefore, exposed as contingent, constituted and open to change. To a great extent the queer theory industry has been mobilised around a re-reading of the canon's images of heterosexual desire to show moments of instability, deviation and mobility. Deleuze, however, offers a quite distinct model of reading, both of the literary work in *Difference and Repetition*, and of art in general in *The Logic of Sensation* and (with Guattari) in *What is Philosophy?* In *The Logic of Sensation* (2003) Deleuze describes all art as the repetition of the history of art, but always with a struggle to release sensations from their subjection to figuration and repetition. There is no such thing as a bare canvas, for we are already composed and dominated by clichés. The future can come, not through the assertion of greater and greater individuality, but only in a destruction of the personal to release the figure. This would not be the figuration *of* some repeatable form, but the delineation or process of differing from which this or that determined figure is drawn. In *Difference and Repetition* Deleuze draws upon Shakespeare's *Hamlet* and Proust's *Remembrance of Things Past* to describe the profound syntheses of time that go beyond the body that is composed of habits, and the self that is composed of memories. The act in *Hamlet* exists above and beyond Hamlet's individual existence; it is a pure potentiality, something that he may or may not live up to, actualise or bring into the present. The future, or the opening of the new, can come about not through Hamlet drawing upon himself, his desires or his personal past, but by living out or allowing that power to differ which exists above and beyond him:

> As for the third time in which the future appears, this signifies that the event and the act possess a secret coherence which excludes that of the self; that they turn back against the self which has become their equal and smash it to pieces, as though the bearer of the new world were carried away and dispersed by the shock of the multiplicity to which it gives birth: what the self has become unequal to is the unequal in itself. In this manner, the I which is fractured according to the order of time and the Self which is divided according to the temporal series correspond and find a common descendant in the man without qualities, without self or I, the 'plebeian' guardian of a secret, the already-Overman whose scattered members gravitate around the sublime image. (Deleuze 1994: 112)

Here, for Deleuze, the art of theatre is not about the representation of plots, individuals and desires, but somehow giving form to a power of the pure past. Beyond the habitual repetitions which organise a body – 'this is what I do' – and beyond the repetitions that constitute a self – 'I am who I am by being the same through time' – drama exposes this higher repetition which destroys the self and its world of co-ordinated actions: 'Drama has but a single form involving all three repetitions' (Deleuze 1994: 115). The task of art is the presentation of this higher power, and reading the work of art is intuiting this power of time. In Proust the art of the novelist lies in presenting a self with its habits and recollections, and then presenting the pure potentiality from which that self was actualised: the past not as it was actually lived and recalled, but as it never was, but only *could be*, 'in a splendour which was never lived, like a pure past which finally reveals its double irreducibility to the two presents which it telescopes together: the present that it was, but also the present which it could be' (Deleuze 1994: 107). Against a critical reading, which would look at the ways in which art or literature queers the pitch of the normal, Deleuze offers a positive reading in which temporality in its pure state can be intuited and given form as queer, as a power to create relations, to make a difference, to repeat a power beyond its actual and already constituted forms.

References

Bersani, L. (1995), *Homos*, Cambridge, MA: Harvard University Press.

Butler, J. (1987), *Subjects of Desire: Hegelian Reflections in Twentieth-Century France*, New York: Columbia University Press.

Butler, J. (1990), *Gender Trouble: Feminism and the Subversion of Identity*, New York: Routledge.

Butler, J. (1993), *Bodies that Matter: On the Discursive Limits of 'Sex'*, New York: Routledge.

Deleuze, G. (1990), *The Logic of Sense*, trans. Mark Lester, New York: Columbia University Press.

Deleuze, G. (1994), *Difference and Repetition*, trans. Paul Patton, London: Athlone.

Deleuze, G. (2003), *Francis Bacon: The Logic of Sensation*, trans. Daniel Smith, London: Continuum.

Deleuze, G. and Guattari, F. (1994), *What is Philosophy?*, trans. Hugh Tomlinson and Graham Burchill, London: Verso.

Habermas, J. (1992), *Postmetaphysical Thinking: Philosophical Essays*, trans. William Mark Hohengarten, Cambridge, MA: MIT Press.

Irwin, T. H. (1988), *Aristotle's First Principles*, Oxford: Clarendon.

Kant, I. (1990), *Foundations of the Metaphysics of Morals and, What is Enlightenment*, trans. Lewis White Beck, 2nd edn, rev., New York: Macmillan.

Langton, R. (1998), *Kantian Humility: Our Ignorance of Things in Themselves*, Oxford: Clarendon Press.

O'Neill, O. (1989), *Constructions of Reason: Explorations of Kant's Practical Philosophy*, Cambridge: Cambridge University Press.

Wollstonecraft, M. (1975), *A Vindication of the Rights of Woman*, ed. Carol H. Poston, New York: Norton.

Chapter 2

Thirty-six Thousand Forms of Love: The Queering of Deleuze and Guattari

Verena Andermatt Conley

TO QUEER: to deviate from expecting norm, to make strange. Example of bad word that has been turned around.

http://dictionary.reference.com/browse/queering

American critics often credit themselves for having invented queer theory. It can be argued, however, that French theorists' rethinking of official philosophy and psychoanalysis after 1968 dealt extensively not only with feminisms but with homosexualities. Much of Michel Foucault's work, but also Hélène Cixous's notions of bisexuality and of homosexuality (Cixous 1975), or Jacques Derrida's various staging of male couples – Derrida-Genet or Socrates-Plato (Derrida 1974 and 1980) – explored the destabilisation of a self and of what today are called 'non-normative sexualities'. It is, however, especially in the writings of Gilles Deleuze and Félix Guattari that the question of homosexuality as queering, that is, as becoming and as an ongoing differing of difference, is raised. From *Anti-Oedipus* to *A Thousand Plateaus* (Deleuze and Guattari 1977 and 1987), queering is discussed and performed in the context of the philosophers' attack on 'normality' and enforced behaviour in a capitalist, institutionally bourgeois disciplinary society. Deleuze discusses it openly when he writes about his desire to impregnate state philosophers by way of anal penetration. In his translator's preface, Brian Massumi quotes the couple: 'I imagined myself approaching a [philosopher] from behind and giving him a child that would indeed be his but would nonetheless be monstrous' (Deleuze and Guattari 1987: 276). For his part, Guattari discusses homosexuals engaged in non-genealogical, 'monstrous' becomings. 'Queering' in the sense of Deleuze and Guattari goes beyond a simple insertion of a gay subject in an existent society. The philosopher and the analyst champion queering as becoming so necessary for the continual invention of terms such as women and homosexuals. A radical move that breaks down all oppositions imposed by state thought and its various representatives (family, school, law or army), queering produces becomings that go beyond normative couplings to invent new connections be it with humans, animals, vegetals or machines.

Deleuze and Guattari's queerings function at the level of singularity and collectivity, of aesthetics and ethics. They make numerous references to literary texts. An aesthetic queering of singularities is accompanied by temporary manifestations of militantism that would help transform society. At no point do the philosophers simply want to integrate a gay population into the status quo of present society. Their work escapes much of the present discussions in the Anglo-Saxon world that takes as its point of departure the division between a desire for rights to established values – such as marriage – and of queering, that is, of making strange all of present society (Warner 1999). What can be called queering in the texts of Deleuze and Guattari is predicated on a queer revolution – sexual and social – and the becoming-revolutionary of the queer. It can be said that all of Deleuze's writing with Guattari functions as a kind of homosexual experimentation. In addition, queering is addressed variously throughout their individual writings. We will see how such queering functions in the texts by Deleuze and Guattari and ask how we can read their theories today.

Just as Derrida experimented with homosexuality through writers like Jean Genet, so Deleuze entered into becomings with Guy Hocquenghem, a gay French writer whom he met after 1968. It is in a preface to a novel by Hocquenghem, never translated into English, *L'Après-Mai des faunes* (Hocquenghem 1974) – a title that for a French reader bears unmistakable literary references to Mallarmé – that Deleuze muses on homosexuality as queering. From the texts of an openly gay writer and activist influenced (among others) by Deleuze's theory, the philosopher in turn elaborates on homosexuality as queering. Homosexual struggles are associated with the margins and a becoming-minoritarian. For Deleuze, homosexual identity does not exist. As is the case for other minorities, gay identity is always established by, or in connection with, a majority. To fix gay *identity* is to try to stabilise what has to be radically destabilised. It would be laughable to pretend to know even what gay identity is.

Deleuze argues that homosexuals like other minorities – women, colonised people – have to question these identities *and* turn away from their own questioning in an ongoing fashion. They have to enter into a permanent revolution. In Hocquenghem, Deleuze finds a writer who searches not for a 'gay identity' or for 'being-gay' but for *becoming* gay. Since this becoming is linked to complex socio-historic structures, every book has to write it out in a different way. To become gay has to do first and foremost not with identity but with desire. Homosexual desire has to be distributed and mobilised otherwise from book to book. It is continually transforming itself, and thus for Deleuze, there can be no pre-existing identity from which to transform oneself. There is only a label given by the majority that the gay person takes over. He – in the case of Hocquenghem – is both gay and not gay. He is in a constant becoming that goes through desire.

Writing in the early 1970s, Deleuze develops a notion of 'vitality' as a liberation of desire. A dominant order stifles desire. It controls individual and collective desire through institutions be it philosophy or, especially, psychoanalysis. Deleuze argues against a psychoanalysis that 'normalises' the subject by reducing everything to an Oedipal scenario. As an institution, psychoanalysis normalises desire and excludes difference. By doing so, it limits creativity. Psychoanalysis has recourse to interpretation and focuses on words. Deleuze argues for the necessity to introduce semiotic chains that would valorise not only words but other regimes, signifying *and* asignifying, such as gesture and sensation. *Experimentation* instead of a reductionist interpretation should support all forms of desire and not exclude gay practices the way Freud did when he classified them as 'abnormal'. Queering as becoming has to reinstate a vital desire that experiments with innumerable sexualities. The homosexual is not fixated on his past but on the present and turned toward the future. He is in touch with invention and an opening of spaces. Deleuze discovers in Hocquenghem a homosexual desire that is not defined as 'a regressive interiority but through an Outside, whose characteristics are present' (Deleuze 2004: 285). The philosopher finds this in a special movement of cruising, a mode of encounter, exchangeability and mobility of roles, even in a kind of betrayal against his own class, that is, that of men.

In addition to desire, queering must produce utterances (*énoncés*). Deleuze makes it clear that to produce a real and *not* a capitalist pseudo-desire entails producing new utterances. It is a matter of undermining the order-word (that is, an utterance that bears an effect of authority or law) of a hegemony in an ongoing movement of becoming. To desire then is not to long for something but to produce new ways of feeling, perceiving and conceiving. Gay people have to invent different ways of desiring that do not pre-exist. Just as women, for Deleuze, have to become more and more 'woman' (Deleuze and Guattari 1987), so then homosexuals have to become more and more homosexual. Deleuze brings forward a historical dimension when he declares that the production of utterances, *enoncés*, inserts difference in gay writers. 'Of course, Hocquenghem does not sound like Gide, or Proust [. . .]: but style is politics – and so are generational differences, and the different ways of saying 'I' [. . .]' (Deleuze 2004: 285).

For Deleuze, it is from this new style – that is, from a way of creating assemblages (*agencements*) – that homosexuality in the 1970s can produce utterances that do not carry or write *on* homosexuality. Such a gesture would put homosexuals back squarely into the majority. In order to be able to say something and to produce change, gays have to be part of a minority or, even more so, of a becoming *minoritarian*. Only in that capacity can they escape a hypocritical, normativising majority. Gays have to make pronouncements on sexuality itself *and* de-normativise it. At the same time, their critique has to bear on the *entire* social field. By escaping the heterosexual model and the localisation of this model, gays can be leading a micropolitics of desire that changes what organises, dominates and represses all of society including military organisations. In this ongoing queering, homosexuality truly liberates itself, Deleuze concludes, when, by being marginal, it has 'no *social utility* whatsoever' (Deleuze 2004: 286, emphasis in text). A utilitarian model tends to be exploitative and thus, being close to capital, disables real desire. Relations of force, often expressed in couples such as man-woman, straight-gay, master-slave, have to be made unstable and reversible. The lack of usefulness makes of these couplings something aesthetic, inventive, without a 'project'. To be 'useful', would be tantamount to entering into an existing society defined by hierarchies of categories and dominant, often expressive desire. To break with it one cannot enter into it but think its Outside.

With echoes of Michel Foucault and through his work on gay writing Deleuze shows how Hocquenghem cannot be content with putting oneself in the margin but one has to go on to undo the 'nominalism' of homosexuality. For Deleuze – and Guattari – language exists only as a dominant order. It is not communication but prescription. Language is the centre that invents the margin and not vice-versa. This spatial ordering defined by centres and margins is a recent invention in history and cannot be naturalised as 'having always existed' (Deleuze 2004: 286). It is a question, for Deleuze, of undoing homosexuality as a 'state of things'. When homosexuality is a word, it has to be taken literally, *pris au mot* (Deleuze 2004: 286). Deleuze quotes, not without inserting a slight critical distance, Hocquenghem's own neo-Hegelian remarks: 'It is by making shame all the more shameful that we progress' (Deleuze 2004: 286–7).

Praising the fact that FHAR (*Front homosexuel d'action révolution-naire*), the group Hocquenghem helped found, explored its relations with other minoritarian movements, such as the MLF (*Mouvement de libera-tion des femmes*), Deleuze argues against the closure of a group on itself. A collective group has to connect with others, evolve and even disband without sadness or nostalgia. Of importance is the avoidance of sclerosis, that is, of repetition of the same. By way of Hocquenghem, Deleuze insists on a homosexuality that will open itself up 'to all sorts of possible new relations, micro-logical or micro-psychic, essentially reversible, transver-sal relations with as many sexes as there are assemblages (*agencements*), without even excluding new relations between men and women: the mobility of particular S&M relations, the potency of cross-dressing, Fourier's thirty-six thousand forms of love, or the n-sexes (neither one nor two sexes)' (Deleuze 2004: 287). Deleuze recalls how Proust already advocated a 'multiple homosexuality' that would include transsexual communications with flowers and bicycles. He praises in Hocquenghem the allusion to a homosexual 'transmutation' that would not be interme-diary but a part of a world transferred into and onto another. This trans-mutation is what Deleuze and Guattari describe elsewhere in relation to the wasp and the orchid as 'a capture of code, [. . .], a veritable becom-ing [. . .]. The two becomings interlink and form relays in a circulation of intensities pushing deterritorialisation further' (Deleuze and Guattari 1987: 10). Homosexual becomings function in similar ways.

Queering is not based on recognition in a dialectic. For Deleuze no homosexual subject clamours for rights. Rather, the 'new' homosexual affirms himself or herself by saying that no one *is* homosexual. Homosexuals are still being named as such by a majority in power but they are already elsewhere. There are only homosexual productions of desire and assemblages (*agencements*) that produce utterances (*énoncés*). Deleuze makes it clear that in the 1970s divided-subjects à la Gide or even guilt-ridden subjects à la Proust are of times past. Queering implies a specific homosexual desire with homosexual utterances. One has to go back through a deeper and broader history of homosexuality to give it back all the otherness it contains and of which it had been stripped. This cannot be found in an unconscious elaborated by a repressive, official psychoanalysis but only through the progression of a sexual becoming that is always to come. Deleuze elaborates these forms of homosexual desire and becoming in a post-1968 climate that is under the sign of a vital desire and a cultural revolution that condemns the state, state thought and its representatives, the school, the family or the law. Any utilitarian project is also associated with the state.

In 1993, in his preface to a new English edition to Hocquenghem's earlier text, *Homosexual Desire*, first published in France in 1972, Michael Moon writes about the proximity between the French gay writer and poststructuralist theory without mentioning Deleuze's preface to a later book. He puts Hocquenghem squarely in the ferment of the 1960s and provides provocative historical minutiae of this romanticised and bygone period. The numerous details about provocation and activism that often invited police action bring forth a side of Hocquenghem and his group, FHAR, that complement the analytical part of Deleuze. However, Moon's essay testifies to the blatantly militant involvement of many leading French intellectuals – Deleuze and Guattari included – in gay activism. Moon writes:

> Further writings of FHAR members were gathered and published in a book, *Rapport contre la Normalité* (1971, *Report against Normality*), as well as in a special issue of the journal *Recherches* (March 1973). Calling itself a 'Grande Encyclopédie des Homosexualités', and boasting a long roster of 'participants' that included not only such gay-lib stalwarts as Hocquenghem and Pierre Hahn but also Sartre, Michel Foucault, Gilles Deleuze and Jean Genet, the issue included a piece on 'schizo-sodomy' illustrated with Tom of Finland drawings and gay sex graffiti, a thoughtful meditation on the desire of the American comic-strip character Dennis the Menace, a transcription of a long discussion among three young French men about their sexual relations with Arab men and boys, and a foldout cartoon entitled 'La puissance ou la Jouissance?' ('Power or [Sexual] Pleasure'). This special issue of *Recherches* was also seized, and Félix Guattari, its nominal editor, was fined 600 francs for this latest 'outrage against public decency' by the FHAR and their supporters on the intellectual left. (Moon in Hocquenghem 1993: 12–13)

Whether for his outrageousness or his theoretical elaborations that refuse to take gay identity as a point of departure, Hocquenghem who is close to, and inspired by, Deleuze never became very popular in the Anglo-Saxon world. His sense of queering as becoming was ill received or understood by gay theorists who like to insist on identity and gay pride and who often draw a dividing line between queering and rights. It can be said though that Deleuze – as well as Hocquenghem – wrote about homosexuals and becoming in terms similar to many feminists of the same period. Both pay close attention to language and advocate the destabilisation of self and identity. The difficulties with 'trap words' such as *homosexual* but also *lesbian* and *woman*, were discussed and denounced by many feminist writers at the time as well. Monique Wittig who, in her writings, put these words into metamorphosis, has recourse to a kind of queering in *Les Guérillères* (1979). Later, she argues that 'woman' has always been thought from a phallocentric male point of view and therefore lesbians are not women (Wittig 1992). In *The Newly Born Woman*, Hélène Cixous insisted on de-emphasising trap words such as 'man' and 'woman' because of their historical sedimentation. She found salvation in an unlimited exchange as gift and the replacement of nouns with adjectives, 'masculine' and 'feminine' and even attributes of colour. Deleuze's queering as becoming goes beyond homosexuality – though it does not complicate the latter – to include all minorities, to begin with women who insist on changing language in an effort to transform a capitalist, disciplinary society and its institutions.

As has already become amply evident, one cannot think about Deleuze's pronouncements on queering without evoking Guattari, his intercessor. Guattari advocates the necessity of becoming and desire in words that are similar to and even more openly politicised than those of Deleuze. He too underlines the necessity to transform all of society. In *Révolution moléculaire* (Guattari 1977), in a section on *'faire fuir'*, to make flee, to put into flight, he entitles one of the sub-sections – not included in the English translation – *Molecular Revolution: Psychiatry and Politics*, 'Devenir enfant, voyou, pédé,' 'Becoming child, rogue, faggot' (Guattari 1984: 170).[1] The sub-title is provocative and not without shock value, both through its choice and its myriad association of other words. Guattari wants to produce lines of flight and advocate transversal thinking that move beyond the limits. Words like child, *voyou* (rogue) or the more derogatory *pédé* (fag) for 'homosexual' – used by Deleuze – have to be put in flight. To become, they have to be subjected to a generalised queering that would take a 'bad' word and transform it even further. A majority established these words as categories and binary oppositions that control the ways a social body thinks of its milieu. They have to be disconnected from the group in which they were imprisoned. In the parlance of Guattari, they have to be put in flight and their desire liberated so that the child, the *voyou* or the *pédé* can become. These words, when taken literally, will become in ways unknown to the majority. They will be carried off in a becoming-minoritarian. The child can free him or herself from a reductionist and constraining Oedipal scenario. Similarly, the rogue or gang leader – with direct echoes of the Black Panthers – whom Guattari sees somewhat romantically as struggling for social justice, and the homosexual who had been labelled abnormal can now invent their flights.

This majority cannot be thought outside socio-historic power formations that are sexual and economic. Already in 1977 Guattari senses an impending shift toward an increasing consumer society that is about to channel desire in ways that reinforce a voluntary servitude: 'In fact, people serve only to enframe, to "channel" – in the sense of information theory – a process of semiotisation that, increasingly, goes through television, cinema, records, comic strips, etc., without assembling such machinic processes according to collectively assumed finalities; one ends up with a kind of generalised, semiotic intoxication' (Guattari 1984: 171–2). More as an analyst than a sociologist, Guattari shows how people are 'mentally equipped' (172) so that they perform certain tasks and agree willingly to conform to social organisations. Their egos are modelled by unconscious representations that enter in complicity with repressive dominant formations.

To this, Guattari opposes 'a collective assemblage of the social that no longer looks to make people enter into pre-established frames in order to make them adapt to universal and eternal finalities but that accepts the finite and historically delimited aspect of human enterprises' (172). He, like Deleuze, introduces a historical dimension in his thinking on becoming 'pédé.' He orients a liberation of a desiring energy such as the desire to live from institutions into an assemblage (*agencement*) of people, of functions, of economic and social relations toward a generalised politics of liberation (173). In the wake of communism he continues to argue that the entirety of the social compact has to search for new ways of being in common. He sees this happening in 1977 with an increasing awareness of a transversality, of problems such as urbanism, bureaucracy, neurosis, micropolitics in the family and, last but not least, in ecology. It is not only specialists who should militate but all of society should bring about a shift in what he will later call an ongoing transformation of sensibility, desire and intelligence (Guattari 2000). One should not apply readymade methods but become *analytically militant*. Guattari argues for a continuum between theory, practice and militantism. A constructivist, he wants to build something living, not only with one's family members but with friends, militants and oneself. Everyone has to transform the relations with their own body and with themselves. As Deleuze puts it in his preface to his friend's *Psychanalyse et transversalité*, Guattari is not preoccupied with the unity of a self (*moi*). Rather, the self is something that has to be dissolved under the double assault of political forces (Guattari 1972, my translation). For Guattari, there are not two economies, one libidinal and another political. There are only flows of desire that are one and the other (Guattari 1972). To those who interject that this is not a revolution, he answers that it is a question of a different revolution. It's a question of ending *all* forms of alienation, those of workers, women, children, sexual minorities, atypical sensibilities, the love of sounds, colours, ideas. What Guattari continues to call a 'revolution' in whatever domain, goes through a preliminary liberation of *an energy* of desire (Guattari 1972: 175). Only something transversal and a chain reaction that goes through the existing stratifications will catalyse an irreversible process of calling in question the power formations to which the present society is enchained.

Guattari takes his own discipline to task. Focusing on the limit between normal and pathological, psychoanalysis has entered a political field. It is part of a capitalist system of production established according to these norms and serves as a model for life and desiring. Psychoanalysis tries to structure itself according to scientific models from biology to linguistics; it has even sought refuge in literary activity. The problem is that psychoanalysis thinks its practices are in collusion with dominant models of power and goes against liberating desire. It takes over and frames human beings from birth on. Having relayed in the social domain religious and philosophical quarrels of other times, it has become hegemonic and aims at controlling madness, dreams, deviations, art, history, even occurrences in the everyday such as a slip of the tongue (245–6). In the dominant society of 1974, every non-meaning has to be interpreted and homosexuality is classified as perversion. It is explained as a fixation at an infantile stage, that is, a pre-genital or polymorphic stage. This is how, under the guise of an objective description, 'a normal desire is imposed that disqualifies that of the child, the homosexual, the mad person and, closely related, that of woman and of a young person who has not fully accepted the conjugalo-familial perspective, etc.' (246).

Revolutionary struggle has to do away with dominant models and, especially, the model of models – capital – that reduces desiring multiplicities into an undifferentiated flux of workers and consumers. To do away with struggles based on binary oppositions one has to recognise the plural character of desiring commitments, of possible hyphens between revolts and revolutions. Such a struggle would have to take into consideration minorities of all kinds without prior normative rules. For such a conversion to happen, one has to be rid of psychoanalytic models of repression based on Oedipal scenarios and castration. No struggle will be possible that does not focus on desire. Desire is made captive by psychoanalysis in the service of capitalism that opposes a dangerous subjective desire and a rational self on the side of reality with which one has to negotiate (247). For Guattari, a desire liberated from power is more real than the delirious rationalism of planners. As long as there exist no micro-politics that introduce shifts in an official desire, one cannot but repeat the same model and, as a result, no liberation is possible for minorities. In a short section, 'Becoming Woman' – included in the English translation – that follows the one on '*pédés* and *voyous*', fags and rogues, Guattari explains why he coined the contested expression, 'becoming woman'. As the prototype of a minority and insofar as she enters into dominant binaries between man, woman, such as strong, weak, rich, poor, active, passive, she also has the opportunity of escaping the dominant order and of entering into becoming. This is the case for woman as a sexual body, not as a social body. The latter, caught as she is in society by marriage and maternity, has forfeited that chance. As the prototype of becoming, woman as sexual body can inspire homosexuals and other minorities to become. This kind of becoming is only open to those who are outside of any category.

For Guattari, the focus is placed on the micro-politics of desire. Critical of the emphasis structuralism places on the signifier, he declares that language is always shaped by a specific social and political model. The social field is not determined by an economic infrastructure, nor is the semantic field by a signifying structure. To analyse and change complex socio-historic structures one has to put in question myriad forms of power that control the social fields at all levels. Those in power order the rights of the person as well as categories of race and sex, and age groups. Yet even before language, there exists a multitude of micro-political levels. This is why it is all-important for a micro-politics to intervene in power and change dominant significations (241–2). Micro-politics help transform sexual minorities as long as one does not distinguish between objectivity and subjectivity (248). To an interpretation with words, Guattari opposes experimentation with 'signs, machinic functions, assemblages of things and people' (248). For Guattari, the undoing of the self comes with an emphasis on desire, a politics that thinks across disciplines and a micro-politics that precedes language. A transformation of homosexuals cannot come about without simultaneous undoing of state power for which an ongoing experimentation with people, things and machines is tantamount.

When writing about homosexuals Deleuze and Guattari were intensely aware of doing so in a time of what they called a generalised becoming-minoritarian. Both knew they were writing, as they had argued for subjectivity in general, in a world in ongoing transformation. Guattari was continually rewriting his texts in order to deterritorialise them according to changing socio-historical contexts. The world of their published reflections – as we can read in the preface of Michael Moon – is no longer ours today. We may wonder how Deleuze and Guattari would rewrite their notions of becoming as queering today. With an even greater intensification of capital, most women and gays have bought into capitalism, the supreme order to which, at this point, as Etienne Balibar notes elsewhere, no organised resistance is possible. Already Guattari showed how many gays constitute themselves as 'corporate groups'. Gay desire – like that of many other groups – has been recuperated by capitalism. It has become a cottage or even a consumer industry. In spite of this appropriation, a noticeable and ongoing transformation of sensibility, desire and intelligence is witnessed due in no small part to micro-politics. Some of the rhetoric of the FHAR, such as the touting of sexual encounters with Arab boys, or Guattari's romanticisation of street gangs, ruffles sensibilities today. It also strikes a contemporary reader as strange that Deleuze and Guattari carry on an almost masculinist and homogenising discourse by focusing on homosexuals and *pédés* exclusively without any mention of lesbians, bisexuals or transsexuals. In the United States, since the 1970s, that is, since the time when Deleuze and Guattari wrote the texts quoted above, significant transformation has taken place both in the way gays relate to themselves and the way others relate to them. Psychiatry has modified its stance that treated homosexuality as abnormality; now popular culture displays more of a gay sensibility on television, film and video, all the while the demand for rights, though often denied, is never abandoned. With AIDS, the importance of freeing the energy of desire, of becoming and reinventing the term through experimentation and the creation of new assemblages has, if not disappeared, at least lost some of its momentum.

In a way, both the philosopher and the analyst are close to some of the pronouncements of Judith Butler and Eve Kosofsky Sedgwick who draw inspiration from poststructuralist theory. From *Bodies that Matter* to *Undoing Gender* and elsewhere Butler makes clear that homosexual 'identity' is a mirage. It is always imposed by a dominant social order. Of importance for her is the need to re-signify words and to reinvent identity – or identities – in ongoing fashion. As Deleuze writes, Hocquenghem does not say I the way Gide or even Proust did. Butler and others insist on the necessity of reconciling a certain desire and re-signification with rights. Today's society is no longer that in which Deleuze and Guattari wrote their essays on queering and that the media, celebrating a forty-year anniversary, re-signify in consumerist terms as the 'summer of love' through appeal to the anniversary of Sergeant Pepper's Lonely Heart Club band. With the waning of the state and its institutions, repressions no longer function the same way. The scourge of AIDS has made distant memory of the anti-establishment buzz words of the 1960s; communication is no less affected by globalisation, the withering of the state, electronic transmission and the undoing of many traditionally symbolic boundaries. Deleuze and Guattari were keenly aware of some of these impending transformations. They were also aware of an intensification of capitalism that exploits strategies of marketing to spell a waning of desire as it was written about in the 1960s, the moment when the slogan was *'Puissance ou Jouissance'*, 'Power or Sexual Pleasure'.

Today, when – often as a result of consumerism – essences have been replaced with social conventions. Subjects and citizens have asked for the right to dwell, to move, to be, to represent, to speak. Other rights are being added, such as the right to experiment with institutions – the right to marriage, adoption, benefits, the right to 'come out' in institutions like the military – and to explore homosexual, lesbian, bisexual, transsexual desires and a generalised queering. For this we can recall Guattari's exhortation to be *analytically militant*. The terms are held in an unstable relation. The militant does not follow a pre-traced party line. He or she invents and experiments instead of interpreting what already exists.

We are far from the context in which Deleuze and Guattari wrote on homosexuality and queering. However, it is productive to think of the stress they placed on desire to change society. Some of it has been accomplished. There prevails a new sensibility, a new desire, even a new intelligence that functions transversally, across many disciplines that range from urban planning to education, art, even fashion and food. All of these can implement novel forms of subjectivation. Yet desire today goes for the most part through forms of global capitalism that produce, as Deleuze and Guattari insist, stupendous quantities of misery. We pay attention to words in a sexual context but not to how they are structured by a social-economic discourse. Minorities become majorities and enter the discourse of marketing. We forget the words of Guattari to the effect that in capitalism economic and sexual flows are of the same currency. Queering risks taking place more at the level of a pseudo-desire that does not, as in the texts of Deleuze and Guattari, search for sexual *and* social becomings. We should not, however, in Guattari's terms, mummify the philosopher and the analyst's theories. Rather, we should 'open them up onto further constructions that are just as provisional, but more firmly grounded in the solid earth of experience. What matters, in the last resort, is how a theory is used' (Guattari 1984: 253). In spite of a certain romanticism and utopianism associated with their thirty-six thousand forms of love, Deleuze and Guattari's exhortations to rethink our desires and direct them away from existing power structures in order to change the latter can make us think and dream less of missed opportunities than of future becomings.

References

Butler, J. (1993), *Bodies that Matter*, New York: Routledge.
Butler, J. (2004), *Undoing Gender*, New York: Routledge.
Cixous, H. (1986), *The Newly Born Woman*, trans. B. Wing, Minneapolis: University of Minnesota Press.
Deleuze, G. (2004), *Desert Islands and Other Texts, 1953–1974*, trans. M. Taormina, New York: Semiotext[e].
Deleuze, G. and Guattari, F. (1977), *Anti-Oedipus*, trans. R. Hurley, M. Seem and H. Lane, Minneapolis: University of Minnesota Press.
Deleuze, G. and Guattari, F. (1987), *A Thousand Plateaus*, trans. B. Massumi, Minneapolis: University of Minnesota Press.
Guattari, F. (1972), *Psychanalyse et transversalité*, preface by G. Deleuze, Paris: Maspéro.
Guattari, F. (1977), *Révolution moléculaire*, Fontenay-sous-Bois: Recherches, 'Encore'.
Guattari, F. (1984), *Molecular Revolution, Psychiatry and Politics*, trans. R. Sheed, New York: Penguin.
Guattari, F. (2000), *The Three Ecologies*, trans. I. Pindar and P. Sutton, London: Athlone Press.
Hocquenghem, G. (1974), *L'Après-Mai des faunes*, Paris: Grasset.
Hocquenghem, G. (1993), *Homosexual Desire*, trans. D. Dangor, introduction by M. Moon, Durham: Duke University Press.
Kosokfsky Sedgwick, E. (ed.) (1997), *Novel Gazing: Queer Readings in Fiction*, Durham: Duke University Press.
Warner, M. (1999), *The Trouble with Normal*, New York: Free Press.
Wittig, M. (1979), *Les Guérillères*, trans. D. Le Vay, London: Women's Press.
Wittig, M. (1992), *The Straight Mind*, Boston: Beacon Press.

Note

1. The English translation, *Molecular Revolution: Psychiatry and Politics* (1984), is an edited compilation of two volumes: Guattari's *Psychanalyse et transversalité* (1972) and his *Révolution moléculaire* (1977).

Chapter 3

The Sexed Subject in-between Deleuze and Butler

Anna Hickey-Moody and Mary Lou Rasmussen

Schizoanalysis is the variable analysis of *n* sexes in a subject, beyond anthropomorphic representation that society imposes on this subject, and with which it represents its own sexuality. The schizoanalytic slogan of the desiring-revolution will be first of all: to each its own sexes.

(Deleuze and Guattari 1983: 296)

[T]he notion of the subject carries with it a doubleness that is crucial to emphasise: the subject is one who is presumed to be the presupposition of agency [. . .] but the subject is also subjected to a set of rules or laws that precede the subject [. . .]

(Judith Butler in Meijer and Prins 1998: 285)

The 'set of rules' to which Butler refers in the latter quote above are the same structures that make up the 'senselessly privileged' psychoanalytic subject which Deleuze and Guattari urge their readers to move beyond (Deleuze and Guattari 1983: 298). Deleuze and Guattari critique the ways in which capitalism axiomatises[1] the psychoanalytic subject. Psychoanalysis sutures myth to capitalism and subjectivity, heterosexuality to family and sociability. Psychoanalysis co-constructs homosexuality and madness, neither of which offer any escape from the psychoanalytic theatrical stage of capitalism. Rather, homosexuality and madness are co-constitutive of the neurotic, psychoanalytic pole of capitalism. As such, homosexuality and madness have their own traps: madness embodies the schizophrenic social movement in a state too extreme to be useful; homosexuality can operate within a circuit of production-consumption that is excessively closed. Deleuze and Guattari argue for a movement towards: 'new regions where the connections are always partial and nonpersonal, the conjunctions nomadic and polyvocal, the disjunctions included, where homosexuality and heterosexuality cannot be distinguished any longer' (Deleuze and Guattari 1983: 319). On the one hand, this reads like a manifesto for queer theory. On the other hand, this is dangerous territory. Identities, politics and social visibility are at stake. Not to mention lifestyles and sexual pleasure. It seems almost as if Deleuze and Guattari would have women dump their girlfriends and fuck chairs outdoors in order to affect a flow in which 'non-human sex mingles with the flowers' (Deleuze and Guattari 1983: 319). While we do not think this is the kind of social action schizoanalysis calls for, we do want to grapple with the work of Judith Butler to offer a located way of thinking 'queer' in relation to Deleuze and Guattari.

Deleuze and Guattari understand much about the politics of producing subjectivity: we often create psychoanalytic types in ourselves. We submit to myth as a form of social control. As little factories of myth reproduction, we are the new Ophelia: women who want to marry our mothers, men who desire union with the Father. We re-invent thousands of *Hamlet* and *Oedipus Rex* complexes. Butler asserts the difficulty of moving beyond such a double-bind in which the subject is an effect of a set of laws that precede it: psychoanalytic, mythic, tragic, cultural laws – laws which are re-invented and re-imagined across generations. In the introductory quote above, Butler reminds us that an answer is not always to be found by looking *beyond* the subject. What Butler is saying here is that it is important to both work with the notion of the subject and, at the same time, to be able to look beyond the subject. In emphasising the importance of working within and beyond the subject, Butler draws on her own approach, which intends to work the legacy of humanism against itself. She then contrasts her approach to Latour and Haraway's approaches, which emphasise a trans-human agency, especially in their use of the term 'actor' and their focus on exchanges within networks. There are parallels here with schizoanalysis: in which the schizoanalyst is an agent that effects productive flows beyond the increasingly personalised limits of capitalism. In creating space for such resonances to be discussed, this chapter identifies select schizoanalytic elements in Butler's work and makes room for further encounters between Deleuze and Butler.

Deleuze and Guattari deterritorialise psychoanalytic ideas, while Butler reworks them; both want to craft sexual subjectivities that refute majoritarian readings of gender and sexuality. These projects have many forms of cultural and political utility; to our minds the modes of resistance they generate need not follow one path. For Deleuze and Guattari, crafting sexual subjectivities contrary to majoritarian ideas of gender and sexuality is a means of folding the social field and libidinal investments of groups into practices that distort and disfigure capitalist modes of production. But simultaneously we must reckon with the tendency of capitalism to re-code escaping flows. The personal isn't just political: it's marketable. The exercise of folding the social field and libidinal invest-ments of groups into daily life in ways that decode and deterritorialise capitalism and associated Imaginary structures is one of the tasks of schizoanalysis. We can understand this call to intervene in interfaces of capitalist production and subjective desire as a broad impetus of the schizoanalytic project. They explain:

> . . . decoding and the deterritorialisation of flows define the very process of capitalism – that is, its essence, its tendency, and its external limit. But we know that the process is continually interrupted, or the tendency counter-acted, or the limit displaced, by subjective reterritorialisations that operate as much at the level of capital as a subject (the axiomatic), as at the level of the person's serving as capital's agents (application of the axiomatic). (Deleuze and Guattari 1983: 320)

We can intervene in the economies of value created by capitalism, one of which is the value accorded to sexual reproduction and heterosexual family units. Possibilities for schizoanalytic political intervention are found in making a productive, new whole from an assorted collection of parts. Libidinal economies need to be re-worked and re-channelled, as an answer to the question:

> What are your desiring machines, what do you put into these machines, what is the output, how does it work, what are your nonhuman sexes? (Deleuze and Guattari 1983: 322)

A queer schizoanalysis realises what we 'put into' desiring machines is already a combination of autopoetic structures that maintain investment in deconstructing, or reconstructing, heteronormative ideas. Such aware-ness makes plain the constructed and binary foundation of heteronor-mative ideas. Secondly, our intention is to make new machinations of desire that rework, inspire and feed back into queer aesthetic, political, sexual and philosophical practices. We are not convinced that studying 'nonhuman sexes', on their own, is an entirely useful way of thinking through '. . . our desiring machines, [and] what [we] put into these machines' (Deleuze and Guattari 1983: 322), what their output is and how they work. We insist that queer theorising about the ethics and aes-thetics of humanity and sexuality is an area that continues to require much attention. We argue in favour of the enduring importance of study-ing the desiring machines that produce/regulate our sexual identity, our experience of sexual pleasure and the social significance of sex.

Our chapter responds to the tensions outlined above: between, on the one hand, the political impetus for fleeing from psychological and sexual types, and on the other hand, the need to engage with, and harness the political utility of, embodied ways in which such flight is incorporated into lived subjects. That is, to re-think the ways in which tropes of sexed being become part of the fabric of our subjectivities in ways difficult to escape. We examine selected resonances between the work of Butler (1993, 1997) and possibilities for deterritorialising or destratifying the heteronormative sexual subject presented by the work of Deleuze and Guattari (Deleuze 1991, 1995; Deleuze and Guattari 1983, 1987). As we note above, Deleuze and Guattari are renowned for their scathing critiques of psychoanalysis – yet Butler takes up psychoanalytic concepts in her consideration of sexual subjectivity. Such differences in conceptual tools, and in the ontological frameworks of desire that these respective theorists mobilise, are two of several grounds that have informed a contemporary culture of scholarship that considers Deleuze and Butler to be antithetical. In this chapter we do not dispute such fundamental ontological differences, but we question the utility of opposing strategic unions between these theorists. Why can't we use Butler with Deleuze to create new possibilities for queer theory? Indeed, there are resonances in the meta-textual politics of DeleuzoGuattarian theory and Butler's sexed subjectivity that deserve consideration. With a view to furthering such inquiry, the authors explore possibilities for certain types of critically queer unions between Butler, and the joint work of Deleuze–Guattari. Such unorthodox unions echo the Deleuzian methodology of practising 'philosophy as a sort of buggery or (it comes to the same thing) immaculate conception' (Deleuze 1995: 6). One such union, in thought, or on a plane of immanence, might involve Butler's concept of the lesbian phallus, taking concepts created by Deleuze–Guattari from behind, and generating queer theory for the new millennium.

We recognise that Deleuze and Guattari's work offers valuable methods for leaving behind renderings of queer theory preoccupied with being anti straight and non-normative, and which seem incapable of decentring the subject. One such example of Deleuze–Guattari inspired queer theorising is Mark Graham's study of the relationships between bodies and things (Graham 2004), a study which assumes 'a clear boundary between objects and persons must be abandoned and that persons do not finish at their skins' (2004: 299). Graham conceives of a sexuality removed from the constraints of 'oedipal imperatives and heterosexist assumptions about the gendered nature of sexuality'. Such an approach demonstrates the limitations of not taking sexual assemblages seriously enough (2004: 302), through illustrating that such assemblages extend beyond individual identity. Gender and sex are of the world, not just the person. This sentiment is exemplified by Deleuze and Guattari's (1983: 293) statement that: 'The truth is that sexuality is everywhere: the way a bureaucrat fondles his records, a judge administers justice, a business-man causes money to circulate; the way the bourgeoisie fucks the prole-tariat; and so on.'

We see value in Deleuzian inspired queer theory to the extent that it prompts an awareness of the degree to which sexuality and sexual poli-tics are part of everyday life. We are disturbed by a lack of generosity within Deleuze Studies towards Butlerian inspired queer theory; a senti-ment somewhat evident in the editors' drive to develop a post-Butlerian queer theory founded upon a 'new image of thought outside that of rep-resentation: a material thinking-image which will be able to provide the term "queer" with an active (that is, productive and positive) rather than a reactive force (queer as the negative, the anti-straight, the non-normative, an exclusively deconstructive practice)'. We are not sold on the chorus that suggests:

> You've got to accentuate the positive
> Eliminate the negative
> Latch on to the affirmative
> Don't mess with Mister-In-Between.

Rather, we argue the utility of theorising in the company of Deleuze and Butler, coupling the negative and the affirmative, messing with Mister-In-Between.

In her essay 'The End of Sexual Difference' (2004: 195) Butler consid-ers Braidotti's 'Metamorphosis'. She agrees with Braidotti's diagnosis that her work might be situated within a 'theology of lack', a lack pre-occupied with 'melancholy, mourning, conscience, guilt and terror'. She dryly suggests that 'this is what happens when a Jewish girl with a Holocaustal psychic inheritance sits down to read philosophy at an early age, especially when she turns to philosophy from violent circumstances'. While Butler accedes to being a 'theologian of lack', we wonder if queer theory will be as useful in the absence of lack. What is lost when 'the the-ology of lack' is regarded merely as 'a reactive force'? Lack *produces* much as it is a *response to* a given state of affairs. Lack is part of a million different desiring machines that produce new material forms. With this in mind, we argue for a positive engagement with the possibilities afforded by lack and a re-assessment of approaches to theorising lack. Contemporary queer theory needs to think about what 'lack' does, to trace the trajectories in thought that lack effects and to affirmatively claim the usefulness of lack as a concept.

Queer theorising inspired by Deleuze and Guattari would benefit if it refused to jettison the located and embodied notions of agency developed by Judith Butler. We contend that the binary opposition between Deleuze and Butler is becoming a 'habit of thought'[2] (Deleuze and Guattari 1996: 105–6): a knee-jerk reaction or affective response that prohibits any theoretical union between these theorists. Deleuze and Guattari (1996: 106) articulate the relationship between concepts and habits in thought stating:

> Wherever there are habits there are concepts, and habits are developed and given up on the plane of immanence of radical experience: they are 'conventions'. That is why English philosophy is a free and wild creation of concepts. To what convention is a given proposition due; what is the habit that constitutes its concept? This is the question of pragmatism.

Habits have concepts. The habitual practice of reading Deleuze against Butler needs to be re-worked through the development of new concepts. The ontological divide between Butler and Deleuze is a ballast around the neck of contemporary thinkers who are concerned with the problematics of gender, sexuality and agency as articulated in political subjectivities. Feminist scholars with an interest in sexual subjectivities, for example, see the earlier works of Braidotti (1991), Grosz (1994) and Jardine (1985), have found Deleuze's work problematic, partially because his ontology is not easily mapped over existing knowledge structures. While grounded in critical political projects, such misgivings have somewhat impeded positive encounters between Deleuze's work and feminist studies of sexed subjectivity. Recent forays into queer theory have effected more productive unions between Deleuze and Guattari's work and the possibilities and politics of 'queer'. Diarmuid Hester (2006), Michael O'Rourke (2005, 2006), Jeffrey Cohen and Todd Ramlow (2006) are breaking new theoretical ground and beginning to produce material that suggests there is value in thinking Judith Butler with Gilles Deleuze. In continuing this theoretical project, in this chapter we consider how Butler's ideas of performativity and the lesbian phallus might resonate with Deleuzian schizoanalysis.

Love your Lack

In an essay exploring 'the queer-in-motion of queer studies and of Deleuze' (2006: para. 2), Jeffrey Cohen and Todd Ramlow (2006) interrogate Butlerian and Deleuzian notions of 'becoming' (2006: para. 13). Cohen and Ramlow argue that Butlerian 'becomings' be perceived as 'a process formed of alliances with and through others, a process not collapsible to either side of a self/other binary, a process always in motion, changing (performatively) in multiple contexts' (Cohen and Ramlow, 2006: para. 13). Such a reading of 'becoming' in Butler is juxtaposed to Deleuze and Guattari's multiplicity which they argue is 'the very condition of minoritarian micro-politics and is propelled by multiple and simultaneous becomings' (Cohen and Ramlow 2006: para. 13). Deleuze and Guattari's concept of becoming (1987, 1996) takes matter, and corporeality, as a site of transformation and constant, internal differentiation. The self is always becoming different from itself. Within Deleuze and Guattari's thought, the human body is an effect of its own movements and processes of connection. The body does not precede the flow of time through which it becomes. Deleuze and Guattari suggest that we do not begin as fixed subjects who then have to know a fixed world. Rather, they argue that there is experience and *from* this experience we form an image of ourselves as distinct subjects. All life is a series of 'foldings'. Every cell, every organism (and the human body) are folds of the milieu of life. Our bodies are the becoming-actual of all our virtual possibility, a limit set in chaos that is a resolution of infinite speeds. Subjectivity is an effect of our processes of becoming. While Cohen and Ramlow are disposed to consider resonances between Butler and Deleuze through notions such as becoming, others such as Rosi Braidotti (2006a & b) may be more sceptical about such readings. For instance, in her recent paper 'Affirming the Affirmative', Braidotti rejects Butler's claims to connections with Spinoza, arguing that:

> The conatus as pure affirmative affectivity . . . has nothing to share with the logic of irreparable loss, unpayable debt and perpetual mourning, which is at the core of the psychoanalytic and deconstructive ethics that Butler espouses . . . In contrast to this tradition . . . I read Deleuze & Guattari as neo-vitalists who affirm the force of the affirmative and posit an ethics based on the transformation of negative into positive passions. (Braidotti 2006b: para. 18)

Deleuzian thought might be perceived as coterminous with Braidotti's movement towards 'compulsory optimism' (Rothe 2006), and the affirmation of the affirmative. But this should not be the case, as an ethics based on transformation cannot be conceived outside relationships with lack, melancholy and mourning.

The project of affirming the affirmative is apparent in Sasha Lambevski's (2004) essay 'Movement and Desire', an essay focused on liberating queer theory from 'the oedipal prison'. This escape takes the form of a study of 'microsocial sexual rearrangements'. For Lambevski, these 'rearrangements' are important objects of study because they can help us see the limits of ideology and categorisation in accounting for flows of desire. These rearrangements demonstrate that:

> . . . sexuality belongs neither to the subject nor to the world exclusively. As such it is not ownable, quantifiable, recognisable, or amenable to critique. It is a flow attached to a nomadic desire . . . (Lambevski 2004)

This theorisation of sexuality is echoed in Braidotti's focus on the idea of 'sustainability'; a means of countering theoretical moves to produce queer theoretical over-codings for new capitalist flows. In making her case for sustainability, Braidotti (2006b: para. 7) says that:

> I do not think that a naive celebration of global queerification on the one hand and the reference or the return to a universal on the other are inevitable or even necessary. On the contrary, I want to argue for a more specific and grounded sense of singular subjectivities that are collectively bound.

It is our contention that Deleuzian and Butlerian inspired queer theory, jointly considered, can make productive contributions to consideration – and production – of a 'grounded sense of singular subjectivities that are collectively bound'. Global queerification of capitalist flows does not have to be synonymous with queer theory. Quite the contrary, in fact, queer can be aligned with 'a re-grounding of the subject in a materially embedded sense of responsibility' (Braidotti 2006b: para. 7). As Braidotti's article title suggests, 'positive passions' are key, alongside a feminism that 'need not be critical but can be inventive and creative . . . experimenting with thinking is what we all need to learn' (Braidotti 2006b: para. 31).

This emphasis on affirmation is not necessarily antithetical to Butler's ethics. In offering this reading we are mindful of Butler's rethinking of her melancholic view of subject formation in *The Psychic Life of Power* (1997), departing from her emphasis on the force of Nietzchean punishment toward a Foucaultian ethics which 'focuses on the peculiar creativity in which morality engages and how it is, in particular that bad conscience becomes the means for manufacturing values' (2005: 15, 16). Vikki Bell characterises this trajectory in Butler's work 'as tracing the paths by which different becomings are actualised' (Bell 2006: 217). The creative task that underpins Butler's ethics is found in thinking through the means by which values are manufactured.

However, too much emphasis on creativity as affirmation is, to Butler's mind, symptomatic of ahistoricity. She argues:

The 'ever new' possibilities of resignification are derived from the postulated historical discontinuity of the term. But is this postulation itself suspect? Can resignifiability be derived from a pure historicity of 'signs'? Or must there be a way to think about the constraints on and in resignification that takes account of its propensity to return to the 'ever old' in relations of social power? [. . .] Neither power nor discourse are rendered anew at every moment; they are not as weightless as the utopics of radical resignification might imply. (Butler 1993: 224)

Butler and Braidotti disagree on the possibilities of 'radical resignification'; in fact Butler is scathing about the possibilities attributed to strategies of 'radical resignification'. Here we depart with Butler, concurring with Braidotti in perceiving the benefits of affirming the affirmative; but we do wonder about the tendency to 'eliminate the negative'. If one is to understand singular subjectivities as collectively bound, surely it is important to consider the ties that bind. What are the prospects for a 'materially embedded sense of responsibility' when desire is not conceived as 'ownable' (Lambevski 2004) or 'amenable to critique' (Lambevski 2004). We want to occupy a realm in between Butler and Deleuze in which affirmation, resignification, lack and melancholy articulate different aspects of our theoretical work.

In a recent discussion of the Butlerian idea of 'performative knowledge' (2006), Bell endeavours to trace what she perceives as some of the links between Butlerian and Deleuzian thought. Implicit within her discussion is a critique of certain readings of Butler's oeuvre that situate it as at odds with Deleuzian theorising (for instance, see Braidotti 2006a & b; Colebrook 2000). Bell's project is sympathetic to our attempt to emphasise the theoretical utility of reading Butler alongside Deleuze. In her discussion of 'performative knowledge' Bell focuses on how notions of co-extensivity come to play in the work of Deleuze and Butler. Below, Bell situates Butler's understanding of 'the subject' as refusing a split between language and bodies:

In place of the certainty that I am – the cogito – is an argument for 'co-extensivity'. 'Thinking' is only confirmation that an individual exists within a discursive world; 'the subject', in this rendering, is co-extensive with his or her outside in the sense that they are produced by historically varying conditions that are in turn sustained by their produced elements. (Bell 2006: 214)

For Bell, Butler is not a representational thinker, but rather a thinker whose focus is on particular lines of flight, lines 'associated with knowledge, power and subjectification that encircle and produce the effect of interiorities' (Bell 2006: 217). For Bell, these lines are part of Deleuze's dispositif. To our mind, these lines of flight are also central to investigating Deleuzian inspired questions. One such question, which might productively lend itself to a Butlerian focus on knowledge, power and subjectification, is Moira Gaten's inquiry: 'What is the relation between the collective assemblages which constitute the body politic and the sexual politics of language?' (2000: 70). Such a spirit of inquiry inspires us to articulate selected schizoanalytic aspects of Butler's work.

Schizoanalytic Aspects of Judith Butler's Work

We begin this section with a proviso. We are not suggesting that Deleuze and Guattari's schizoanalysis and Butler's lesbian phallus are ontologically compatible. Almost the opposite, in fact, as we have noted. The concepts of desire that are mobilised by Butler, Deleuze and Guattari are different. Butler takes up a psychoanalytic concept of desire alongside a Hegelian notion of the dialectic and Foucaultian reading of power. Deleuze and Guattari develop a post-Freudian, post-Marxist ontology of desire that conceives flows of desire in a manner comparable to Foucault's heterogeneous flows of capillary power. Desire, like power, is everything. It's everywhere: it is positive, productive and generative and is not only formed in relation to lack or sexuality. One of our key points is that it is this very incompatibility, this irreconcilable difference, which makes a union between Deleuze and Guattari and Butler so compelling and so useful – if they were already the same, why would we need both of them? Working the differences between Deleuze, Guattari and Butler offers one of the most dynamic scholarly trajectories available to contemporary queer theory.

More than inquiring into the productive nature of the *differences* between Deleuze, Guattari and Butler, scholars need to adopt some self reflexivity in their approach to working with these theorists. In the specialised fields within which we write, the ontological differences between Deleuze, Guattari and Butler are complex and profound. To a school teacher, an artist, a lawyer or well-educated professional outside our area of specialist study these differences are not so obvious. In fact, to the well-educated professional, the meta-politics of these scholars are not dissimilar. Within academic institutions Deleuze, Guattari and Butler are almost always employed to argue the importance of minoritarian bodies and to bring awareness to issues relating to minorities. Beyond a hagiographic focus on the theorists themselves and their philosophical structures, their writings are used in ways that effect similar politics. This is the most pressing and immediate reason to acknowledge that a union of sorts already exists between them. It is an accidental union, a meta-textual, meta-ontological union, yet it shows up an 'outside' to theory, from which Deleuze and Guattari and Butler are more aligned than might be thought within their respective fields of scholarship. This point is significant if we are to work with theory in ways that impact outside the academy and, as tertiary educators who are often pushed to justify the relevance and significance of theory in our curriculum, we are pragmatic about the role of difference in the ontological frameworks of Deleuze, Guattari and Butler. Yes, they are antithetical and, furthermore, these differences need to be explicated and mined. However, outside their respective ontologies, there is also a meta-political agenda at stake. In spite of Deleuze's adamant disassociation from 'left' politics, his writings are increasingly taken up in ways that advance or argue for minoritarian subjects, as is the work of Judith Butler.

As concepts, Deleuze and Guattari's schizoanalysis and Butler's lesbian phallus articulate the conviction that psychoanalytic models of power dominate the ways in which subjectivity is imagined and performed by individuals. Both concepts advance critiques of the role of psychoanalysis in contemporary cultural imaginaries, suggesting that this prominence is not a good thing and should be challenged. Part of this psychoanalytic model of subjective creation is the effect of psychic interiority, an assemblage of connections which reproduces an unconscious closed off from contact with the real and closed in upon itself; *psychoanalysis constructs the unconscious*. In opposition to this psychoanalytic production of the unconscious, schizoanalysis involves the production, release and affirmation of flows of desire. This desiring-production occurs in the individual body, yet it also occurs in large social assemblages and machines. Here, it is not what desire represents that is of importance, but rather the ways in which flows of desire are organised, in relation to capitalism, within the socius.

Schizoanalysis and the lesbian phallus may both be critical of the role of psychoanalysis, but these critiques can also take very different forms. For Janell Watson, these divergent strategies for undoing capitalism and heterosexism provide important insights into the development of political subjectivities. Drawing on the work of Guattari, Watson (2005) theorises the notion of 'Polyphonic Subjectivity', a notion somewhat akin to the fractal movement of subjectivity taken on by Deleuze and Guattari, who state:

> Let's not rush in to introduce a term that would be like a phallus structuring the whole and personifying the parts, unifying and totalising everything.

Everywhere there is libido as machine energy, and neither the horn nor the bumble bee have the privilege of being a phallus: the phallus intervenes only in the structural organisation and the personal relations deriving from it, where everyone, like the worker called to war, abandons his machines and sets to fighting for a war trophy that is nothing but a great absence, with one and the same penalty, one and the same ridiculous wound for all – castration. This entire struggle for the phallus, this poorly understood will to power, this anthropomorphic representation of sex . . . is where desire finds itself trapped, specifically limited to human sex, unified and identified in the molar constellation. But the desiring-machines live on the contrary under the order of dispersion of the molecular elements. And one fails to understand the nature of partial objects if one does not see therein such elements, rather than parts of even a fragmented whole. (Deleuze and Guattari 1983: 323)

Operating in a manner very similar to the productive critique inherent in schizoanalysis, the lesbian phallus draws upon the belief that metaphysical constructions – as well as material acts – produce sexual subjects. Indeed, Deleuze and Guattari and Butler make similar arguments about the cultural power and popularity of the Oedipal triangle: see for example, Butler's work in *The Psychic Life of Power*, and Deleuze and Guattari's position in *Anti-Oedipus*. Yet perhaps Deleuze and Guattari cast their theoretical net too wide? In focusing on an array of socioeconomic forms of production (barbarians, savages and civilised men) that subvert the automatic production of Daddy-Mommy-Me and associated heterosexual practices, they almost gloss over or bypass critical applied understandings of the labour involved in constructing queer subjectivities that actively displace heterosexual assumptions, ideals and everyday practices.

Butler first introduces the idea of the lesbian phallus in *Bodies That Matter* in a chapter entitled 'The Lesbian Phallus and The Morphological Imaginary'. Here Butler sets out to rethink the idea of the phallus, via Sigmund Freud and Jacques Lacan. This investigation of the 'imaginary construction of body parts' leads her to argue: 'To be a property of all organs is to be a property of no organ, a property defined by its very plasticity, transferability, and expropability' (1993: 63). In short, Butler is attempting to create a theoretically useful fiction that allows readers to think differently about the circulation of power. Such a project is important, she argues, because 'what is needed is not a new body part, as it were, but a displacement of the hegemonic symbolic of (heterosexist) sexual difference and the critical release of imaginary schemas for constituting sites of erotogenic pleasure' (1993: 91). For Butler, this strategy of displacement allows us to 'consider that "having" the phallus can by symbolised by an arm, a tongue, a hand (or two), a knee, a thigh, a pelvic bone, an array of instrumentalised body-like things' (Butler 1993: 88). Butler's lesbian phallus is very much open to variation and plasticity. We are reminded of Deleuze and Guattari's (1987) 'Body without Organs', an elaboration of Artaud's (1976: 571) suggestion that: 'When you will have made him a body without organs, then you will have delivered him from all his automatic reactions and restored him to his true freedom.'[3]

Butler is concerned with matter and representation, not with the hope of excavating a 'real', but rather with highlighting the ways in which imaginaries are constructed, and destabilising anatomy as a referent for sexual desire. Similarly, Deleuze and Guattari's 'partial objects' are one part of all desiring machines. These

> partial objects define the working machine or the working parts, but in a state of dispersion such that one part is continually referring to a part from an entirely different machine, like the red clover and the bumble bee, the wasp and the orchid, the bicycle horn and the dead rat's ass. (Deleuze and Guattari 1983: 323)

This theorisation of partial objects helps us to imagine the unending possibilities inherent in desiring machines. It refutes totalising and unifying sexual structures. In concluding her discussion of this concept Butler notes that 'to speak of the lesbian phallus as a possible site of desire is not to refer to an *imaginary* identification and/or desire that can be measured against a *real* one; on the contrary it is simply to promote an alternative *imaginary* to a hegemonic imaginary and to show, through that assertion, the ways in which the hegemonic imaginary constitutes itself' (1993: 91). Butler, Deleuze and Guattari show up the constructed nature of 'the whole' and our libidinal investments in particular ideas of the whole.

The lesbian phallus is part of Butler's greater project within *Bodies That Matter*, a project focused primarily on understanding relations of power, and how these relations are complicit in 'the production of sexed morphologies through regulatory schemas . . . to show how power relations work in the very formation of "sex" and its "materiality"' (1993: 16–17). In a fairly Deleuzian register, this project is characterised by Butler as 'less a theory of cultural construction than a consideration of the scenography and topography of construction. This scenography is orchestrated by and as a matrix of power; a matrix that remains disarticulated if we presume constructedness and materiality as necessarily oppositional notions' (1993: 28).

While Butler has positioned her scholarship as neo-Spinozist, rather than Deleuzian, we glean elements of Deleuzian schizoanalysis in ideas such as the lesbian phallus, or Butler's take on 'cross-dressing' as a kind of performance or masking that 'characterises the mutual lure of the orchid and the wasp' (Flieger 2000: 59). By providing the tools for better understanding the techniques through which the body is framed and formed, Butler allows for certain questions to emerge, questions that resonate throughout her work. These questions interrogate constructions that are understood as artificial, but nonetheless crucial. Two questions prompted by such a line of inquiry are recited below:

> How do tacit normative criteria form the matter of bodies? And can we understand such criteria not simply as epistemological impositions on bodies, but as the specific social regulatory ideals by which bodies are trained, shaped and formed? (1993: 54)

For us, doing research on disability and sexualities within the broad field of education, such lines of questioning continue to provide fruitful lines of inquiry (see Rasmussen 2006; Hickey-Moody, Harwood and Rasmussen 2007). Such lines of questioning open up possibilities for Deleuzian thinking about unimaginable and as yet unthinkable queer partial objects:

> For what can one do . . . With respect to that which can only be seen and heard, which is never confirmed by another organ and is the object of Forgetting in memory, of an Unimaginable in imagination, and of an Unthinkable in thought – what else can one do, other than speak of it? Language is itself the ultimate double which expresses all doubles – the highest of simulacra. (Deleuze 1990: 284)

Queer, Partial Conclusions

In closing, we would like to note that, in a manner akin to Deleuze and Guattari, Butler seriously engages with theorists who are critical of the legacy of humanism. In responding to a question about the significance of Haraway and Latour's work on hybridity and the nonhuman Butler states:

> I prefer to work the legacy of humanism against itself, and I think that such a legacy is not necessarily in tension with those who seek to displace humanism through recourse to vocabularies that disperse agency across the ecological field. They are two ways of undoing the same problem, and it seems important to have scholars and activists who work at both ends of the problem. (Butler in Meijer and Prins 1998: 285, 286)

Gilles Deleuze and Judith Butler are theorists who stand alone in their own rights. Respectively, they have large scholarly followings. While Butler suggests that she opposes Deleuze because she finds 'no registration of the negative in his work, and . . . feared that he was proposing a manic defence against negativity' (2004: 198), in the same paper Butler notes that she regularly receives essays and comments from people who insist that she is Deleuzian (2004: 198). In keeping with such contradictory messages, we are not arguing that Deleuze and Butler's positions should be seen as a neat fit. However, we do argue for a theoretical utility in thinking Butler and Deleuze side by side in imagining the future of queer theorising.

References

Sole authored texts by Butler

Butler, J. (1993), *Bodies That Matter: On the Discursive Limits of Sex*, New York: Routledge.
Butler, J. (1997), *The Psychic Life of Power: Theories in Subjection*, Stanford, CA: Stanford University Press.
Butler, J. (2004), 'The End of Sexual Difference', *Undoing Gender*, New York: Routledge, pp. 174–203.
Butler, J. (2005), *Giving an Account of Oneself*, New York: Fordham University Press.

Sole authored texts by Deleuze

Deleuze, G. (1990), *The Logic of Sense* (French 1969, trans. Mark Lester and Charles Stivale), New York: Columbia University Press.
Deleuze, G. (1991), *Empiricism and Subjectivity* (French 1953, trans. Constantine Boundas), New York: Columbia University Press.
Deleuze, G. (1995), *Negotiations* (French 1990, trans. Martin Joughin), New York: Columbia University Press.

Jointly authored texts by Deleuze

Deleuze, G. and Guattari, F. (1983), *Anti-Oedipus – Capitalism and Schizophrenia* (French 1972, trans. Robert Hurley, Mark Seem and Helen Lane), Minneapolis: University of Minnesota Press.
Deleuze, G. and Guattari, F. (1987), *A Thousand Plateaus: Capitalism and Schizophrenia* (French 1980, trans. Brian Massumi), Minneapolis: University of Minnesota Press.
Deleuze, G. and Guattari, F. (1996), *What is Philosophy?* (French 1991, trans. Hugh Tomlinson and Graham Burchell), New York: Verso.

Secondary texts

Artaud, A. (1976), 'To Have Done with the Judgment of God', *Antonin Artaud Selected Writings*, ed. S. Sontag, Berkeley, CA: University of California Press.

Bell, V. (2006), 'Performative Knowledge', *Theory, Culture and Society* 23(2) pp. 214–17.

Braidotti, R. (1991), *Patterns of Dissonance: a Study of Philosophy in Contemporary Culture*, Cambridge: Polity Press.

Braidotti, R. (2006a), *Transpositions: On Nomadic Ethics*, Cambridge: Polity Press.

Braidotti, R. (2006b), 'Affirming the Affirmative: On Nomadic Affectivity', *Rhisomes* 11/12 http://www.rhisomes.net/issue11/braidotti.html [Retrieved 9 January 2007]

Colebrook, C. (2000), 'Questioning Representation', *Substance* 92, pp. 47–67.

Cohen, J. J. and Ramlow, T. R. (2006), 'Pink Vectors of Deleuze: Queer Theory and Inhumanism', *Rhisomes* 11/12 http://www.rhisomes.net/issue11/braidotti.html [Retrieved 9 January 2007]

Conley, V. A. (2000), 'Becoming – Woman Now', *Deleuze & Feminist Theory*, I. Buchanan and C. Colebrook (eds), Edinburgh: Edinburgh University Press, pp. 18–63.

Flieger, J. A. (2000), 'Becoming-Woman: Deleuze, Schreber, and Molecular Identification', *Deleuze and Feminist Theory*, I. Buchanan and C. Colebrook (eds), Edinburgh: Edinburgh University Press, pp. 38–63.

Gatens, M. (2000), 'Feminism as "Password": Re-thinking the "Possible" with Spinoza and Deleuze', *Hypatia: A Journal of Feminist Philosophy* 15(2) pp. 59–75.

Goulimari, P. (1999), 'A Minoritarian Feminism? Things to Do with Deleuze and Guattari', *Hypatia* 14(2) pp. 97–120.

Graham, M. (2004), 'Sexual Things', *GLQ: A Journal of Lesbian and Gay Studies* 10(2) pp. 299–307.

Grosz, E. (1994), *Volatile Bodies: Toward a Corporeal Feminism*, Bloomington, IN: Indiana University Press.

Hester, D. E. (2006), 'A Monstrous Triptych: Cooper, Acker, Palahniuk' Unpublished MA Dissertation. *The English Research Institute*. Manchester Metropolitan University.

Hickey-Moody, A. C., Harwood, V. and Rasmussen, M. L. (2007, in press), 'Taking a Seat on the Pink Sofa', *Queer Youth Cultures*, S. Driver (ed.), New York: SUNY.

Jardine, A. (1985), *Gynesis: Configurations of Women in Modernity*, Ithaca: Cornell University Press.

Lambevski, S. (2004), 'Movement and Desire: On the Need to Fluidify Academic Discourse on Sexuality', *GLQ: A Journal of Lesbian and Gay Studies* 10(2) pp. 304–8.

Meijer, I. C. and Prins, B. (1998), 'How bodies come to matter: An interview with Judith Butler', *Signs* Winter 23(2) pp. 275–86.

Mercer, J. (1944), 'Accentuate the Positive' ["Ac-Cent-Tchu-Ate the Positive"] (Lyrics). For the film *Here Come the Waves*, Paramount Pictures, USA.

Miller, H. (1939), *Hamlet*, Puerto Rico: Carrefour.

Morris, M. (1996), 'Crazy Talk is not enough', *Environment & Planning D: Society & Space* 14 pp. 384–94.

Musser, A. (2006), 'Masochism: A queer subjectivity?', *Rhisomes* 11/12 http://www.rhisomes.net/issue11/musser.html [Retrieved 7 January 2007].

O'Rourke, M. (2005), 'Queer Theory's Loss and the Work of Mourning Jacques Derrida', *Rhisomes* 10, Spring 2005 http://www.rhisomes.net/issue10/index.html [Retrieved 19 December 2006]

O'Rourke, M. (ed.) (2006), 'The Becoming-Deleuzoguattarian of Queer Studies', *Rhisomes* 11/12, Fall 2005/Spring 2006 http://www.rhisomes.net/issue11/index.html [Retrieved 2 December 2007]

Rasmussen, M. (2006), *Becoming Subjects: Sexualities and Secondary Schooling*, New York: Routledge.

Rothe, J. (2006), 'Lodz, Braidotti and Butler' An online discussion of a dialogue between Braidotti and Butler at the 6th European Gender Research Conference: Gender and Citizenship in a Multicultural Context, University of Lodz, Poland, 31 August–3 September 2006. See http://www.weave-network.eu/index.php?option= com_joomlaboard&Itemid=27&func=view&id=64&catid=22   [Retrieved   9 January 2007].

Toscano, A. (2005), 'Axiomatic', in *The Deleuze Dictionary*, A. Parr (ed.), Edinburgh: Edinburgh University Press, pp. 17–18.

Watson, J. (2005), 'Schizo-Performativity? Neurosis and Politics in Judith Butler and Felix Guattari', *Women: A Cultural Review* 16(3) pp. 305–20.

Notes

We would like to extend our thanks to Surya Parekh for his comments on an earlier draft of this chapter.

1. An axiom is a self-evident truth that requires no proof, or a universally accepted rule. 'Axiomatic' is a word Deleuze and Guattari use to explain the inherent value of objects in relation to their contexts. In very broad terms, an 'axiomatic system' is one in which the value of labour and material is produced by the system: the axiom is what drives the system and it is a product of the system. See A. Toscano (2005), 'Axiomatic', in *The Deleuze Dictionary* A. Parr (ed.), Edinburgh University Press, pp. 17–18.

2. Concepts are often the products of habits in thought. Deleuze and Guattari state: 'The English nomadise over the old Greek earth, broken up, fractalised, and extended to the entire universe. We cannot even say that they have concepts like the French and the Germans; but they acquire them, they only believe in what is acquired – not because everything comes from the senses but *because a concept is acquired by inhabiting, by pitching one's tent, by contracting a habit*' (Deleuze and Guattari, 1996: 105, authors' emphasis).

3. The Body without Organs is also found in the German language version of Marx's *Economic and Political Manuscripts of 1844*. The English translation does not include the phrase Bodies without Organs, but the German version does.

Chapter 4

Every 'One' – a Crowd, Making Room for the Excluded Middle

Dorothea Olkowski

Do you long for the power of a concept of self? Simply repeat after me, 'I think, therefore I am', and all the doubting, thinking and being of the *cogito* are yours, your persona. Given the multitude of forces at work, each ready to claim sovereignty, we might have to embark on a more hazardous outing, another spin through the world which puts philosophical intuition into play and which recalls us to our finitude in order to construct logics and languages influenced by the unperceived, unknown past that nonetheless inhabits us, like light rays diffracting into spectra. (Olkowski 2007: 22–3)

The Brittlestar and Classical Dynamics

Physicist and philosopher Karen Barad has given us an account of an amazing sea creature, the Brittlestar, an invertebrate related to starfish, a creature that has no eyes, but is all eyes. The approximately ten thousand spherically domed calcite crystals covering the five limbs and central body of the Brittlestar function as microlenses that collect and focus light directly onto nerve bundles which are part of the Brittlestar's diffuse nervous system, giving it compound-eye capability (Barad in press). The Brittlestar's microlenses are optimised to maximise visual acuity enabling them to discern predators or discover hiding places. However, all of this activity takes place in a creative tension between the resolution of detail and diffraction effects and between geometrical and physical optics. Scientists, she notes, are studying the Brittlestar in the hope of mimicking its technique for producing vision. Of special interest is the information that the Brittlestar is a creature without a brain; it is simply a visualising apparatus, a metamorphosing optical system. As Barad forcefully notes, 'there is no *res cogitans* agonizing about the postulated gap (of its own making) between itself and *res extensa*. There is no optics of mediation, no noumena/phenomena distinction, no question of representation'

(Barad in press). Instead, the Brittlestar is the model of *intra-action*, constantly breaking off and regenerating its bodily boundaries as it enfolds bits of its environment within itself and expels parts of its own body into the surrounding environment. In this way, the Brittlestar cannot be said to exist as an autonomous entity positioned inside a spacetime frame of reference, neither that of a Euclidean container nor even that of a dynamical manifold specified by classical science. There is no pre-existent container or manifold within which the creature exists and moves along spacetime co-ordinates while its body is made and remade. Instead, the Brittlestar might be said to undergo what I would call a spatio-temporalisation, what Barad refers to as 'space-time-matter-in the making' (Olkowski 2007: 33–40; and Barad in press).

To truly understand the Brittlestar and its ongoing spatio-temporalisation calls for new ontological and epistemological structures. The pure *cogito* can only be enacted in the binary sphere where it remains independent of extension. It knows only the content of its immediate thoughts, those that can be intuited clearly and distinctly in the present moment without the aid of memory, sensation or even reason. In order to go beyond this immediacy, it must call upon divine intercession. But even then, it remains committed to the idea of the world in the mind while ignoring or effacing that aspect of the mind that is in the world. Barad argues that knowing is not a human-dependent characteristic but a feature of the world in its differential becoming, that *the world articulates itself differentially*, performing and articulating what matters, whereby different material intra-actions produce different materialisations of the world. Moreover, differentiating is not about othering/separating, but about making connections and commitments. Thus Brittlestars are not pure bits of nature or blank slates for the imprinting of culture but are engaged in making a difference in a world of continuous differential becoming (Barad in press). The implications that can be drawn from the study of the Brittlestar are numerous. But among them are certainly the ideas that nature makes and unmakes itself experimentally and that nature's differentiations of its own material were *never binary*. In this, Barad's onto-epistemology strongly resembles that of Gilles Deleuze.

Classical physics developed the rules for differentiating complicated functions by starting from the formula for a curve and calculating the formula for the gradient (or steepness) of that curve by taking small differences in the x and y directions and computing the gradients of the resultant straight lines – the gradient function is called the derivative of the original function (Devlin 1994: 90). 'The crucial step . . . was to shift attention from the essentially static situation concerning a gradient at a particular point P to the dynamic process of successive approximation of the gradient [of the curve] by gradients of straight lines starting at P' (Devlin 1994: 87, 88). From this, Deleuze makes 'a complete determination with regard to the existence and distribution of . . . [regular and singular] points which depends upon a completely different instance', an instance characterised in terms of a field of vectors (Devlin 1994: 44).[1] The goal here is to explicitly link differential equations and vector fields. A vector is an abstract entity that has magnitude and direction in a plane or in three-dimensional space, or in a space of four or more dimensions in vector space, from which may be projected an infinity of possible trajectories in spacetime (Devlin 1994: 44).[2] A vector field is defined, by Deleuze, as the complete determination of a problem given in terms of the existence, number and distribution of points that are its condition. This corresponds fairly well to the more or less standard mathematical definition where a vector field is defined as associating a vector to every point in the field space. Vector fields are used in physics to model observations, such as the movement of a fluid or the transformations of Brittlestars, which include a direction for each point of the observed space. In mathematics (specifically linear algebra), the rules of association, commutation and distribution define vector space without reference to magnitude or directions. Thus they may be utilised in a variety of fields whose terms are not material or physical as well as in the material and physical realm.[3]

The rules governing vector fields, association, commutation and distribution are the least restrictive set of linear rules that remain commutative, that is, for binary operations, any order is possible.[4] These rules have their equivalents in logic where association is an expression of logical equivalence permitting the valid regrouping of simple propositions; it governs the relations, which is to say, the connections between subject and predicate (Kant 1965: 108). In syllogistic terms, this would be expressed as the categorical relation.[5] Deleuze argues that the rules for vector space apply to nature and so nature itself is associative, commutative and distributive, where mere association – as opposed to unity – means that the laws of nature distribute parts which cannot be totalised, and that nature is conjunctive, expressing itself as this and that, this or that, rather than as Being, One or Whole. The claim is that we can never have knowledge of nature as a whole. Divine power is nothing but nature's diverse parts (places, species, lands and waters); each self is not identical to any other; and every 'body' comprising the world consists of diverse matter. As such, nature is associative, commutative and distributive and our knowledge of nature is derived from understanding these immanent, regulative functions. If nature's immanent, regulative functions are associative, commutative and distributive, each of these, as mathematical or logical operations, reflects a view of nature as the power of things to exist one by one without any possibility of them being gathered together in a unity (Deleuze 1990: 266–7). Following these rules, whatever has been added together can be taken apart and reformulated. Thus, becoming is everywhere and the claim made for Brittlestars, that they are 'living breathing mutating lensing systems that transgress the sacrosanct divides between organic and inorganic, machine and animal, epistemé and techné, matter and intelligibility, macro and micro', is one with the claim that they might be 'desiring-machines', connecting, then disjoining and differentially conjoining former binaries in the creation of difference. Thus, as Barad observes, researchers of these creatures are not external observers but they are engaged in the co-constitution of 'we' and 'they'; they are entangled, and as 'subject' and 'object' are mutually constituted. Similarly, the bodies of Brittlestars are not passive materiality awaiting the meaning-giving acts of culture and history, for 'intelligibility and materiality are not fixed aspects of the world, but rather intertwined agential performances' (Barad in press). When bodies are performances not things, the specific embodiment of an entity, whether Brittlestar or human being, is that of 'the being of the world in its dynamic specificity' (Barad in press).

Brittlestar Sensibility?

And yet, Barad's encouraging reformulation, even as it breaks up linear causality, binary thinking and being through constant *intra-action* in differential becoming, remains within the limits of that structure of differential becoming, as does the concept of differentiation set out by Deleuze. In Barad's formulation as in Deleuze's, mind is a specific material configuration, or as Deleuze argues, an assemblage of affects and percepts connecting, disjoining and conjoining with one another. As Barad defines it, differential becoming implies the repetition of a significant pattern for which there will be a variety of differences among its phenomena. For both, contingency lies in particles; every assemblage of particles produces a different world, a different entity, an unpredictable entity, but within the range of a particular pattern oriented by an attractor (Rouse 2004: 147). An attractor is defined as a set of states, invariant under the dynamics, which neighbouring states in a given basin or arena approach asymptotically in the course of dynamic evolution (http://mathworld. wolfram.com/Attractor.html).[6] This model underscores the difficulty if not impossibility of distinguishing object and world or subject and object. Barad makes reference to quantum physics, and the idea that the position of any entity characterises the entire arrangement or assemblage within which it exists. Thus that within certain arrangements only position and not momentum can be determined because that system has no definite momentum apart from the intra-actions of phenomena with the environment (Rouse 2004: 149). However, even in experimental situations where it is difficult to identify a phenomenon by means of a repetitive pattern in an environment, it is still the *intelligible* pattern of the experiment that reveals the *unintelligible* complexity of the environment (Rouse 2004: 149). Thus intelligence and intelligibility formally account for the Brittlestar's ongoing differential self-articulation, *but do not take the Brittlestar's own sensibility into account*. From the point of view of intelligible differentiation, which is a view from 'outside', Brittlestar sensibility is unintelligible. The structure described by Deleuze is strikingly similar. Every subject or object is an event, *nothing but* the result of contingent affects and percepts which are themselves independent of and exceeding any living being, standing on their own, simply expressing a pure sensation – freeing it from objects and from states of a subject (Deleuze and Guattari 1994: 163–7). In addition, every event is an effect of concepts, prospects and functives (the objects of logic and mathematics). That is, forms of content (structured materialisations) and their forms of expression (structures) intra-act, constitute and define one another. Were the world not an ongoing process of trajectories differentiating themselves, there would be no intelligence either. It seems then that the binary thinking that arose most powerfully with the conception of an *ego cogito* has at last been overcome. And the implication of this is that all binaries, including those powerful cultural signs such as male-female, heterosexual-homosexual, rational-emotional, active-passive, and so on, have come undone. Deleuze, in particular, is quite specific about the mechanism by which this occurs.

Citing the Cartesian will to distinguish doubt from certitude, Deleuze notes that making such a distinction presupposes the good will of the thinker and the good nature of thought, that is, the expectation that identity, analogy, opposition and resemblance will be accompanied by the 'I think', such that I conceive, I judge, I imagine, I remember and perceive become the four branches of the *cogito* and 'difference becomes an object of representation always in relation to a conceived identity, a judged analogy with other genera, an imagined opposition of predicates or a perceived similitude' (Deleuze 1994: 137–8). Difference, differentiation and even repetition are lost to recognition in a concept, distribution through analogy, reproduction in imagination and resemblance through perception (Deleuze 1994: 145). These aspects of the *cogito* do nothing to disturb thought; they are clearly objects of recognition whereby thought recognises itself in things and in the comfortable certainties of the *cogito*. What is problematic is that truths generated in this manner are, in fact, no more than hypothetical, they assume or presuppose exactly what is in question and therefore lack certainty, if that is what is meant by absolute necessity (Deleuze 1994: 139). What forces us to think differently is possible through a violent disjunction in the logical sense of this term. Deleuze points out that in *The Republic*, amid the violence of Socrates's encounter with the sophist Thrasymachus, Socrates recalls the Idea of justice, an Idea not able to be remembered on the empirical level. Yet, influenced by empirical, moral motives, Plato misses the opportunity to cast aside common sense and the empirical, and thereby clouds *thought*. Faced with the claim that something is both just and unjust, Plato insists on making sense of the empirical realm and insists on the law of non-contradiction and the law of excluded middle. The former establishes that for any proposition, that proposition and its negation are never both true, and the latter, that for a given proposition and its negation, at least one must be true (Hass 2002: 75). As Marjorie Hass has argued, symbolically, logical contradiction is a structural relation of dominance and erasure because it constructs difference in terms of exclusion (2002: 76). The law of excluded middle or contrariety is less hierarchical insofar as a single term may have a variety of contraries that need not indicate the lack of a specific property, so that if both contraries are asserted, the system does not collapse. Yet, Plato and Aristotle generally presume that the contrary of a term is not a pluralistic set (such as bad, sad or unrepentant, for the term good), but that the contrary of good is nongood, reinstating privilege and hierarchical unity (Hass 1998: 35–6).

Deleuze, as such, seems to use the idea of contrariety in this latter sense, as commensurate with non-contradiction. For Socrates, contrariety disrupts common sense and compels even the Socratic soul to probe, to problematise, 'arousing thought in itself' (Plato 524e).[7] But in the end, the sensible discordant encounter with contrariety must be harmonised. Coaxing Thrasymachus to become gentle, to cease being angry, Socrates upholds the law of non-contradiction and the law of the excluded middle, thereby affirming binaries and their hierarchical structures. Seeking to escape this fate, although caught up in the same logical system, Deleuze proposes something other. As we noted above, he proposes a spacetime, a manifold, in which nature is associative, commutative and distributive, where association is opposed to unity, and the laws of nature *distribute parts* which cannot be totalised, so that nature is conjunctive, expressing itself as this *and* that, this *or* that, rather than as Being, One or Whole. That things exist one by one without the possibility of being gathered together is the expression of purely external relations of association within this spacetime field, an immanent field. Such relations are further characterised in terms of the chance collisions of particles that exist one by one and are not unified or governed by a divine or transcendental principle. Instead, they are connected by means of differential relations where the construction of vector fields are organised by the functions of differential calculus. In other words, Deleuze proposes a purely *formal* model, bypassing the empirical and commonsensical.

In order to overcome the limits imposed by Socrates's refusal of contrariety and non-contradiction, Deleuze proposes an image of thought *unsullied by the opacity of physical existence*, that is, an image set free from recognition, similarity, identity and analogy. Qualitative opposition within the sensible is quickly tamed by common sense which knows that contraries cannot coexist in the object. The simultaneity of contraries which violates the logical law of excluded middle, according to Deleuze, *can only be thought*; it can only be thinking. It is *thought* that is pure difference, differentiating itself in a continuous trajectory. It will be the same for memory, imagination, language, for all so-called faculties. This transcendental empiricism is empirical only insofar as it designates as imperceptible and unthinkable that which takes place at the empirical level and thereby immediately transcends it (Deleuze 1994: 144). Opposition (contrariety), resemblance, identity and analogy are effects of this thinking in the empirical realm where common sense and the law of non-contradiction prevail. For the faculties, there is only violence, the violence of not harmonising or unifying one another, instead *disjoining* all that they encounter. Disjunction of the faculties is their *discordant harmony*. This is how its elements exist one by one without the possibility of being gathered together. First, thought undergoes its clash with the unrecognisable sign, the *being* of the sensible, not sensibility itself. The sign defies common sense and good sense, which is the 'coexistence of contraries, the coexistence of more and less in an unlimited qualitative becoming', which can never be sensible, which is always only given as a sign (Deleuze 1994: 141).[8] Then, in place of one's own sensibilities, there is the violated 'soul', the fractured I that is forced to pose a problem and in the trauma of this violence to forget anything that can be recalled, anything seen, heard, imagined or thought, in order to think and recall that which has *never been empirical*, which is transcendental with respect to both sensibility and memory, thus, what is essentially nonsense and forgetfulness. In the midst of this original violence, the faculties themselves are forced to their limits, meaning they are forced into discordant harmony, their *disjunction*, the open-ended disorder of the faculties, so that each may pursue its own 'essential' projects, the transcendental projects of thinking, willing or imagining (Deleuze 1994: 140–1).[9] If a faculty is forced to its limit, this does not imply that it reaches some end, but rather that it moves forever, closer and closer, towards some point without ever crossing it.

Transcendentally, in a purely formal sense, in the realm of thought, binaries are overcome and the formal Idea, rather than determining that something is male or female, animal or vegetable, remains *indeterminate*. But does this translate into an empirical world for which we can say the same, for which Barad seems to want to claim the excluded middle? For Deleuze, outside of the formal transcendental realm of thinking, willing and judging, we succumb over and over again to non-contradiction and the law of the excluded middle. Yet, following Barad, it seems that the terms 'difference' and 'diverse' are concepts resonating in the world, and that they inhabit the sensible realm, those states capable of being formalised by the differentiating continuum of the transcendental sphere. Care must be taken, for Deleuze, all particles enter into the indeterminate Idea and its n-dimensions consisting of variables or co-ordinates. There they maximise the sets of relations between changes in variables and become defined as elements, effects of sets of relations, which do not change until the Idea itself alters its order and metric, until a new Idea is posed. The notion of limit in mathematics certainly implies this.[10] Although the conception of the problematic Idea that undergoes continuous differentiation/differenciation is a conception that undermines the recognition, representation, habituation, equalisation nexus of classical, modern thought, replacing it with the Idea of difference and the diverse, an important question remains. Does it contribute to conceptions of intra-activity beyond the formal and external description of particles? Does it characterise the Brittlestar's own sensible existence (Deleuze 1994: 245)?[11] Let us briefly examine this.

It has been remarked that,

> We are used to the idea that a physical theory can describe an infinitude of different worlds. This is because there is a lot of freedom in their application. Newton's physics gives us the laws by which particles move and interact with one another, but it does not otherwise specify the configurations of the particles. Given any arrangement of the particles that make up the universe, and any choices for their initial motions, Newton's laws can be used to predict the future. [. . .] Newton's theory describes an infinite number of different worlds, each connected with a different solution to the theory, which is

arrived at by starting with the particles in different positions. However, each solution to Newton's theory describes a single universe. (Smolin 2001: 42–3)

Every trajectory in each universe is defined by laws that specify the movement and interaction of particles. But even for dynamical differential systems, the rules of motion are given, what may be contingent are the particular particles themselves, that is, which particles enter into any given trajectory and in what order? Which affects, percepts, concepts, prospects and functives? In an open system, such as that proposed by Barad and Deleuze, as opposed to Newton's closed universe, this cannot be predicted, thus every configuration of particles produces not only a different world, but an unpredictable world. But what does not alter are the rules themselves that specify the movement and interaction of particles. Moreover, in these worlds, space and time are given not emergent. They are the pre-given, pre-existent manifold, and time is simply a parameter of *any space whatever*, a fourth dimension, a means for differentiating different spaces, but not an emergent and unpredictable reality. Where the spacetime manifold is always, already given, creation per se disappears insofar as predictability is a requirement of the system.

We have noted Barad's proposal that for quantum physics, such predictability seems to disappear, since the position of any entity characterises the entire arrangement or assemblage within which it exists thus that within certain arrangements only position and not momentum can be determined because that system has no definite momentum apart from the intra-actions of phenomena with the environment (Rouse 2004: 149). But is this uncertainty not merely a function of our starting point, the fact that even a differential system operates as a classical system in a pre-established continuous spacetime manifold? Is it not possible that from another perspective, something else altogether may be taking place? In other words, if we want the excluded middle to operate not only formally (logically, mathematically) determining entities from the outside, but also, physically, sensibly, from within, then we must find a model of sensible life that makes this possible. Let us begin then with a brief questioning of sense and sensibility, in order to think about the problems arising with the retreat to a purely formal system that eschews what we will call, not the common sense empirical, but the sensible. And let us consider positing, not an empirical individual subject to non-contradiction and the law of excluded middle, but a vulnerable sensible intuition that is not merely a singular event, a singular agent, an effect of formal processes, but is itself a new structure in which what point of view exists does so as a crowd.

The Past Light Cone of an Event

Many readers will be familiar with the image of a cone the philosopher Henri Bergson utilised to characterise ontological memory, that memory created by the imperceptible influences of states in the world on an individual sensibility. The cone describes a situation in which the entire past coexists with each new present in relation to which it is now past. Describing this in terms derived from the theory of general relativity, Bergson states that 'memory, laden with the whole of the past, responds to the appeal of the present state by two simultaneous movements, one of translation, by which it moves in its entirety to meet experience, thus contracting more or less, though without dividing, with a view to action; and the other of rotation upon itself by which it turns toward the situation of the moment' (1988: 168–9). The light cone is a well-known structure in physics. It assumes particular importance in the theory of general relativity. General relativity tells us that the speed of light is invariant and nothing (no causal effect and no information) travels faster than the speed of light. 'The causal past of an event consists of all the events that could have influenced it. The influence must travel from some state in the past at the speed of light or less. So the light rays arriving at an event form the outer boundary of the past of an event and make up what we call the *past light cone of an event*' (Smolin 2001: 58). By drawing a light cone around every event, we may specify all the causal relations affecting it. Doing this with every event would yield the causal structure of the universe. This is significant insofar as 'most of the story of our universe is the story of the causal relations among its events . . . [but crucially and unlike differential dynamical systems] the causal structure is not fixed . . . it evolves, subject to laws' (Smolin 2001: 59). The question is, of course, how? 'How many events are contained in the passage of a signal from you to me . . . How many events have there been in the whole history of the universe in the past of this *particular* moment?' (Smolin 2001: 60). Or, how many events constitute a point of view, making it not an individual subject to the law of non-contradiction but a crowd for which the law of excluded middle obtains? The answer to these questions depends on the nature of spacetime.

Barad and Deleuze assume that space and time are continuous. This means that they can be (at least in thought) divided infinitely, that there is no smallest possible unit of space or time. This implies that for any event, at least on the level of particles, it could always be faster and the number of events, being infinitely divisible, could be infinite. Such assumptions are non-physical, since no physical person or thing can travel faster than the speed of light nor can it be infinitely divided. However, another emergent approach to this question is worth considering, that is, the idea that space and time are discrete.[12] If space and time are discrete, they cannot be infinitely divided and the number of events or states may be very large, but it is still finite. What this suggests is that continuous or smooth spacetime may be useful illusions but that the world consists of discrete sets of events that can be counted (Smolin 2001: 61–2). Referring back to the conception of light cones, rather than a single cone, a single event, let us think about a causal network of interconnected states for which every perspective and every state consists of a multiplicity of cones linked to one another, influencing one another, 'combinatorial structures' that have been called 'spin networks', networks giving rise to situationally-organised, intra-active behaviour.

Such a concept is the work of a young physicist, Fotini Markopoulou, who is searching for a physical description of the universe, thus one that is not based on the physically impossible but mathematically conceivable notion of infinite divisibility of continuous spacetime. What Markopoulou proposes is a causal structure of spacetime that codes, not the view from outside, that Barad and Deleuze utilise, but rather, what an observer inside the universe can observe (Markopoulou 1999: 1). Arguing against classical models precisely because, as Barad points out, they lead to uncertainty, Markopoulou suggests utilising causal sets (large collections of causal relations), sets of events in *discrete* spacetime partially ordered by causal relations. Moreover, Markopoulou proposes to work with *evolving* sets that give the causal past of each event as well as the causal structure of each event in a causal set. She further suggests that evolving sets satisfy a particular algebra called Heyting algebra which utilises a non-standard logic whose historical development has been related to understanding the passage of time. This logic is called Intuitionistic logic and unlike standard symbolic, binary logic it does not forbid the so-called 'excluded middle'. Whereas the classical Boolean mathematician believes that a statement x is true or false whether or not she has proof for it, Intuitionism does not allow proof by contradiction. Thus, from the onset, it does not consider x to be true or false unless there is a proof for it. In other words, if x may be true tomorrow or false tomorrow, without a proof the option is open, thus Intuitionistic logic is suited to time evolution, where certain physical statements become true at a certain time (Markopoulou 1999: 34–5).

In this manner, the logic used by observers to describe what they see has been modified. Moreover, any single observer is able to know only a subset of true facts regarding their universe (Markopoulou 1999: 1).

What is crucial here for my point is that 'a theory with internal observables is fundamentally different than a theory describing a system external to the observers', as the former obey Intuitionistic logic and the latter obey so-called Boolean logic and observe the law of non-contradiction (Markopoulou 1999: 2). Of equal importance is the idea of a theory that refers to observations made from 'inside'. For physicists, this means inside the universe, and such observations can only be partial, that is, they contain information that is in the causal past of an observer in a particular region of spacetime. They do not contain information about the so-called future, information that should be obtainable from a classical dynamical perspective. In terms of light cones, this means that information that constitutes a particular point of view intra-acts within the boundaries of any light cone where space and time are not taken to be infinitely divisible or infinitely extensible. Even though we are operating entirely within the realm of linear causality, there is not single wave function for the entire universe, that is, what is being measured or described is the evolution from each spacetime to another spacetime. Spin network graphs have been used to model quantum spatial geometry and events in a causal set that are *evolving*, yielding a quantum causal history (Markopoulou 1999: 3). One significant implication of this model is that unlike dynamical systems, the manifold of spacetime is not pre-given. Rather than the Brittlestars dynamically changing form of content and form of expression which takes place in a pre-established spacetime manifold and is produced or assembled from outside by the elements of that manifold, the model of quantum causal histories specifies that spacetime and the states that evolve, the stage and the actors, evolve together (Markopoulou 2002: 3). This is particularly useful for the exploration of states that occur at a scale where classical physics fails, the Planck scale of quantum states, and additionally, it allows for the construction of a point of view that is not at all an individual but can only be called a crowd, a point of view according to which different observers 'see' or 'live' partly different, partial views of the universe, partial views which nonetheless overlap. How can this be?

If the causal past of an event consists of all the events that could have influenced it, these influences travel from some state in the past at the speed of light or less. We have noted that the light rays arriving at an event form the outer boundary of the past of an event and make up the past light cone of an event. Under these conditions, the causal structure of states evolves and the motion of matter is a consequence of that evolution. And we have asked, following this model, what if continuous differential spacetime (so-called smooth space) is just a useful illusion?

What if, from the perspective of a different system, the world can be said to be composed of discrete states, states on a very small scale, but nevertheless, states discontinuous with respect to both space and time on that very small scale? Under such conditions, what might be observed? Is it possible that this structure and these processes might involve the construction of a vulnerable and sensitive contingency, an ontological spatiotemporalisation, an ever-changing perspective made up of a crowd of perspectives in the heterogeneity of space and time? Such a perspective, if it is thinkable, if it is real, could manifest itself as a sort of history, but a complex causality, layers and layers of states, always susceptible to realignment, to patterns and particles resolving in a point of view that is the effect of a crowd of influences and itself contributes to a crowd of influences. These conical flows of information, often imperceptible, influence one another, and in this they influence the sensibility of all things.

Given that this is something extremely difficult to situate, it is much more likely to be overlooked. If it is the manner in which states (including very tiny states) influence and alter one another, this implication is that these states influence and alter sensibility, all sensibility. These influences are not the objects of perception nor of consciousness; they cannot be experienced as increases or decreases of power, as the raising or lowering of intensities. They are, at least, capable of receptivity. If they are noticed at all, it is usually only insofar as they are *felt*, felt as pleasure and pain, discomfort and distress. Their influence on sensibility comes via a sensory system, thus they do not constitute a personal memory. This might be the way Brittlestars evolve in an absolute, immediate, nonconscious consciousness, an ontological unconscious whose passive existence no longer refers to an individual or to a being but is unceasingly suggested in the reflection, refraction and dispersion of light, in a spectrum. But how are we to study and understand such states? What is our access to this felt pleasure and pain and in what manner might it indicate the existence of states that influence and alter our sensibility and that of Brittlestars? Researchers in the cognitive sciences have been examining precisely these questions. Thus let us turn to some of their work in order to study the influence of such very small states that are felt as pleasure and pain.

It has of course been well noted that within the cognitive science tradition the 'temptation to conflate emotional feelings and cognitive processes remains rather too prominent' and that scientifically important distinctions can be made between affects and cognitions (Panksepp 2005: 11).[13] Although the precise dividing line between affective sensations and cognitive processes is difficult to draw, there are credible ways to distinguish them (Panksepp 2005: 32). The great mystery is how feeling occurs and influences bodies. The French physiologist Michel Cabanac, now working in Canada, affirms the necessity of differentiating not only affective sensation and cognition but also sensation and perception. Although psychologists made this distinction as early as the eighteenth century, it was blurred by the otherwise important advances in the study of perception by the Gestaltists who incorporated sensation and content into global experience. Given the tendency of such theorists to refer almost exclusively to auditory and visual perceptions, which are the principal channels of communication among humans, other sensory inputs which are less complex were ignored (Cabanac 1995: 403). Another difficulty in characterising sensation comes from the attempt to characterise sensation in terms of its attributes. Certainly, sensation has attributes but which ones? Is it quality and intensity, duration and extension, clearness, affectivity? And what about attributes such as vision that have their own attributes like light and colour or sound which has pitch and volume? As we can see, a simpler descriptive model of sensation might well be called for, since not all sensations have all attributes and some sensations may have attributes that exceed the definitions (Cabanac 1995: 404).

Cabanac proposes an alternative model based on the idea of multidimensional scaling, that is, sensation as a multidimensional response to a stimulus. Cabanac's abstract model incorporates four dimensions, quantity or intensity, quality (the nature of the stimulus), affectivity (usefulness with respect to pleasure and displeasure), and duration, insofar as temporal synthesis is intrinsic to all affective sensations. If temporality is a fourth dimension of a multidimensional structure, then it can be understood, as we have maintained, as a stage that emerges only with and in terms of its contents or actors and does not pre-exist them. In identifying the quality, Cabanac urges us to focus on the sensation itself in addition to the receptor organs. This is facilitated by separating the idea of sensitivity from that of sensation. Thus *sensitivity* can be defined as the capacity of an afferent neuron to detect a physical or chemical change at its endings and to transmit this information to nervous centres where the sensor may be an organ or simply a free nerve ending, or not identifiable at all. Afferent pathways may consist of as few as one neuron or a chain of them. On the other hand, *sensation* is defined in terms of cognition. 'The brain possesses properties that can no more be explained by its neuronal constituents than life can be explained by the atomic or molecular properties of the constituents of the living cell. Consciousness is one such property and sensation can be defined as the emergence of sensitivity into consciousness' (Cabanac 1995: 407). The important implication here is that sensitivity and thus sensation are not limited to the five senses but may occur at any point in the body with a few minor exceptions. Many afferent pathways are limited to a bundle of a few neurons whose meagre input is overwhelmed by that of the classical senses, which also have the advantage of large, fast and frequent spikes in their 'A' fibres rather than the weaker 'C' fibres of other neurons (Cabanac 1995: 409). Although neurons are larger than Planck scale, neurons consist of highly ordered networks comprised of microtubules and other filamentous structures which organise cellular activities. Paramecium sensory input and movement, cell division ('mitosis'), cell growth, synapse formation and all aspects of co-ordinated functions are accomplished by microtubules, cylindrical polymers of the protein tubulin arranged in hexagonal lattices comprising the cylinder wall. It has been speculated that these qualify as quantum phenomena. Additionally, insofar as there are neurons in the human body that may be triggered by even a single photon (a quantum event), it may be reasonable to assume that quantum sensitive neurons are playing a significant role in the construction of sensitivities (Penrose 1989: 400–1; Hammeroff and Penrose 1996: 507–40; Cabanac 1995: 408). The speculative implication of this would be that every 'one', every so-called individual is constructed as a crowd by the many but not infinite influences of intersecting light cones over time.

Cabanac maintains that any afferent pathway is a potential sensitivity, yielding everything from visceral sensations in the limbs, neck and chest to heartbeats, movements in the abdomen and other physical urges (1995: 412–13). The list of potential sensitivities may extend to a sensitivity for speed and even for time. Moreover, the lack of adequate words with which to describe the more ephemeral sensitivities serves as a barrier to acknowledging them. Since peripheral sensors adapt quickly to circumstances, the intensity of a sensation can be understood in terms of the frequency of spikes arriving at the centres. Cabanac connects the affectivity of sensation directly to the experience of pleasure and displeasure. Pleasure-displeasure may occur on the sensory level as the enjoyment of a stimulus. It may also involve aesthetics, desire in the sense of a fulfilled need and accomplishment. The last three require greater understanding and would seem best characterised as intentional sensations. Cabanac places pleasure and displeasure on a single affective gradient from the extremely negative or distress to the extremely positive or delight. It is, ultimately, the *wisdom of the body* that engages the organism in its own sensations and leads it to seek pleasurable sensations and avoid unpleasurable ones (1995: 415). But the affective dimension is a contingent one, meaning whether a given sensitivity is felt as pleasure or displeasure varies with the internal state of the subject, for the subject tends towards relative equilibrium whether it results from pleasure seeking or autonomic responses (shivering or sweating for example in the case of cooling or warmth).

One of the great advantages of conceptualising non-intentional feelings in this way is precisely its simplicity. If it is the case that any afferent fibre may arouse a sensation, it does not require a high level of behaviour or rationality for the body to make use of its own feelings of pleasure and displeasure (Cabanac 1995: 414). Furthermore, pleasure and displeasure are linked to the well-being and happiness of the organism. Of course, pleasure, along with feeling in general, has never been a topic that philosophers have embraced, bringing into play, as it does, the morals of pleasure opposed by the morals of duty (Cabanac 1995: 415). Yet, the value of pleasure/displeasure is one with the view that our knowledge of the world and our intentional relation to the world is 'filtered' by the so-called chemicophysical window of our own sensitivities and then again by the biological and cultural formations of our brains. As Cabanac expresses this, what we think about sensitivity and sensation might well influence how we think and, I would add, what we think. This latter because sensation links us to our environment in a way that does not preclude cognition but gives rise to it. It may be the case that phylogenetically, sensitivities emerged into consciousness as sensations when they proved useful to the organism. They allowed the organism to become aware of environmental stimuli in a multidimensional rather than singular context. Not just vision, smell, sound and touch, but myriad possible sensibilities, interrelated and influencing one another, making it possible to discern what in the environment might be useful and what might be harmful, constituting that organism's duration, its immanent temporality, making it possible for organisms to anticipate and to change. *Without this nothing new would occur.* If organisms possess similar neurons and afferent pathways, and if these pathways transmit information to the brain from the common environment, then the conclusion is that all conscious events are likely to have the same or a similar structure. There is no question but that this is a highly speculative thesis, constructed on speculative theories in physics and cognitive science, but nevertheless it seems to be a much more hopeful theory. To state that every living thing is a point-of view that is constructed *from within* through its vulnerable sensitivities, and that it is not constructed as a singular entity, but as a crowd, seems to hold profound implications for our self-understanding as well as our social, political and environmental constructions. For, the very same information that constructs 'me' may also be said to be constructing 'you', for everywhere in the universe there are photons, light rays coming from the past, influencing us, constructing us, so that we are, every one of us – a crowd.

References

Barad, K. (in press), 'Queer Causation and the Ethics of Mattering', in *Queering the Non/Human*, ed. N. Giffney and M. J. Hird, Aldershot: Ashgate Press.

Bergson, H. (1988), *Matter and Memory*, trans. N. M. Paul and W. S. Palmer, New York: Zone Books.

Cabanac, Michel (1995), 'What is Sensation? Gnoti se auton,' in *Biological Perspectives on Motivated Activities*, ed. Roderick Wong, Northwood, NJ: Ablex, pp. 399–417.

Copi, I. M. and Cohen, C. (1990), *Introduction to Logic*, New York: Macmillan.

Deleuze, G. (1990), *The Logic of Sense*, trans. Mark Lester with Charles Stivale, Constantin V. Boundas (ed.), New York: Columbia University Press.

Deleuze, G. (1994), *Difference and Repetition*, trans. Paul Patton, New York: Columbia University Press.

Deleuze, G. and Guattari, F. (1994), *What is Philosophy?*, trans. Hugh Tomlinson and Graham Burchell, New York: Columbia University Press.

Devlin, K. (1994), *Mathematics: The Science of Patterns, The Search for Order in Life, Mind, and the Universe*, New York: Scientific American Library.

Hameroff, S. and Penrose, R. (1996), 'Orchestrated Objective Reduction of Quantum Coherence in Brain Microtubules: the "Orch OR" Model for Consciousness', in *Toward a Science of Consciousness – The First Tucson Discussions and Debates*, ed. S. R. Hameroff, A. W. Kaszniak and A. C. Scott, Cambridge, MA: MIT Press.

Hass, M. (1998), 'Feminist Readings of Aristotelian Logic', in *Feminist Interpretations of Aristotle*, ed. Cynthia Freeland, University Park: Penn State University Press, pp. 19–40.

Hass, M. (2002), 'Fluid Thinking, Irigaray's Critique of Formal Logic', in *Representing Reason, Feminist Theory and Formal Logic*, eds Rachel Joffe Falmagne and Marjorie Hass, New York: Rowman and Littlefield, pp. 71–88.

Kant, I. (1965), *The Critique of Pure Reason*, trans. Norman Kemp Smith, New York: St Martin's Press.

Lane, R. D. and Nadel, L. (eds) (2000), *Cognitive Neuroscience of Emotion*, Oxford: Oxford University Press.

Markopoulou, F. (18 November 1999), 'The internal description of a causal set: What the universe looks like from inside', arXiv:gr-qc/9811053 v2: 1–35.

Markopoulou, F. (20 December 1999), 'An insider's guide to quantum causal histories', arXiv:hep-th/9912137 v2: 1–4.

Markopoulou, F. (7 November 2002), 'Planck-scale models of the universe,' arXiv:gr-qc/0210086 v2: 1–19.

Olkowski, D. (2007), *The Universal (In the Realm of the Sensible)*, Edinburgh and New York: Edinburgh and Columbia University Presses.

Panksepp, J. (March 2005), 'Affective Consciousness: Core Emotional Feelings in Animals and Humans', in *Cognition and Consciousness*, 14(1) pp. 30–80.

Penrose, R. (1989), *The Emperor's New Mind*, Oxford: Oxford University Press, pp. 507–540.

Penrose, R. (1996), http://www.quantumconsciousness.org/penrose-hameroff/fundamentality.html%06

Plato (1997), *Republic*, trans. G. M. A. Grube, revised C. D. C. Reeve, in *Plato, Complete Works*, Indianapolis: Hackett Publishing.

Rouse, J. (Winter 2004), 'Barad's Feminist Naturalism', in *Hypatia, Journal of Feminist Philosophy*, 19(1) pp. 142–61.

Smolin, L. (2001), Three Roads to Quantum Gravity, New York: Basic Books.

http://www.answers.com/topic/vector-space

http://mathworld.wolfram.com/Attractor.html

http://mathworld.wolfram.com/VectorField.html

http://www.quantumconsciousness.org/penrose-hameroff/fundamentality.html%06

http://www.vias.org/simulations/simusoft_vectorfields.html

Notes

1. See also http://www.vias.org/simulations/simusoft_vectorfields.html and http://mathworld.wolfram.com/VectorField.html
2. 'If you have a collection of entities called vectors, an operation of addition of two vectors to give a third vector and an operation of multiplication of a vector by a number to give another vector, and if these operations have the [appropriate properties, they are associative, commutative, distributive and closed under vector addition], then the entire system is called a vector space' (Devlin 1994: 44).
3. For a concise definition, see 'vector space'. *Britannica Concise Encyclopedia*. Encyclopædia Britannica, Inc., 2006. Answers.com 29 Jan. 2007. http://www.answers.com/topic/vector-space
4. For example: [(p v q) v r] may be replaced by [p v (q v r)] and [(p . q) . r] may be replaced by [p . (q . r)] (Copi and Cohen 1990: 692).
5. For example: (p v q) and (q v p) as well as (p . q) and (q . p) may replace one another (Copi and Cohen 1990: 694).
6. An asymptote is a line that continually approaches a given curve but does not meet it at any finite distance (http://mathworld.wolfram.com/Attractor.html).
7. Without contrariety and contradiction, would Platonic thought have developed?
8. It is the same clash as that decried by Plato, but this time without the resolution in harmony.
9. Without this forcing, Deleuze believes that we remain ignorant or minimally habituated.
10. See http://www.coolmath.com/limit1.htm for a graphic and simple discussion of the concept of limit in calculus.
11. Different/ciation indicates both the state of differential relations in the Idea and the qualitative and extensive series in which they are actualised.
12. Discontinuous spacetime belongs to the classical system of continuous spacetime. Discrete spacetime is part of the conceptualisation of quantum.
13. Citing R. D. Lane and L. Nadel.

Chapter 5

The Adventures of a Sex

Luciana Parisi

In queer theory the question of what is sex has been rethought in terms of the biological plasticity of the body as evidenced, for example, by hormone and genetic ambivalences neutralising the distinction between masculinity and femininity, female and male, leading to a notion of fundamental queerness of all sexes. The importance of such a notion lays in its indirect suggestion that sex, as the natural source of (culturally constructed) gender, does not coincide with the immutable fixed order of nature. On the other hand, however, a more explicitly political tendency in queer theory has reshaped the indirect claim for a fundamental queer biologism and has rather argued for the centrality of the discursive apparatus of power forming the complexity of sexual identities through practices of performativity. Here, the bio-logic of queerness is explained in terms of a gendered materiality, constantly being reconfigured by discursive apparatuses. For queer theory, such discursive exercises of power – or bio-power having material effects on the body-sex – is constantly open to resistance by the subversive performativity of signs, leading to ruptures in meanings, positions, roles of the gender-sex identification.

The centrality of performativity in queer theory has been recently re-elaborated in terms of posthuman material-discursive intra-actions, suggesting a new alliance between science and ontology (Barad 2005). However, this article suggests that the question of how does sexuality become queer remains still largely unaddressed in such posthuman queer theory, to the extent that sex, or what is given in sexuality, remains anchored to the primacy of gender as phenomena-in-things (Barad 2002), in the same way as materiality remains determined by the performativity of material-discursive apparatuses.

This article argues that notions of relational ontologies developed in the context of posthuman theories of performativity are not abstract enough to engage with the experiential adventures of a body-sex. Drawing on the philosophy of abstract materialism developed in the works of Gilles Deleuze and Felix Guattari, this article explores queer sexuality through the notion of the abstract machine as enabling us to conceive the pure experience, event and dramatisation of many sexes without falling back onto the ontological constitution of queer sexuality. The article will then argue that to affirm a queer ontology in the light of Deleuze and Guattari's philosophy of immanence (immanent desire), one may need to engage with the virtual worlds of many sexes implicated in the individuation of a multiplicity of sexuality producing utterances, styles, politics that do not revolve around the being queer itself.

0. Fundamental Queerness

> Hocquenghem can be everywhere on the spiral and say all at once: homo-sexual desire is specific, there are homosexual utterances, but homosexual-ity is nothing, it's just a word, and yet let's take it literally, let's pass through it, to make it yield all the otherness it contains – and this otherness is not the unconscious of psychoanalysis, but the progression of a future sexual becoming. (Deleuze 2004: 288)

In the preface to Hocquenghem's book *L'Après-Mai des faunes*, Deleuze explicitly warns against the psychoanalytical declaration that in the end 'we are all unconscious latent queer' (284). For Deleuze, Hocquenghem's book is concerned with homosexuality, but, at the same time and in opposition to the psychoanalytical bio-universality of sexual identity, it is a book that clearly claims 'no one is really homosexual'.

In this short preface, Deleuze emphasises that for Hocquenghem desire has nothing to do with the wholeness of Oedipal sexuality, the universal narrative of the family triangle. Indeed desire here represents nothing. It has no primary subject or object. Desire can only assemble, without constituting wholes: machinic breaks, partialities, discontinu-ities make desire. Deleuze thus suggests that queer desire only remains specific to a peculiar relationship with the Outside whose characteristics are present in staying not primarily with the same sex (that is, we are all queer and want to be recognised by the social order as such) so as to resist heteronormativity, but in embracing the non-reproductive order of sex (that is, the bio-social order of reproduction) by inventing, rather than constituting, sexuality. Such an invitation to invent sexuality appealing to a future of sexual becoming, however, is not quickly to be confused with the projection for a new future for queer politics, since this kind of future is already incorporated by the capitalisation of desire through the imperative 'you can now be whatever you want to be'.

Rather, a future of sexual becoming here entails the more implicit task of the production of novel utterances and modalities that do not and must not revolve around being queer itself. The becoming of sexuality thus demands neither the belief in a liberating future nor the impossibility of reaching a more inclusive social order, since these can only operate through the Oedipal law of the symbolic. The future of sexual becoming instead entails the activities of microsexual variations that are already here acting on a present spanning towards an immediate past-future, determined not by the psychobiology of sexual identity, but by the agitating activities of virtual sexes ready to invent a future in the everyday.

As Deleuze explains, in Hocquenghem's book utterances of sexuality define two political modalities. In the first place a modality about sexuality in general. The homosexual has nothing to do with phallocentrism since its sexual modality above all denounces the phallocentric repression of femininity. The point here, as Deleuze highlights, is not to reinsert any pseudo-signifier or symbolic relation that could erect homosexuality (and queer sexuality) to the status of transcendence through which all sexes can be explained. Indeed, the political identification with the very word homosexual, with the very margin-position is here denounced as a mere function of nominalism. '[. . .] language is not information or communication, but prescription, order and command. You will be on the margin. It's the centre that makes the margin' (286). Assigning a social status to intolerable sexuality makes it tolerable. What deviates from the law becomes constitutive of the law. And yet, Deleuze points at how a word by just being a word produces specific utterances, 'acting as if . . . out of defiance [. . .]. We will act as queens because we want it [. . .] We will take you at your word' (286). In this way, Deleuze points out, homosexuality will not close itself within an already constituted self, but will remain open to all possible implications, a micrological, microphysical reversible sex, a transmutation of sexes from one order to another, from flowers to motorcycles, 'an intensive continuum of substances' (287). In short, this book for Deleuze is an invitation to extract sexes from the stratification of desire into the whole of Sex, able to state – as an order-word – that 'in the end everyone's a little gay'. Rather, Deleuze suggests that the new homosexual can at last say: 'nobody is homosexual. [. . .] There is no more homosexual subject, but homosexual productions of desire, and homosexual assemblages that produce utterances, proliferating everywhere . . .' (288).

In this short preface, Deleuze denounces all attempts at identifying specific yet collective modes of desire with one sexuality and rather

points at how desiring assemblages become producers of a singular multiplicity of sexes never integrated into a whole. However, it may be
important to specify here that Deleuze's and Deleuze and Guattari's philosophy of immanence does not aim at liberating desire from an all-
constraining form of sexuality. This will imply confusing the field of
desire – of production and destruction, composition and decomposition
of assemblages – with an ultimate moral subject of desire. What the philosophy of immanent desire has to offer to the ontology of queer sexuality entails no ontological whole – all being is located in bio-psychical
essence or discursive constructions or in their intra-action – for sexual
identity. A philosophy of immanent desire rather demands an engagement with a material, at once abstract and concrete, metaphysics of a
multiplicity of sexes implicating the transformation of mental, affective,
social, political, aesthetic modalities. Such metaphysics has no bottom
ground to refer back to, no genealogical tree to evolve from, no bio-
ontology of sex to achieve. Instead, it can only be implicated in processes
of continual variations of sexes – a series of veritable adventures of sex –
whose conditions are not set primarily by a causal grid, a structure able
to filter what lies outside of itself, but rather by virtual activities, larval
bodies, agitating particles involving the becoming of an always collective desire: a swerve in the continual sequence of events, or a *clinamen*,
as Lucretius called it, which breaks off from the linear trajectory of the
arrow of time. For Deleuze, such a swerve points to an original determination in the direction of the movement of the atom, which remains
however unassignable or inaccessible in its actual taking place. This is
an intensive field of remarkable points – a multiplicity – of any causal
series, a 'lex atomi' that acts as guarantee of an irreducible plurality of
causes and exclusion of any totalised understanding of causality producing some universal destiny.[1] Lucretius stresses the random nature of
the swerve in blocs of spacetime, precisely to expose the possibility of
declining: a heterogeneous individuation in the process of being individuated, a becoming of the continual series of singular assemblages of
desire.

With this premise, this article will endeavour to ask if it is possible for
queer sexuality to be thought as an immanent philosophy of desire. In
particular, the article will discuss the centrality of the ontology of performativity – be it discursive or material-discursive – in queer theory and
consider whether this offers a challenge to psycho-bio-logic queerness as
the ultimate constitutor of all modalities of sex. Can the ontology of performativity provide a politics of future sexual becoming that defies the
bifurcation of culture from nature, gender from sex?

1. The Imperative of Performativity

Queer theory has strictly drawn on post-structuralist feminism to challenge precisely the biological ground of sex at the core of psychoanalysis, and the ontology of nature. Queer theory has taken the post-structuralist opportunity of undoing the biological fixity of sex so as to expose the artificiality of a sexuality, which is always already mediated by language, discourses and the order of the symbolic. While some feminist theories have turned the biologism of psychoanalysis into a productive materiality for a sexual difference that cannot be contained in the order of representation, and thus reversing sexual bio-pathologies into the metaphysical affirmation of a dark feminine sex, as in the unique concept of the matter-mater-matrix by Luce Irigaray,[2] the post-structuralism that has come to dominate gender politics in queer theory has fully rejected such biologism, elevating the question of material sexuality into a structural model of psychic mental relations forming the symbolic order of gender. In such a structure of signs, signifiers and objects can be arbitrarily linked without any need to be rooted in substance. There is no biologism that can explain in a cause-effects chain the relation between sex and gender. Indeed sex, any natural ultimate cause of sexual identity, does not exist outside, but within the text, the realm of culture, mediated by language and discursive formations. By disentangling queer sexuality from the law of nature, always mediated by the cultural realm of the symbolic, queer theorists have suggested, contra the psychoanalysis dictum 'everyone's a little gay', that there is no natural order to sex. Rather sex cannot but remain temporary and ambiguous in the fractured structure of signifiers, which produce sex through and in performativity. Most queer theory has been influenced by such a concept of performativity, introduced by Judith Butler and derived from the work of Derrida (1990; 1993).

It is this concept (an onto-methodological concept) that may need to be revisited were we to open queer theory to a metaphysics of immanent desire, implicating an *abductive field of machinic experience* involving the direct alliance of affects, concepts and percepts, what Deleuze and Guattari define as a machinic desire made of eventuations and becomings.

In *Gender Trouble*, Butler brings together Derrida's concept of performativity and Foucault's claim about the productive effects of regulatory power so as to put forward a notion of identity qua performativity. Butler proposes that we understand gender not as a thing or as a set of free-floating attributes, not as an essence, but rather as a 'doing', 'gender is itself a kind of becoming or activity [. . .] gender ought not to be conceived as a noun or a substantial thing or a static cultural maker, but rather as an incessant and repeated action of some sort' (1990: 112). In *Bodies That Matter*, Butler argues for a linkage between femininity, queer and materiality to explore the conditions, power encroaching the body. Such materiality is above all understood in its classical sense of generation or origination, or causality (31). In her view, such material cause is not separable from its historical formations and the shifting of meanings. A body is never just given but is rather produced. This is an iterative production specifically understood in terms of the performativity, a 'specific modality of power as discourse' (187).

Hence, performativity is neither wilful nor just arbitrary. A specific historicity of discourses determines their power to enact what discourses name (187). This is how the material is normalised: through reiteration, repetition of speech and signs. And yet it is precisely such reiteration of signs, or arbitrary signifiers arranged in a grid of power that determines social positions through restrictive representations and ideological social encodings, which allows Butler to open up and subvert the grid. By undoing the signs by the same means of reiteration, performativity 'opens the signifiers to new meanings and new possibilities for political resignification'.

It is clear that Butler's work both emphasises how the norm materialises (or animates) the body, through resignification, speech acts that bring into being what they name. Performativity therefore defines the production of discourses as they occur through a certain kind of repetition, which installs (sets into practice) the effects of certain ontologies. Performativity shows the conditions under which certain biological differences become norms of sex in certain historical periods. At the same time, it uproots sexual identity from the bio-cultural imperative of natural sex through the transgressive and subversive repetition of signifiers. In this sense, it has been argued that performativity is inherently queer (Sedgwick 1993) since it does not offer an identity, but a modality of sexual transformation entangled to the productive transformation of discourses. However, one may ask to what extent such transformation is not already prescribed by the discourses, the structures and the ideologies that produce it. In short, whether the volatility of queer sexuality, its subversive practices of reiteration, are not mere reiterations of predetermined positions encroached in the semiotic structure of the symbolic, ultimately unable to account for the material activities of signs-bodies, autonomous from the constituted whole of the text forever writing the script for sexual identities within the technocapitalist imperative of performativity.

1.1. The quantum mechanics of post-human queerness

Most recently a focus on the implications of technoscience for gender and queer theories has clearly shifted the central concept of performativity towards new critical territories. The emphasis on the performative nature of signs qua signifiers, it has been argued, has indeed left the legacy in queer theory of a passive body-sex, a mere container of socio-cultural significations.

Recently, Karen Barad (2005) has argued for a post-humanist conception of performativity for queer studies.[3] While Butler's theory of performativity privileges signifying structures of power as the ultimate shapers of identity, a doing without the doer, Barad proposes to engage with the material activities of performativity mediated not by signifiers but always relative to an observer. She argues for a notion of agency that exposes the repetitive intra-actions between the material and the discursive, tackling the ancient ontological question about the conditions that enable an object to be defined as real.[4]

In particular, borrowing from the theory of quantum mechanics as developed by Neils Bohr, Barad sets the scene for a performative metaphysics able to challenge the separateness between the observer and the observed. She draws from Bohr's distinction between the interaction of independent entities (or relata) and intra-action of relata-within-phenomena. For Bohr, relata are not prior to intra-active components. Rather, specific intra-actions make relata dependent on phenomena (200). In what she calls 'my agential realist elaboration of Bohr's epistemological inseparability between observer and observed', Barad derives that 'phenomena are the ontological inseparability of agentially intra-acting "components"' (200). This is to specify that intra-active phenomena are ontological prior to given or pre-existing relata. It is only through the performative repetition of intra-action that an agential cut able to configure a separation between objects and subjects can occur. There is nothing that pre-exists such intra-actions or relations that exclude all transcendent supplement – an exterior point of measurement. Here causality is re-worked in terms of agential realist ontology, a 'realist understanding of the nature of apparatuses . . . play[ing] . . . a crucial role in the production of phenomena' (201).

In particular, Bohr's notion of apparatuses as dynamic reconfigurations of the world is here borrowed to suggest that these are nothing but themselves phenomena (202). Similarly, phenomena are 'produced through agential intra-action of multiple apparatuses of bodily production' (202). As specific causal material enactments, these agential intra-actions, which include as opposed to Butler's performativity, a relation between humans and nonhumans, culture and nature, are phenomena that constitute reality. For Barad, Bohr's explanation of the way phenomena are inseparable from objects (the intra-action between specific physical arrangements) warns against the relativism of a theory of performativity that exclusively locates action, change, dynamics in the discursive arrangement of signs, leaving behind the complex agential realist activities, which defy any splitting of the material from the discursive.

From this standpoint, she argues that 'meaning is not ideational but rather specific material (re)configuration of the world, and semantic indeterminacy, like ontological indeterminacy, is only locally resolvable through specific intra-actions' (203). By re-working Butler's performing bodies to include non-human agencies as constitutive of the reality of matter, Barad proposes a concept of performativity beyond its anthropomorphic limitations. Thus reality is not delimited to the linguistic or discursive acts or to the human-centred vision of the body. 'Performativity is not understood as iterative citationality (Butler) but rather iterative intra-activity' (212).

By giving back historicity to matter, rather than imposing human history on matter, Barad claims that 'reality is not composed of things-in-themselves or things behind phenomena, but "things-in-phenomena"' (202). This implies that specific intra-actions produce, perform and enact a changeable being: a materiality of continual change is derived from actual intra-actions between the constitutive components of matter. The discursive therefore is always already part of the material intra-production of phenomena that is particular physical arrangements that give meaning to certain concepts rather than others (204). These apparatuses, resonating but not matching with the Foucaultian discursive practices, are material reconfigurations that produce material phenomena, a dynamic relationality that is locally determined in a particular phenomenon, through specific causal intra-actions (205). In short, Barad re-works, in the light of early quantum physics, the material-discursive practice of gender performance as entailing specific iterative enactments, agential intra-actions, through which matter is differentially articulated (207).

By assigning no priority to given entities or discursivity, Barad points at how intra-actions are constraining activities that do not determine the future, but rather remain uncertain, depending on the intra-activities of phenomena, which entail human, non-human, cyborgian forms of agency: a pluralist enactment or doing. In other words, Barad's posthuman metaphysics of performativity works to defy the belief in an ultimately external observational point. Performativity entails enacting intra-actions that are not in the world, but are of the world (213).

2. Machinic Materialism

From this standpoint, Barad suggests that queer theory needs to embrace a relational ontology that rejects the metaphysics of things and the relativism of effects and that is yet able to account for the 'role we play in the intertwined practices of knowing and becoming'. Her detailed engagement with quantum mechanics importantly points to a novel approach to materiality and nature in an attempt to problematise both objective realism and subjective constructivism. This enables Barad to propose a new notion of queerness not simply derived from nature but produced by the intra-action of phenomena in things. Quantum mechanics is here not simply conceived as a discursive representation of the behaviour of atoms used to explain human culture, but as itself implicated in an apparatus of knowledge produced out of the agential realism of phenomena. This has important consequences for the formulation of the relation between sciences and culture vis-à-vis a materiality of culture. No longer a materiality filtered by the semiotic chains of signification, but a materiality of agency, an agential realism that accounts for all kinds of phenomena as always already occurring in things. Hence, this implicit conception of quantum queerness seems to suggest that the intra-actions of phenomena, far from being divorced from the real at the limit point of human perception, are instead already part of the real up to constitute a veritable agencial realism encompassing both human and non-human and thus excluding all possibilities of defining queerness from one external point of view, for example a hetero-normative point of view of sex.

Barad's 'relational ontology', defining the ontology of being queer as an intra-active performativity of phenomena-in-things, replaces Butler's semiotic-discursive performativity and thus introduces a new mode of conceiving queerness, now enlarged to non-human agents. It may be useful at this point however to explore further the implications of such ontology in the light of Deleuze's and Deleuze and Guattari's abstract or incorporeal materialism.

While Barad's relational ontology is implicated in a phenomenal account of real intra-actions which themselves produce phenomena, the abstract materialism of Deleuze and Guattari points not at the phenomena as constitutor of reality, but at the distinctive yet coexisting planes of virtual and actual materialities as felt in experience, otherwise termed abstract machines.

Deleuze and Guattari's abstract machine includes not agential realist intra-activities, but the occurrence of *singular events*, not a performative iteration and enactment of phenomena, but *throbs of experiences* in duration, not the posthumanist shift towards the reality of signs, but a *pragmatics of abduction* fusing together conception, perception and action, an onto-method of dramatisation of virtual sexes, the a-humanist experience of abstraction. Similarly, abstract materialism may question the extent to which Barad's elevation of quantum mechanics from epistemology to metaphysics does not risk reiterating the discursive approach to science, which she refuses, insofar as by rejecting what is given in materiality, that is abstract bodies, she also rejects what is implied in quantum mechanics: the event of experiencing quantum, imperceptible, larval bodies before these acquire the qualitative properties of phenomena.

Before discussing these distinct material metaphysics further, it may be useful to discuss Deleuze and Guattari's notion of the abstract machine first.

> An abstract machine in itself is not physical or corporeal any more than it is semiotic; it is *diagrammatic* (it knows nothing of the distinction between the artificial and natural either). It operates by *matter*, not by substance; by *function*, not by form. The abstract machine is pure Matter-Function – a diagram independent of the forms and substances, expressions and contents it will distribute. (1987:141)

In as much as there is nothing eternal or ideal about machines, nothing universal that can be deducted to explain the concrete, similarly there is no concrete induction, nothing bio-physical, from which to derive an abstraction. On the contrary, Deleuze and Guattari suggest that abstraction only entails the primacy of complete assemblages, the gelling together of pre-individualities, a felt continuum that embeds discrete bodies within a field growing by its edges, adding and subtracting components: an ontogenetic process in which all elements play a part and yet no element can form a whole. The abstract machine entails an engineering patchwork of partialities passing from one state to another, fusing and breaking into each other, and yet belonging-together at points of transitions, which are less irreducible dots than inflections, critical thresholds, curvatures of imperceptible continuities. In other words, an abstract machine entails a mathematical topology of matter, whereby beneath the continuity and discontinuity of forms and substances, expressions and contents, entire populations of passional signs grow by connections.

This is not simply to be conceived as a bottom-up generation of material forms triggered by the intra-actions between phenomena. Rather, the composition of an abstract machine entails the togetherness of heterogeneous regions of spacetime that are virtually real and yet not realised. Far from implicating an agential realism, all be it a composite agency made of phenomena-in-things, an abstract machine rather distinguishes between degrees of intensive and extensive materiality. It is not possible to account for becoming in an all-encompassing identity, analogy or verisimilitude between phenomena and things.

What is at stake for an abstract machine is exactly an account of the amodal connection, the gap, interval, hiatus, between the autonomy of the abstract and the concrete. What the machine does, or rather what machinic connection deploys, is the process by which becoming or novelty can be possible again, without being explained away by the perennial primacy of phenomena, the seamless intra-activity between phenomena and things. One may indeed wonder: what exactly are the conditions for such intra-activity between phenomena-in-things so that it happens again and again?

Deleuze and Guattari's machinic materialism is instead directly concerned with what is given, that is, what is there in potential to be experienced: how does an abstract relationality become unfolded again to become concrete? The point here is less that matter is made of parts that intra-act to constitute reality, invoking a quasi-empirical inductive method, but rather what counts here is to affirm that between parts there is a multifolded dimension of *lived abstractness*: the insides of and spaces between atoms, the atomic and subatomic particles are separated by voids larger than they themselves are, where each particle's own inside is itself a virtual folding. The space in which atoms relate to each other is infinitely divisible yet continuous, a fuzzy quantity, an inexact cipher, an incomputable materiality, which is nonetheless held-together by virtual populations at the interval from one transition to another, entering singular composition, folding inside out according to certain pressures, gradients, inflections. This machinic relation is primarily diagrammatic insofar as numbers of connection are primarily numbering affections passing from one state to another, deploying a phase space that corresponds not to a spatialised extension (for example, phenomena-in-things), but to an intensive spatium, an abstract quantity or quantum. Here a sense of adimensional blocs of spacetime comes into play, a multiplicity of Aions.

It is evident that the abstract machine determines not an ontology constituted by the intra-action of parts that are here and now, the activities of actuals on actuals. If abstract machines entail immediacy, this is certainly not induced by the instantaneous direct perception between present phenomena-in-things. Rather, such immediacy can only address the immediate momentum running just before and after the present. This momentum can also usefully be defined by William James in terms of a 'specious present',[5] a dilated discreteness of infinitesimal durations: the merging of a bloc of spacetime just gone and a bloc of spacetime just arriving in the relaxed bloc of spacetime of the present. In this sense, what lies in the intra of intra-actions is a gap or interval that does not match with the agential realism of discrete phenomena. Such an interval is instead an abstract continuum, a virtuality composed of remarkable infinitesimal points, exposing the imperceptible activities of crowds no matter at what scale. And yet one may wonder, if an abstract machine defines without determining what is given in potential (that is, virtual materiality) and what can become actual (concrete materiality), then how can it be that the abstract machine at once accounts for the discrete and the continuum without imposing another external point of view on the activities of matter? How can the abstract machine engage with concrete experience without resorting to an absolute metaphysics that unites discreteness, as it were, from above?

Deleuze and Guattari's philosophy of immanence leaves no doubt that this may be the case. In particular, the concept of the event clearly points out that a virtual world is implicated in every subject as a field from which a point of view, for example a manner or modality, distinguishes itself. Against Aristotelian essentialism, these mannerisms are modalities of transformation of worlds extended to the cosmos, but not for such cosmos to encompass all modalities summed into One totality (Deleuze 1993: 60–1). Indeed, such cosmos is never a whole but a machinic multiplicity of worlds continuously composing and breaking down. And yet these mannerisms cannot be disentangled from the virtual constellations of worlds that make an event possible. But how exactly does an event come about?

Deleuze provides a precise notion of the event by drawing at once from the monadic metaphysics of Leibniz and the processual thought of Alfred North Whitehead. With Whitehead, Deleuze defines an event as always encompassed by larger and smaller events ad infinitum; an infinitesimal division here is used to account for the infinitesimal continuum of material worlds. The world of events is therefore continuous and yet, for Whitehead, only discontinuity can account for the becoming of being (or conscrescence) and make possible the distinction between the coming into being of an event and the event itself.

Against what Whitehead saw as the pervasive belief in the seamless continuity of time, the constant flows of eternal becoming, he proposed, by appropriating quantum mechanics, an atomic theory of time, defining the event as the onset and perishing of an actual occasion. Hence the event specifically accounts for the dawn and sunset of experience when it commences and reaches a completion. It terminates by passing from one state, actual occasion or present, into another, past.[6] Thus every actual event is implicated in the event just gone, which however can only go once completed, once from the arrow of time a new path is taken, at a point inflection, the infinitesimal curvatures of the *clinamen*. The past-present defines the onset of the event and the present-future the transformation; the occurrence of an actual experience entails a semi-open cycle of birth and perishing. What becomes here is not the actual experience but the continuity between one occurrence and another. The famous Whiteheadian formulation – the many become one and are increased by one[7] – implies that a chaotic multiplicity of past events, eternal objects of a disjunctive diversity, become one, not a pregiven one, but enter into an actual occasion as an inventive process of occurrence. Here pre-individual bodies tend to become present anew, rubbing against each other so as to actualise anew; a field of compossible worlds becomes incompossible once the constellations of virtual universes enter into one extension or the other.

Extension indeed, as Deleuze points out, is the first component or condition of both Whitehead's and Leibniz's definition of the event (1993: 77). Here extension entails the connection of wholes and parts. '[I]t is when one element is stretched over the following ones, such that it is a whole and the following elements are its parts' (77). A second definition for events is their intrinsic, intensive properties, such as a certain texture, colour, timbre of a sound. A third definition is the individual, which for Whitehead entails creativity, the production of novelty, the becoming or concrescence of elements into a novel assemblage, 'the production of novel togetherness'. ' "Creativity" is the principle of *novelty*. An actual occasion is a novel entity diverse from any entity in the "many" which it defines' (Whitehead 1978: 21). Such novelty entails not simply a link between parts, an intra-action between agencies, but the activity of prehensions.

The notion of prehension is at the core of Whiteahead's metaphysical enterprise for invention of a new empiricism; an empiricism detracted from the priority of sensory discrete perception.[8] Prehension is not sense perception. It determines neither a cognitive act of observation nor a sensory-motor response. Prehension may be better described as enactment, a propensity to feel thought before sensing, or an abstract sensation that is non-sensuous, an affection that coincides not with here and now but with a vector connecting here with there, immediately before and after. Prehensions define the individual unity of the event. 'Everything prehends its antecedents and its concomitants, and by degrees, prehends a world' (Deleuze 1993: 78). The ear is a prehension of sound. The eye a prehension of light.

> The vector of prehensions moves from the world to the subject, from the prehended datum to the prehending one (a 'superject'); thus the data of a prehension are *public* elements, while the subject is the intimate or *private* elements that expresses immediacy, individuality and novelty. (78)

However, prehensions are never just prehensions of something. Each prehension is a prehension of prehension (the feeling of or before feeling) and the event is only but a nexus of prehensions. Each new prehension forms an individual unity and thus becomes the datum for the next prehension. The objectification of one prehension and the subjectification of another are what compose an event. Thus an event is at once potential and possible, virtual and actual, abstract and concrete. Each event is at once implicated in the becoming of another event and in its own becoming (78).

Like Leibniz's monads, prehensions are active expressions of the datum prehended: 'the form in which the datum is folded in the subject, a feeling, or manner . . .' (78). According to Deleuze, Whitehead re-echoes the problematic already dear to Leibniz concerning the investigation of the conditions that allow the objective world to become subjective: the convergence of divergent series as producer of novelty. Such conditions however do not occur without the ingression of pure potentialities in the event. In this sense, the notion of events not only challenges the object-subject 'bifurcation of nature', but also provides a metaphysics of concrete experience, which is not derived from the intra-action between things-phenomena as mediated by inferential signs, but expresses quantic signs in terms of felt, prehended continuities between states of matter, the becoming of occurrences of abstraction.

The abstract machine thus entails extensive connections, intrinsic qualities, prehended unities, experienced virtualities, a felt abstraction implicated in the smallest and largest events, a discontinuous repetition of continuity, a becoming of assemblages.

As previously seen, Barad's posthuman performative ontology instead is predicated upon the iterative patterns of physical phenomena located in phenomena themselves and constituting patterns of local intelligibility by means of the 'prosthetic performativity of the agencies of observation'. These involve further patterns of intra-action, whose conceptual-discursive character is determined by a perceptual identification operating not via sense perception but by means of an inferential web. As Joseph Rouse in his article 'Barad's Feminist Naturalism' explains: 'Discursive practices as characterized by a pragmatically inferentialist semantics (see Brandom 1994) are thus an indispensable component of any intelligible phenomenon, and a crucial part of Barad's "agencies of observation" '.[9] Rouse clarifies that for Barad's agential realism, meaning and its interpretation are thoroughly material phenomena starting with a mark on bodies 'whether these are movements, vocalizations, or inscriptions'. These marks on bodies are 'the material indications of phenomena'. An inferential and not perceptual intra-action with marks on bodies (establishing a reference frame, marking off and counting equal unit division, standardising the units, and so forth) is at stake in the iterative practice of material-discursive performance. The configuration of intra-active phenomena implies the iterative function of inferential semantics: a shift from linguistic performativity still involving a given subject, to a semantic performativity now involving the priority of semantic interpretations towards a material system.

But how, one may wonder, does such semantic performativity come about? What are the conditions of such quasi-memetic transference of meaningful signs or marks on bodies in different contexts, so quickly disposing of the materiality of prehensions?

Despite invoking posthuman materialism, what seems to remain excluded from such iteration of signs is precisely a materialism of continuity: prehensive activities serving neither to direct attention to the physicality of the senses nor to the mind so that it can add its representation to the formation of the world. As Whitehead argues, the relation between perception and knowledge involves the prehensive activities of thought, an abstract or non-sensuous grasping or affective tonality relating the object and the subject, the knower and the known through a primary process of prehensive events (1933: 176–8).

Deleuze, together with Whitehead and Leibniz, addresses the materiality of continuity in terms of psycho-mental prehensions marking the conditions for the expression of the constitutive relations of the world in its creative process, its adventures of becoming (the concrescence of many worlds into one with the addition of one). And this is not simply because the datum is always a construct, a sort of phenomena in the object, but more fundamentally because the continual process relocates, rather than simply inferentially situate in a locus, every datum in a world of pure activity or pure experience. Hence prehensions are themselves power-beings, synthesisers of asymmetric forces into the production of a higher yet infinitesimal unity, which defines the adventurous construction of novelty.

Hence what does not cease to repeat in the passages of events is the prehensive immanence of thought. Brian Massumi calls this sensation: the point of conversion where perception unfolds into thought and thought infolds into perception. Sensation is 'the registering of the multiplicity of potential connections in the singularity of a connection actually under way' (2002: 64). The thought-perception continuum operates recursively. It is a refrain where every moment extends beyond itself in a way that is thought and felt, anticipated form of a yearning or tending (65).

Iteration here has nothing to do with a repetition derived from the intra-active enactment of phenomena. Rather '[t]he different components conserve their heterogeneity, but are nevertheless captured by a refrain' (Guattari 1995: 17) which couples them together. The refrain is the multirhythmic interval produced not by the intra-action of the components, but by the relationship's infinitesimal relation to itself first. For Deleuze and Guattari, the interval between events is part of the production of novel events qua experiences. This entails neither the performativity of discursive apparatuses on bodies nor the intra-active performativity of material-discursive phenomena.

Iteration rather points at the persistent variation of pure experience. In *The Critical and The Clinical* (Deleuze and Parnet 1997: 86–7), Deleuze draws on the radical empiricism of William James to remind us that experience is better to be understood in terms of texture: the fabric of experience entails the construction of a patchwork, sewing and stitching elements or throbs, quantum throbs, of experience from next to next, by means of the intermediary series. As James puts it: 'Experience itself, taken at large, can grow by its edges. That one moment of it proliferates into the next by transitions which, whether conjunctive or disjunctive, continue the experiential tissue, cannot, I contend, be denied' (1912: 42). Throbs of experience rather than agential realist entities entail the continual experiencing of virtuality, a lived abstractness, a real bundle of relations: space as a relation of linkage, time as a continuous relation of enveloping. Here is how experience must always start: with a multiplicity of felt and not inferential thought, interlaced and superimposed upon each other in all directions, revealing themselves as one follows them.

It is here perhaps that queer theory can benefit from Deleuze and Guattari's philosophy of immanent desire act to expose not simply what is queer, what are the phenomena that constitute queerness, but how, who, when queer: the conditions of pure experience enveloped in an intensive spatium preceding and exceeding the constitutive quality of sexuality derived from the limits of the intelligible, of phenomena-in-things. In other words, the contribution that the philosophy of immanence can offer to the production of a philosophy of queerness lies in the capacity to affirm the events of intensive determinations of experience as conditions of experience. Here, the irreversible nature of duration endures (the common duration between distinct changing phenomena does not change but endures) independently of the observer's choice of system of reference or phenomenal constructivism. Here repetition is possible only in the immediate direct feeling of abstract blocs of space-time: sensations of rhythms repeat in the successive series of vibrations bound together by inner continuity of intensive spatium.

3. Coda on Dramatisation: How, Who, When Queer?

Beyond experience, intensive spatium defines a prior condition of experience. In the essay entitled 'The Method of Dramatization', Deleuze suggests that a good question to engage with the intensive determinations of experience is not what is this? But who? How much? How? When? can this happen (2004: 94). In short, the method of dramatisation entails pure differential activities governed not by the semantic web of signs but belonging to the passions of larval remarkable regions or points, deploying entire fields of individuation. These are prior conditions under which specifications occur: intensive sexes and not sexual identities, larval sexes and no agents of sex, rhythmic sexes and not repetitive sex.

For Deleuze, what is virtually present ceaselessly dramatises through repetitions and resonances directly intervening in physical, biological and psychic dynamisms by a process of individuation where each difference is already virtually differentiated. Dramatisation therefore entails the productive activities of a yet to be actualised individuation. It concerns the agitations of pre-individual particle-forces that coincide not with this or that sexuality, with being queer, with the experience of being queer. What indeed queerness is implicated into is the dramatisation of virtual sexes, the spatio-temporal constellations of sexualities defining how queerness is given in sexual experience, a multiplicity of sexes that do not revolve around being queer itself.

Here dramatisation entails not the performativity of material-discursive signs, phenomena-in-things constituting sexuality or queerness as the intra-action between the real and the phenomenal, the web of activities defining agential reality in history, which accounts for the specificity of the complex relations between human and non-human, natural and artificial components under a specific situation: the observational cut. This posthuman performativity indeed addresses not the discursive apparatus that enables sexuality to enter a regime of repeatability of signs that can in turn subvert the discursive structure, but an apparatus that includes the material body as directly implicated in the observational construction of the meaning of how matter comes to matter.

And yet, while posthuman queerness remains preoccupied with the performativity of signs attached to matter and constituting a new ontology for sexuality, the method of dramatisation is concerned with how queerness becomes individuated in the first place, how many sexes are implicated in the abstract machinism of desire? What enters repetition here are not already defined phenomena-in-things, the being queer, but the abstract or virtual microsexual multiplicities ingressing singular compositions, individualities, that correspond to them. '[T]he image of murmuring, or the ocean, or a water mill . . .' (Deleuze 2004: 101), the chaos prehended in an individual unity never dispenses of the chaos but enters a multifolded transformation, an infinite series of inflections or becomings, according to a how, how much, who. In other words, according to veritable specifications of virtual sexes concretely experienced and yet devoid of all fundamental ontologies of sex, queer, homosexual, heterosexual.

The method of dramatisation allows for the pure experience of desiring-machines, the direct prehension of microsexes enveloped in intensive spatio-temporal co-ordinates including the atomic and sub-atomic levels of matter, agitating throughout an intensive spatium, detracting the experience of sexuality from the psycho-biological ground of identification, and thus facing the deepest wound engulfing all kinds of sexes. It is from the obscure depths, the abyss of such an infinite wound that sexuality is dramatised to enter a future of sexual mutation.

For a philosophy of immanent desire to become relevant to queer theory, sexuality has to be housed by intensive spatio-temporal regions expressing the how, how much, when of the becomings of sex. Sexuality is not the ultimate order of the symbolic but the desire primarily implicated in the abstract feeling of what happens to the world, when mental, affective, social, aesthetic assemblages transversally combined across all scales of matter, deploy the singular engineering of each world as an event, a pure occurrence of sex.

References

Barad, K. (1999), 'Agential Realism: Feminist Interventions in Understanding Scientific Practices', from *The Science Studies Reader*, ed. Mario Biagioli, New York: Routledge.

Barad, K. (2005), 'Posthumanist Performativity', *Materialitat Denken*, Bielefeld: Verlag. Originally published in *Journal of Women in Culture and Society*, 2003, 28(3), University of Chicago.

Butler, J. (1990), *Gender Trouble: Feminism and the Subversion of Identity*, New York: Routledge.

Butler, J. (1993), *Bodies That Matter: On the Discursive Limits of 'Sex'*, New York: Routledge.

Deleuze, G. (1993), *The Fold*, Minneapolis: University of Minnesota Press.

Deleuze, G. (2001), *The Logic of Sense*, London and New York: Continuum Books.

Deleuze, G. (2004a), 'Preface to Hocquenghem's *L'Après-Mai des faunes*', *Desert Islands and Other texts 1953–1974*, Los Angeles: Semiotext(e), pp. 284–8.

Deleuze, G. (2004b), 'The Method of Dramatization', *Desert Islands and Other texts 1953–1974*, Los Angeles: Semiotext(e), pp. 94–116.

Deleuze, G. and Guattari, F. (1987), *A Thousand Plateaus, Capitalism and Schizophrenia*, trans. Brian Massumi, London: The Athlone Press.

Deleuze, G. and Parnet, C. (1997), *The Clinical and the Critical*, Minnesota: University of Minnesota Press.

Guattari, F. (1995), *Chaosmosis*, Bloomington/Indianapolis: Indiana University Press.

Irigaray, L. (1985a), *Speculum: Of the Other Woman*, trans. Gillian C. Gill, Ithaca: Cornell University Press.

Irigaray, L. (1985b), *This Sex Which Is Not One*, trans. Catherine Porter, Ithaca: Cornell University Press.

James, W. (1912), 'A World of Pure Experience', *Essays in Radical Empiricism*, New York: Longman Green and Co. pp. 39–91.

Massumi, B. (2002), *Parables for the Virtual, Movement, Affect, Sensation*, Durham: Duke University Press.

Sedgwick, E. (1993), *Tendencies*, Duke: Duke University Press.

Whitehead, A. N. (1933), *Adventures in Ideas*, New York: The Free Press.

Whitehead, A. N. (1978), *Process and Reality*, New York: The Free Press.

Notes

1. For a further explanation of Lucretius's notion of causality, see Deleuze 2001: 303–16.
2. This concept is at the core of Irigaray's early philosophical writing, where she argues for a metaphysics of fluid femininity that is autonomous from the heteronormative ontology of the two sexes. See Irigaray 1985a; 1985b.
3. Barad clearly explains that the notion of performativity adapted by Judith Butler is derived from British philosopher J. L. Austin's study on speech acts and the relationship between saying and doing. Butler's notion of gender performativity indeed proposes an engagement with gender in terms of 'doings' rather than being. While, as Barad points out, Butler articulates the linkage between gender performativity and the materialisation of the sexed body, the work of Eve Sedgwick argues that performativity's genealogy is inherently queer. See Barad 2005: 193. See also Sedgwick 1993 and Butler 1993.
4. In particular, the tension between empiricism and rationalism, relativism and absolutism, nominalism and reality are at play here. Barad is concerned with a

redefinition of objectivity beyond absolute realism to rethink performativity in terms of intra-action between phenomena-in-things. The concept of intra-action derived from quantum mechanics helps Barad to redefine performativity as entailing not just the repetition of signifiers, constituting the discursive apparatus of knowledge, but the repetition of phenomena-in-things – constituting a material-discursive apparatus. Such intrinsic relation between materiality and discursivity is at the core of her re-definition of queerness.

5. The notion of 'specious present' is derived by William James. This notion is intended not just to define the personal experience of a present defined by the moment just gone and the moment just coming, a continuity in discrete spacetime, but also to define a space where distinct minds meet at a speed faster than physical touching. See James 1912: 39–91.

6. On the onset and perishing of actual occasions as entailing its passage from the past to the present and future, see Whitehead 1933: 192–4.

7. On the category of the ultimate and the notions of many and one, see Whitehead 1978: 21.

8. Whitehead specifically formulates the concept of prehension to define a mode of feeling that entails not the primacy of sense perception à la Hume, but occasions of experience that involve our knowledge of the immediate past and future. See Whitehead 1967: 180–1.

9. In this article, Rouse argues that Barad's take on Bohr's emphasis on the apparatus of measurement explains how meaning is produced by reference to any particular physical apparatus, ultimately implying a mutual entanglement in both directions – from the observer to the observed and the other way around. Since the apparatus determines what is being described and measured by means of discursive practices, then Rouse suggests that for Barad the semantic content is inferentialist. In particular, '[w]hat allows the mark of a photon on a photographic plate to measure position, for example, is [its] possible inferential role in a subsequent chain of performances that are held normatively accountable to appropriate intra-actions with the mark'. Such inferential use of concepts such as position, according to Rouse, is a crucial component for the interpretative apparatus belonging to a phenomenon, 'through which a phenomenon becomes intelligible'. See Joseph Rouse (2004), 'Barad's Feminist Naturalism', *Hypathia*, 19(1), pp. 142–61 (http://inscribe.iupress.org/doi/abs/10.2979/HYP.2004.19.1.142?cookieSet=1&journalCode=hyp, last accessed 14 March 2007).

Chapter 6

Queer Hybridity

Mikko Tuhkanen

Queer theory had a good year in 1987. Three texts of major import for queer thinking were published. Leo Bersani's work took an explicitly queer turn in 'Is the Rectum a Grave?,' an essay that rendered the arguments Bersani had formulated during his long career as a literary theorist, beginning from the mid-1960s, relevant to queer thinking energised by the violently phobic reactions to the AIDS crisis. The same year, Judith Butler published her re-worked dissertation, *Subjects of Desire: Hegelian Reflections in Twentieth-Century France*, in which she brilliantly recuperated Hegel's philosophy from the collective dismissal by its numerous critics. *Subjects of Desire* is important for queer theory, for in this book Butler extracted from the theory of the dialectic a politically salient account of Hegelian becoming. It is on this re-worked model of *Werden* that she would three years later, in *Gender Trouble: Feminism and the Subversion of Identity* (1990), erect the theory of performativity, perhaps the single most important concept for the institutional recognition of queer thinking.

The third text I have in mind is Gloria Anzaldúa's *Borderlands/La Frontera: The New Mestiza*. In this text, Anzaldúa elaborates on the theory of being and becoming – terms that I use here advisedly – that she had first articulated in the collective project of *This Bridge Called My Back: Writings by Radical Women of Color* (Moraga and Anzaldúa 1981, 2nd edn 1983) earlier in the decade. Anzaldúa is justly famous for insisting that we always consider racial and ethnic differences in our gender and sexual politics and theories. In this she is not alone but part of an entire movement, of particularly mujeres-de-color critics of (the unmarkedly white) feminism, such as Audre Lorde and Cherríe Moraga, her co-contributors to *This Bridge*. Linda Garber (2001) has convincingly argued that the too-often-unrecognised genealogy of queer theory's major concerns and methodologies leads to the work of thinkers like

Anzaldúa and Lorde. I agree with Garber but would also insist that to effect a return to Anzaldúa's work would give us queer theory largely unrecognisable to its present self. This is because the specificity of Anzaldúa's thinking cannot be grasped through the philosophical perspectives that are currently hegemonic in social sciences and the humanities. I have here in mind the all-but-complete deconstruction of ontology and metaphysics that Elizabeth Grosz, for example, has addressed in her recent work (Grosz 2004 and 2005; see also Haslanger 2000; Oksala 2005). We can understand the historical reasons behind ontology's critical fortunes: the sweep of ontological inquiry has seemed to require the reduction of difference to identity, of multiplicity to a universalism, of the human to the man. Seeking to theorise the nature and conditions of existence, ontology, it is argued, proceeds by obfuscating life's actual variety and complexity, and, as feminism has pointed out, such reduction has traditionally taken place according to criteria where hegemonic particularities are universalised and where other perspectives, such as women's, are rendered partial, inadequate or, simply, inconceivable.

Yet, the (often unacknowledged or unnamed) rejection of ontology makes it difficult, if not impossible, to read much of Anzaldúa's work. Her uncomfortable fit with the most efficiently institutionalised queer approaches can be detected in the work of critics who, taking their cue from Butler's Hegelian-inflected theory of performativity, find her arguments 'utopian' (see Jagose 1994: ch. 6; Raiskin 1994). I propose that we are unable to understand Anzaldúa's philosophy unless we grant that her thinking proceeds from an ontological framework. For example, her insistence on the 'metaphysics of interconnectedness' becomes a naïve generalisation if we do not understand, precisely, the *metaphysical* reach of her argument.[1]

What I here seek is a kind of an involution to 1987, a potential actualisation of Anzaldúa's metaphysics, which I argue has not been seriously considered, perhaps not even recognised, by queer theory's profoundly deconstructive discipline. Taking Anzaldúa's paradigmatic orientation seriously, this essay develops a notion of 'queer hybridity' through her work, especially by placing it in dialogue with theories of mixedness, mestizaje and creolization in African-American and post-colonial theories, which I argue provide a more resonant context for reading Anzaldúa than contemporary queer thinking. Of course, within these fields, one must make further distinctions. In terms of post-colonial theory, I am here thinking of theorists such as Edouard Glissant rather than, say, Homi Bhabha. While Bhabha understands hybridity as 'the effect of colonial power' (Bhabha 1994: 112), for Anzaldúa mestizaje is, in the final analysis, an ontological condition. As Anzaldúa writes in her preface to *this bridge we call home*: 'Biologically, we are a single gene pool with minor variations and superficial cultural and genetic differences; we are interconnected with all life' (Anzaldúa 2002b: 5). While such metaphysics becomes more pronounced in her subsequent texts, it orients her thinking already in *Borderlands/La Frontera*. It is articulated through the notions of both *spirit* and *evolution*, two terms that have been largely greeted with an embarrassed silence in her reception by queer theorists. 'We're supposed to forget,' Anzaldúa tells us, 'that every cell in our bodies, every bone and bird and worm has spirit in it' (Anzaldúa 1987: 36). She suggests in later interviews that this forgetfulness is behind the insistent silence around her arguments about spirituality in academic discussions of her work (Anzaldúa 2000: 7, 144, 161). This silence, one may further note, is matched by the systematic neglect of her evolutionary thinking, which, at best, is considered in metaphoric terms or thought of as a performatively insubordinate repetition of the discourses of racial sciences and the evolutionary schema of José Vasconcelos.[2] The two omissions seem to me connected, both symptomatic of the disorientation caused by the incommensurability of Anzaldúa's paradigm with current theoretical hegemonies. In Anzaldúa, references to *spirit* and *evolution* name the same thing: an ontology of interconnectedness and becoming. I suggest, then, that the embarrassment of such concepts is the embarrassment of metaphysics, perhaps that of an unabashed *monism* in Anzaldúa's thinking. For Anzaldúa, evolution – that is, the world's relentless change and becoming – is enabled by the consistency of being (by *spirit*) and the ontological interconnectedness of bodies, the fact that bodies resonate with others, find themselves partially replicated in other bodies.

I turn to Deleuze's philosophy as a productive point of reference for thinking Anzaldúa's ontology. I am not, of course, the first to suggest this linkage. Deleuze has been cited in Anzaldúa scholarship, as often sympathetically as critically. Most often, his work is referred to in passing to illustrate aspects of Anzaldúa's thinking (Hicks 1991: 109; Kaplan 1990: 360–1; Oliver Rotger 2001: 192 n6; Perles Rochel 2002: 234); at times he is evoked implicitly with the use of terms, such as 'deterritorializations', associated with his philosophy (Hall 1999: 100). Such brief references – often inadequately motivated and contextualised[3] – have in turn elicited criticism, such as Linda Martin Alcoff's, who contrasts Anzaldúa's account of mestizaje's pain and difficulty to what she considers Deleuze and Guattari's romanticised and celebratory nomadology (Alcoff 2006: 257). Agreeing with Alcoff that claiming philosophical connections must be done carefully, I do not seek to identify Anzaldúa's philosophy with Deleuze's. Nevertheless, whatever specific points of harmony, discord, similarity, divergence, correspondence or tension one can locate between the two thinkers, it seems to me imperative to insist on the *paradigmatic* agreement between their projects: diverging from practically all their contemporaries, they are engaged in ontological contemplation.[4] Moreover, it is important to problematise Alcoff's reduction of Deleuze's theories of becoming to slick celebrations of mobility and transformation. She is not alone in dismissing philosophies of affirmation, force and will-to-power as symptomatic of the theorist's privileged immunity to pain, loss and melancholia – or, at worst, of his or her proto-fascism. Yet, Deleuzian affirmation must be understood in its Nietzschean meaning, where what are affirmed are active forces in their characteristic trajectories, where 'the noble affirms the return, not the cessation of desire, and so the return of suffering' (Roberts 1998: 166). Affirmation does not inoculate one against difficulty, suffering or disappearance; neither does it make any particular loss or extinction inevitable. If the philosophy of affirmation embraces the 'fundamental *yes*' of desire and active forces (Deleuze and Guattari 1998: 244), it also affirms the open-ended struggle between such forces. A philosophy of affirmation such as Nietzsche's does not assert the stability and identity of forces but seeks to think how they become through clashes and encounters with other forces. One can argue that, throughout her work, Anzaldúa maps the contact zones of such struggles.[5]

Through Anzaldúa's work, this essay thinks about the potentialities that an ontological turn would open for queer theory. If one of the perceived dangers of ontology has been its seeming affirmation of what exists – and, hence, its allegedly conservative character – clearly with Deleuze and Anzaldúa we move from an ontology of being to that of becoming. Both Anzaldúa's and Deleuze's are ontologies of futurity – ontologies 'rooted in becoming rather than being' (Grosz n.d.: n.p.). Whatever differences, divergences and discords we find between their philosophies, they are both concerned with thinking about the becoming of an interrelated universe.

Interfacing: Anzaldúa's Queer Ontology

[A]ny identity is always riven with forces, with processes, connections, movements that exceed and transform identity and that connect individuals (human and nonhuman) to each other and to worlds, in ways unforeseen by consciousness and unconnected to identity.

Elizabeth Grosz, *Architecture from the Outside*

Anzaldúa's ambitious system posits a 'cosmovisión' (Anzaldúa 2002: 540) that is characterised above all by 'the metaphysics of interconnectedness'. This interconnectedness is actualised in cohering bodies (human or otherwise) that are made up of smaller particles – what Anzaldúa sometimes calls 'subpersonalities' (Anzaldúa 2000: 242) – held loosely together. Because some of these smaller 'particles' are shared with other bodies of various scales and realms, Anzaldúa speaks of bodies' interpenetration: 'The self does not stop with just you, with your body. The self penetrates other things and they penetrate you' (Anzaldúa 2000: 162). She underlines bodies' composite nature, the fact that '[o]ne's own *body* is not one entity':

> you're all the different organisms and parasites that live on your body and also the ones that live in a symbiotic relationship to you. The *mouth*!!! The mouth has tons of bacteria and foreign stuff. Animals live in symbiotic relationships – the cows with little birds picking the ticks off. So who are you? You're not one single entity. You're a multiple entity. (Anzaldúa 2000: 158)

For Anzaldúa, we might say, 'each individual is an infinite multiplicity' (Deleuze and Guattari 1987: 254), a multiplicity that is partially shared with other bodies. Here, 'bodies are made up of parasites, symbionts which infiltrate the systems of the host' (Ansell Pearson 1999: 163). In thus problematising boundaries and categories – particularly in her later work, boundaries not only between human individuals but between the human and the non-human[6] – Anzaldúa is clearly engaged in questioning what Keith Ansell Pearson calls 'the Western tradition of ontotheology', with its 'bias . . . in favour of self-sufficiency and closed boundaries (a conception of life that is not without its political articulations and implications).' In rethinking evolutionary theory by problematising borders, she demonstrates that 'absolute boundaries are radically anti-evolutionary since they entail stasis' (Ansell Pearson 1999: 166–7). In other words, by insisting on the interconnectedness of bodies, Anzaldúa's metaphysics emphasises evolutionary change, its relentless becoming, while at the same time rejecting 'the anthropocentrism that is in-built in so much evolutionary, biological, scientific, and philosophical thought' (Braidotti 2005/2006: para. 21). Hers is a philosophy that, like Rosi Braidotti's 'nomadic eco-philosophy,' 'sponsors a subject that is composed of external forces, of the non-human, inorganic or technological kind. It is territorially based, and thus environmentally bound' (Braidotti 2005/2006: para. 24).

Anzaldúa's philosophy has exerted an obvious (if ambivalent) appeal for queer theorists because of her explicit elaboration of her metaphysics as a system of *queerness*, a queer theory. That is, hers is a metaphysics not only of interconnectedness, but of constitutive crossing, of a movement athwart – *atravesar* – which Eve Kosofsky Sedgwick traces as queer's etymology (Sedgwick 1993: xii). The new mestiza is the point of articulation or expression of this crossing. Emerging '[a]t the confluence of two or more genetic streams, with chromosomes constantly "crossing over" ' (Anzaldúa 1987: 77), she, like queers as *atravesados*, 'supreme crossers of cultures' (Anzaldúa 1987: 84), is a connective point between established entities and identities, seemingly distinct lineages, histories and temporalities. Yet, her profoundly metaphysical stance is likely to render her philosophy unrecognisable to queer theory. Anzaldúa's *atravesados* are not primarily subjects well versed in the performative acts of subversive imitation. Rather, queer crossing in Anzaldúa is an ontological condition, a characteristic of being itself.

This ontology of interconnectedness assumes a universe that is hybridised through *queer bodies*. Anzaldúa finds these queer bodies – or perhaps the same queer body – lodged in otherwise dissimilar cultures with discrete histories: 'I am all races because there is the queer of me in all races' (Anzaldúa 1987: 80). This 'queer of me' is an *unheimlich* body in the precise sense that it is both at home in and an alien to the larger body in which it is located. Anzaldúa seeks such uncannily alien bodies in seemingly self-identical cultures, histories or organisms to show how these bodies are linked to similar ones (or, perhaps, exist in simultaneity, 'at the same time' (Anzaldúa 1987: 77), as equally alien bodies) in other cultures, histories, organisms. For her, the existence of these bodies demonstrates the hybridity of ostensibly separate entities.

In Anzaldúa's metaphysical scheme, this 'queer of me' functions as an *interface*, a common ground that has been abjected from coherent identities (of whatever scale) but that nevertheless resonates with other bodies in those identities and between identities, linking – *but also undoing* – them. In the preface to the 1990 anthology *Making Face, Making Soul/Haciendo caras*, she calls 'inter-faces' 'the very spaces and places where our multiple-surfaced, colored, racially gendered bodies intersect and interconnect' (Anzaldúa 1990: xvi). The dictionary tells us that an interface is, first, a border, 'a surface lying between two portions of matter or space, and forming their common boundary', such as the ones Anzaldúa theorises throughout her work. It is, second, the 'place or means' of 'interaction, liaison, dialogue' between separate and separable entities, and, third and most important, an 'apparatus' connecting these entities 'so that they can be operated jointly' (*OED*).

In Anzaldúa's ontology, then, metastable bodies and identities are interfaced by that which has been abjected from them, that is, their queer bodies. The 'queer of me' as an interface has a double function. It is the site of connection, dialogue and operation between bodies, but also the promise of their mutual undoing – which is to say, their *becoming*. In other words, Anzaldúa locates in the queer interface the promise of becoming, of an evolutionary change through the hybridisation that the new mestiza embodies. This 'bridging' of entities, their hybridisation, enables an evolutionary de-formation of current existence and a becoming-other of what is presently available. The new mestiza is an entity where queer hybridity functions other than through the processes of disavowal and rejection. She constitutes an ongoing hybridisation and becoming in-between cohering entities. In this becoming Anzaldúa locates mestiza strength, characterised by a susceptibility to future conditions, to becoming.

Clearly, on this ontological level, Anzaldúa's reading of queerness is radically ahistoricist, ignoring all the allegedly Foucaultian lessons that other contemporaneous discussions of homosexuality cite:

> Being the supreme crossers of cultures, homosexuals have strong bonds with the queer white, Black, Asian, Native American, Latino, and with the queer in Italy, Australia and the rest of the planet. We come from all colors, all classes, all races, all time periods. Our role is to link people with each other – the Black with Jews with Indians with Asians with whites with extraterrestials. It is to transfer ideas and information from one culture to another. [. . .] The mestizo and the queer exist at this time and point on the evolutionary continuum for a purpose. We are a blending that proves that all blood is intricately woven together, and that we are spawned out of similar souls. (Anzaldúa 1987: 84–5)

Queerness here is not primarily a cultural category but names an ontology of connectedness between and a crossing of temporalities and cultures. In the relentless historicising of social sciences and the humanities, Anzaldúa's new mestiza draws an alien, metaphysical figure. She is a queer hybrid, 'a product of crossbreeding' (Anzaldúa 1987: 81) in a monistic universe 'where all phenomena are interrelated and imbued with spirit' (Anzaldúa 1987: 66). Anzaldúa suggests we understand all locally sculpted forms and situationally formulated names as evolutionary expressions of spirit.

The call for the recognition and utilisation of the fleeting overlaps and momentary alignments between seemingly discrete identity categories is a familiar one, having been deployed by politically minded minority writers and scholars for decades. Kobena Mercer notes in 1989 that 'the essentialist rhetoric of categorical identity politics threatens to erase the connectedness of our different struggles' (Mercer 1994: 218). An acknowledgement and strategic deployment of such connectedness allows one to forge and improvise alliances beyond existing boundaries. As Cathy Cohen writes, 'it is the multiplicity and interconnectedness of our identities that provide the most promising avenue for the *destabilization and radical politicalization* of these same categories' (Cohen 2005: 45). Anzaldúa's texts are frequently cited as examples of the necessity and difficulty of such projects of alliance-making. Yet, what is less often emphasised is that for Anzaldúa the political call for forging alliances that exceed our identity categories is indistinguishable from an ontological description of the world. In Shane Phelan's estimation, *Borderlands/La Frontera* provides us 'a sorely needed ontological account of coalitional identity politics' (Phelan 1994: 58). In this ontology, 'the queer of me' – which the new mestiza consciousness de-abjects, de-disavows – is the elusive potential for actualised, possibly politicised connectedness across and between discrete bodies and identities.

Involution: Anzaldúa's Queer Time

> Returning is being but only the being of becoming.
> Gilles Deleuze, *Difference and Repetition*

> [T]he past can be as malleable as the present.
> Gloria Anzaldúa, 'Haciendo caras, una entrada'

In the scene of a girl child's untimely menstruation that Anzaldúa recounts in both *Borderlands/La Frontera* (Anzaldúa 1987: 42–3) and the earlier essay 'La Prieta' (Anzaldúa 1983: 199), bleeding marks the acknowledgement of both queerness and, because of this crossing, interconnectedness in the narrator's personal history. With her premature haemorrhage at the age of three months the child experiences an alienation from the home, becomes *unheimlich*: 'The bleeding distanced her from others' (Anzaldúa 1987: 43), Anzaldúa writes in the third person, suggesting the trauma of the event (see Anzaldúa 2000: 223).[7] As a doctor pronounces her a throwback to the Eskimo, she turns into, or is revealed as, a queer body, *the queer of me*, that, as she writes later, inhabits distinct cultures and races, linking them. 'The whole time growing up I felt that I was not of this earth. An alien from another planet – I'd been dropped on my mother's lap' (Anzaldúa 1983: 199); 'I was afraid it was in plain sight for all to see. The secret I tried to conceal was that I was not normal, that I was not like the others. I felt alien. I knew I was alien.

I was the mutant stoned out of the herd, something deformed with evil inside' (Anzaldúa 1987: 42–3).

Queerness, like bordering, is for Anzaldúa a site of bleeding: simultaneously a painful breaching of an individual's bodily integrity and a constitutive condition of mutual infiltration or contamination between distinct bodies and speeds, between an organism and the environment. People bleed, as do cultures, ceaselessly extending beyond themselves: 'The US-Mexican border *es una herida abierta* where the Third World grates against the first and bleeds. And before a scab forms it hemorrhages again, the lifeblood of two worlds merging to form a third country – a border culture' (Anzaldúa 1987: 3). At the site of violence, cultures blend into and discolour each other. That which painfully separates also precipitates bleeding, and bleeding joins, amalgamates, hybridises. Bleeding names not only the violence of colonial encounters but also an ontology where blood signals as much a violation as an interrelatedness ('all blood is intricately woven together' (Anzaldúa 1987: 85)) and, because of this connectedness, a becoming and change, life's fecundity.

The sanguine terminology suggests that, given the current tendencies in her reception, Anzaldúa's work may be more productively situated in the varied contexts of post-colonial thinking than the contemporary queer canon, a recontextualisation that would render our perspective more hospitable to metaphysical reflection. Post-colonial theory has remained more susceptible to the thought of ontology than queer theory, perhaps because, from the start, its global, cross-cultural agenda has attuned its theorists and practitioners to the utility and necessity of wide-reaching models. Similarly, the influence of Deleuze's philosophy on a variety of post-colonial writers (see Hallward 2001)[8] goes a long way in explaining their fluency in the metaphysical idiom. For example, both Anzaldúa and Glissant set out from a system of being based on something like a monistic substance, whether it be Anzaldúa's spirit or Glissant's *tout-monde*. While Glissant writes, in *Faulkner, Mississippi*, that theories of being often provide a refuge from the instabilities of becoming that are actualised at sites of crossbreeding (Glissant 2000: 78), his own metaphysical system echoes Deleuze's in prioritising becoming. Similarly, for Anzaldúa, being is the relentless, if painful, becoming of an interrelated universe.

With her ontological claims, Anzaldúa continues a long tradition of transatlantic thinkers for whom *blood* and *bleeding* articulate a suitably militant political, ethical and metaphysical stance. One of the earliest examples in this tradition is the African-American writer and activist

Pauline Elizabeth Hopkins's mobilisation of *blood* as a trope of the nation's (unacknowledged) hybridity. As the biblical title of one of her serialised novels has it, she insists on the fact of humankind's being 'of one blood'. In her lesser-known, self-published tract *A Primer of Facts Pertaining to the Early Greatness of the African Race and the Possibility of Restoration by its Descendants – with Epilogue* (1905), her repetitive mantra 'blood will flow' suggests the irreversible hybridisation of the world, its violence and fecundity.[9] Ultimately, for Hopkins blood's flow does not originate with diasporic violence, on the slave plantation. Rather, it signals an irreducible, originary mixing, a metaphysics of inter-connectedness – the condition of humanity's being 'of one blood'. Similarly, for Anzaldúa, blood's flow may be accelerated at sites of colonial violence, but it goes on with or without such moments of explicit, induced crises: 'All, including the planet and every species', she writes, 'are caught between cultures and bleed-throughs among different worlds' (Anzaldúa 2002: 541; see also Anzaldúa 2000: 21).

Anzaldúa differs from Hopkins in that she is speaking not only of the flow of *human* blood; she describes, rather, cosmic 'bleed-throughs', forms of in-, non- or ahuman connectedness. If blood in evolutionary thinking is used as shorthand to denote genealogy, Anzaldúa's expansion of relatedness beyond the human realm also requires that in reconsidering our models of reproduction, continuity and becoming we go beyond kinship theories. Ontological mestizaje does not take place through vertical reproduction; the new mestiza is not a branch off the family tree, however twisted. We entirely miss the specificity of her condition if we approach it, as some critics have done, through the structuralist framework of regulated sexual exchanges and kinship dynamics (Jagose 1994: 152). Rather, ontological mestizaje proceeds through what might be called horizontal, nonfiliative expansion, through abject(ed) queer bodies. In this way, like Glissant's understanding of creolisation, Anzaldúa's metaphysics goes beyond what we most immediately understand by blood's mobility. In one of her interviews, Anzaldúa comments that, with the new mestiza, '[she] was trying to get away from just thinking in terms of blood – you know, the mestiza as being of mixed blood' (Anzaldúa 2000: 133). If the new mestiza's hybridity is not reducible to the crossing of genealogical lines, hers is, in Glissant's terms, an 'inextricab[ility]' rather than a 'mixture' (Glissant 2000: 84).

Anzaldúa's thinking of life's interconnectedness in spirit brings her system close to Deleuze's reading of Spinoza's single substance. According to Deleuze, in Spinoza's view bodies are composites: 'There are no existing bodies, within Extension, that are not composed of a very great number of simple bodies' (Deleuze 1992: 201).[10] Modes can be seen as coagulations in a field of the single substance, held together by the internal relations peculiar to them. Some bodies that contribute to these singular relations are shared with other modes, in which these parts enter into different relations. Because of these shared bodies – Anzaldúa's 'the queer of me' – modes do not form self-enclosed, sovereign or completely separable entities but overlap with other modes, sharing some of their parts, which each mode submits to a unique relation with other parts. Distinct from one another in their specific internal relations, they are connected through the parts they share (and, ultimately, the single substance of which they are expressions). As Elspeth Probyn notes, Deleuze's 'ideas about bodies shake up assumptions about their boundedness – what we take to be our own and how one body relates to others' (Probyn 2005: 141).

In this context, we must reconfigure relatedness, hybridity and change otherwise than through evolutionary theory's arborescent schema, as Deleuze and Guattari have called it. To contrast Deleuze and Guattari's model of rhizomatic relatedness to that of the genealogical tree is to 'oppose epidemic to filiation, contagion to heredity, peopling by contagion to sexual reproduction, sexual production' (Deleuze and Guattari 1987: 241). Becoming in this model proceeds not through lines of descent but through 'transversal' leaps and connections (Deleuze and Guattari 1987: 11; Ansell Pearson 1999: 170), which can be understood as the movement between bodies that, for Anzaldúa, the 'queer of me' allows. Hybrid forms of life – which, according to Deleuze's reading of Spinoza, *all* modes are – proliferate not through reproduction but by 'expansion, propagation, occupation, contagion, peopling' (Deleuze and Guattari 1987: 239).

Seen in this way, for Deleuze and Guattari as well as for Anzaldúa, hybridity is the ontological condition of all beings, whose lines of flight habit-formation, often happily, prevents. While the ontological violence of bleeding is particularly acute on *la frontera*, its irreducibility to (what Mary Louise Pratt (1991) calls) colonial contact zones becomes obvious in the scene of the infant girl's menstruation. According to the doctor's assessment (which, notably, the narrator does not dispute), in bleeding the *unheimlich* queer becomes 'a throwback to the Eskimo', a mixed, untimely body. Her queerness is an involutionary (re)turn to a different evolutionary moment. Albeit a sign of interconnectedness, bleeding also precipitates the girl child's abjection: in her becoming-queer, she feels that she is 'stoned out of the herd' (Anzaldúa 1987: 43). Bleeding signals a cosmic interconnectedness, which is lived as an experience of singularity and isolation, one's being wrenched out of joint with the environment and its horology. If bleeding marks the girl child's maladaptation, her monstrosity is one of an involuntary untimeliness. When the mestiza emerges as a throwback, her peculiar *facultad* is similarly characterised by a temporal hybridity in that, with her coming-to-awareness, 'dormant areas of consciousness are being activated, awakened' (Anzaldúa 1987: Preface n.p.).

Like for nineteenth-century sexologists, queerness for Anzaldúa disturbs the progression of time. Her theory of shared bodies and evolutionary leaps suggests that sexologists and racial scientists were not wrong in declaring the homosexual woman an irregularity in the evolutionary progression, an aberration in linear time.[11] Yet, for Anzaldúa queerness does not threaten the evolutionary trajectory with degeneration – or rather, she re-evaluates our notions of (de)generation. She seems to understand queer hybridity as *involutionary*, that is, as a productive detour through the past. As a temporal process, involution in biology and physiology signals a movement inwards or back in time and bears connotations of aging and degeneration, a 'retrograde process of development', the very 'opposite of evolution'. As the *Oxford English Dictionary* tells us, it refers to an organ's becoming redundant 'when its permanent or temporary purpose has been fulfilled'. Conceived in terms of purposeful existence, an involute organ can be seen only as a leftover without an effective role in the evolutionary present. Yet, much like Bergson and Deleuze, Anzaldúa re-evaluates such schemas by problematising the usual evolutionary thinking about time, where the past is that which is less differentiated than the present. As Ansell Pearson writes, 'evolution is not only a movement forward but equally a deviation and a turning back' (Ansell Pearson 1999: 46).

The primary denotation of 'involution' is that of an implication, envelopment or enfolding. In biological and physiological terms, involution signals an intricate implication of organisms with their environment as well as other individuals, whether past, extant or emergent: in the *Oxford English Dictionary*'s 'quasi-concrete' illustration, it refers to the existing organism's role as a host or carrier of emergent individuals – 'the future animal exists in the female parent' – or the germinal co-infiltration of 'the universal in the individual'. As such, involution evokes the figure of *the fold*, with which Deleuze articulates 'an *antiextensional* concept of the multiple' (Badiou 1994: 52). Deleuze's, then, is an involutionary ontology, where 'what always matters is folding, unfolding, refolding' (Deleuze 1999: 137). It is in this sense that involution, as a return, 'is being, but only the being of becoming' (Deleuze 1994: 41). Bergson, too, proposes an involutionary understanding of evolution when, in *Creative Evolution*, he insists on the metaphysical connectedness of all beings: 'we shall find [the individual] solidary with each of [his remotest ancestors], solidary with that little mass of protoplasmic jelly which is probably at the root of the genealogical tree of life. Being, to a certain extent, one with this primitive ancestor, he is also solidary with all that descends from the ancestor in divergent directions. In this sense each individual may be said to remain united with the totality of living beings by invisible bonds' (Bergson 1998: 43).

Such involutionary interconnectedness characterises Bergson's, Deleuze's and – as I have been arguing – Anzaldúa's ontology, their understanding of becoming. Deleuze and Guattari speak of life's involutionary turning back, its enfolding upon itself as the ontology of its production: 'Becoming is involution, involution is creative. To regress is to move in the direction of something less differentiated. But to involve is to form a block that runs its own line "between" the terms in play and beneath assignable relations' (Deleuze and Guattari 1987: 238–9). Instead of following sexologists in seeing queer hybrids as throwbacks to earlier evolutionary stages, Anzaldúa similarly describes them as involutes, as unforeseeable mutations that reconfigure the horizon of possibilities by activating the virtual. According to her, queer hybridity allows '*some kind* of evolutionary step forward' (Anzaldúa 1987: 81, emphasis added). Alluding to forms of existence yet to-come with intentional ambiguity, she avoids repeating sexology's programmatic social Darwinism while embracing its problematic of queer (un)time(liness). In this, hers resembles Bergson's argument that evolution, always open and unpredictable, evades all programmes (Bergson 1998: 104–5; Ansell Pearson 2002: 79).

Anzaldúa's thought of the queer's untimeliness similarly echoes postcolonial theory's efforts to problematise the normativity of evolutionary temporality. Colonialism has often established its authority through evolutionary models of time and development. The logic behind terms such as *évolué* – used in the discourse of French colonialism to denote successfully assimilated, 'developed' natives – depends on the social-Darwinist hierarchisation of evolution into a teleological, universal template of progress. An *évolué* is an individual whose 'progress' has been beneficially accelerated and channelled by his willingness to embrace the missionary benevolence of the colonisers and their culture. Négritude writers such as Aimé Césaire and Léopold Sédar Senghor opposed this dynamic by propounding the necessity of the colonial elite to valorise the spirit and history of Africa, to become *griots*, through 'a voyage to ancestral sources' (Senghor 1991: 136). Senghor conceives this return as a movement backward in developmental time, to 'the Kingdom of Childhood'. For Melvin Dixon, this is Senghor's 'master trope': childhood for Senghor represents 'that realm of personal past he claims from the prejudices of Europe and baptizes as *négritude*' (Dixon 2006: 65–6).

Like négritude's, Anzaldúa's system is also one of (re)turning, of turning back and away from the extant historical and cultural moment. Yet, the differences between the two philosophies may be considerable. In seeking to accomplish a 'return to the native land', négritude thinkers arguably relied on a model of origin and authenticity that subsequent critics have problematised – most notable among them Frantz Fanon, who sought 'a . . . secularization of the mystique of negritude with Africa as mediator' (Khanna 2003: 195). If we accept this critique, Anzaldúa's return, in contrast, is an involution – a (re)turn not as much to the past as the virtual. It is a turn to a nonfiliative connectedness. An evolutionary monstrosity, the incipient new mestiza, bleeding across timescales, becomes not an *évolué* but an *involuée*, one that turns back not to the origin or that which once existed – 'Africa' in négritude thought – but to a connectedness whose actualised forms are untimely, yet to-come.[12] In its involutionary mode, Anzaldúa's queer theory 'refuse[s] to grant . . . the past the status of fixity and givenness. The past is always contingent on what the future makes of it' (Grosz 2001: 104). Indigo Violet captures something of this in her commentary on Anzaldúa's theory of 'the force of relation': 'Rather than attempting to re-member a past in search of a sovereign identity limited solely to our communities of origin, we can begin to re-member the past in order to grapple with the interconnectivity of our *mutual* living in America' (Violet 2002: 488). In her turn to the virtual past, the new mestiza's condition is one of becoming – of *queer breeding*. As the *Oxford English Dictionary* suggests, this generation is inherent in involution: involution in algebra designates a process of production, of becoming-more, through self-enfolding; it refers to '[t]he multiplication of a quantity into itself any number of times, so as to raise it to any assigned power', and, consequently, 'in extended sense, the raising of a quantity to any power, positive, negative, fractional, or imaginary'. It is this involutionary condition of becoming that characterises Anzaldúa's queer hybridity.

If, for Anzaldúa, becoming is involutionary, a turning back, for Pauline Hopkins, too, the past is revealed as that which may precipitate a future foreclosed by the nation's disavowal of amalgamation – the abjection of its 'queer bodies' (see Tuhkanen 2007). In *Borderlands/La Frontera*, a recurrent site for such becoming is *miktlán*, the underground realm of the dead, where the queer mestiza finds herself. Similarly, in Hopkins, the virtual past often has a subterranean existence: we find it as we stumble onto the tunnel that secretly joins the master's house and the slave quarters in *Hagar's Daughter* (Hopkins 1901/1902: 215) – carved out by what Robert Young would call 'colonial desire' (Young 1996) – and the forgotten, underground civilisation of Telassar in *Of One Blood*. Valerie Rohy argues that, in her description of the 'uncanny land' of Telassar (Hopkins 1902/1903: 590) – or, we might add, the derelict Enson Hall, the slave mansion that, in the postbellum nation, has earned an 'uncanny reputation' (Hopkins 1901/1902: 228) – Hopkins anticipates 'the psychoanalytic notion of time' that Freud exemplifies in 'The Uncanny'. In Hopkins's work, Rohy writes, 'the elegant linearity of blood lines and time lines is problematized by their status as lines of text whose figurality is inescapable' (Rohy 2003: 229). While Rohy discerns the entanglement of blood (lines) and time (lines) in Hopkins's work – an intertwining equally characteristic of Anzaldúa's thinking – these horologies of blood are, precisely, *not* figural or metaphorical; rather, Hopkins and Anzaldúa elaborate an ontological account of (queer) hybridity and (queer) time. Both Hopkins's 'brotherhood of man' (Hopkins 1902/1903: 713) and Anzaldúa's new mestizaje reconfigure 'blood lines' and 'time lines'. Particularly in Anzaldúa, instead of blood genealogies, we find queer, nonfiliative breeding; instead of linear, developmental time, there is becoming as an involutive enfolding onto the virtual past. Because of this enfolding, 'the past can be as malleable as the present' (Anzaldúa, 1990: xxvii), a malleability that names the potential actualisation of a future to-come.

Conclusion: Tangled Lines of Flight

> What tangled skeins are the genealogies of slavery!
> Harriet Jacobs, *Incidents in the Life of a Slave Girl*

I have been suggesting that Anzaldúa's work may itself be an interface between queer theory and post-colonial thinking. That is, she may provide a way of connecting the two disciplines while at the same time precipitating their becoming in that her work undoes the integrity of both entities.[13] Similarly, it should be clear by now that I detect a significant *accord* – that is, musical harmony or intellectual agreement (see Deleuze 1995: 86, 196 n7) – between Anzaldúa's and Deleuze's systems. Granting all differences and incompatibilities, their philosophies, characterised by metaphysical contemplation, nevertheless meet in their inassimilability to most contemporary queer thinking. It is their paradigmatic orientation that accounts for their marginal positions in the queer canon. Yet, their odd, perhaps ' "slantwise" position' – to evoke Foucault (Foucault 1997: 138) – vis-à-vis queer thinking may also precipitate the latter's reconfiguration.[14]

In developing an ontological notion of (queer) hybridity, Anzaldúa interfaces not only queer and post-colonial theories but also queer and African-American writers. As Werner Sollors (1999) and Robert Reid-Pharr (1999) have shown, a central concern in nineteenth- and early-twentieth-century black letters – of which Hopkins has here stood as an example – was to insist that the condition of 'the future American' was to be one of hybridity, a becoming-mulatto/a.[15] According to Reid-Pharr, nineteenth-century African-American writers '[were] not particularly concerned to express a Black American specificity but instead [were] about the project of representing a real alternative (the mulatto, the yellow, the altogether deracialized) to increasingly rigid narratives of black/white difference' (Reid-Pharr 2001: 73; see also Reid-Pharr 1999). He argues that the third decade of the twentieth century – the Harlem Renaissance – subsequently became an era when 'black intellectuals in concert with white social scientists beg[an] the very difficult cultural and social work of erasing distinction between black and mulatto and rigidifying the distinction between the "purely" black and the wholly "white"' (Reid-Pharr 2001: 46). One might suggest that nineteenth-century black writing comprises unexhausted virtual resources for our efforts to 'become more future-oriented', 'to look toward the future and to find political languages in which it can be discussed' (Gilroy 2000: 335). In her insistent focus on an unforeseeable future, Anzaldúa clearly contributes to the remarkable tradition of 'afrofuturist' thought and imagination, to which Paul Gilroy, toward the end of his book *Against Race* (2000), points as a site of 'imagining political culture beyond the color line'.[16]

A primary way that Anzaldúa engages with the thought of futurity is her evolutionary schema of queer, ontological hybridity. Reid-Pharr is sceptical about hybridity's alleged potential for disruptions. He queries 'whether the excitement with which some scholars approach the possibilities inherent in the hybrid, the mixed, the impure, and so forth is quite as well deserved as one might imagine. The idea that we are all somehow mixed is a notion with which any group of reasonably intelligent undergraduates will agree. The problem stems from the fact this agreement does little to change the actual conditions of living Americans' (Reid-Pharr

2001: 60). In his call for a radically future-oriented politics of post-racialism, Gilroy similarly observes: 'The temporal adjustment that warrants [a] sharp turn away from African antiquity and toward our planet's future is a difficult and delicate affair, especially if we recognize the possibility that the contested colonial and imperial past has not entirely released its grip on us' (Gilory 2000: 335). But in its involutionary mode, this orientation toward the future would not relinquish the past; rather it would reconfigure it in terms of the virtual. Here, Anzaldúa's ambivalent affirmation of mestizaje,[17] like the Deleuzian emphasis on multiplicities, may be an under-investigated resource for both post-colonial and queer theories of becoming. For example, Glissant sees creolisation-as-inextricability as the 'boundless home' of 'multiplicity', 'the suspension of identity' (Glissant 2000: 98). In (what I have tentatively called) Anzaldúa's monism, too, spirit is always splintered and split. For her, as for Deleuze, '[i]nseparable does not mean identical' (Deleuze 1983: 50). The 'inextricable' (Glissant 2000: 84) connectivity of singular bodies, which I have proposed we call queer hybridity, allows the future to emerge as unforeseeable: creolisation entails '[an] unpredictability that terrifies those who refuse the very idea, if not the temptation, to mix, flow together, and share' (Glissant 2000: 30).

Both Anzaldúa and Hopkins argue that the future depends on the de-disavowal, the de-abjection of hybridity, whether intrahuman (Hopkins) or beyond-the-human (Anzaldúa). Mestizaje deterritorialises, allows lines of flight from extant (racial) formations. In this, Anzaldúa echoes nineteenth-century African-American writers, who were consistent in pressing the white memory about the 'tangled skeins' (Jacobs 1999: 594) that crossed and bound the supposedly separate-but-equal constituents of the nation. As Harriet Jacobs and others knew, these skeins – explosively multiplied through the practice of sexual violence on the plantation – were radically inadmissible to the proponents of racial and social hygiene. Importantly, however, such binds often also precipitated flight. As much as a 'skein' flees across the sky, for many slaves the entanglement of blood lines enabled an escape – like the mythical self-alienation of 'flying slaves' – as they stole away from bondage by passing as white, their passport written on their suddenly unmarked skin.[18] As the likes of Hopkins and Chesnutt repeatedly suggest, in wider terms the irreversibly involved and involuted genealogies that snake beneath the nation's official historiography may draw lines of becoming along the subterranean, disavowed tracks of connectedness within and beyond the nation-state's borders. Echoing and elaborating on this tradition, Anzaldúa considers queer hybridity, which is more often than not lived in abjection and disavowal, as a dangerous line of flight, an opening onto an uncertain, painful becoming.[19]

References

Alcoff, L. M. (2006), 'The Unassimilated Theorist.' *PMLA* 121:1 (Jan.) pp. 255–9.

Ansell Pearson, K. (1999), *Germinal Life: The Difference and Repetition of Deleuze*, London: Routledge.

Ansell Pearson, K. (2002), *Philosophy and the Adventure of the Virtual: Bergson and the Time of Life*, London: Routledge.

Anzaldúa, G. E. (1983), 'La Prieta.' In Moraga and Anzaldúa (eds), pp. 198–209.

Anzaldúa, G. E. (1987), *Borderlands/La Frontera: The New Mestiza*, San Francisco: Spinsters/Aunt Lute.

Anzaldúa, G. E. (1990), 'Haciendo caras, una entrada.' In *Making Face, Making Soul/Haciendo caras: Creative and Critical Perspectives by Women of Color*, ed. Anzaldúa, San Francisco: Aunt Lute, pp. xv–xxviii.

Anzaldúa, G. E. (2000), *Interviews/Entrevistas*, ed. AnaLouise Keating, New York: Routledge.

Anzaldúa, G. E. (2002a), 'now let us shift . . . the path of conocimiento . . . inner works, public acts.' In Anzaldúa and Keating (eds), pp. 540–78.

Anzaldúa, G. E. (2002b), '(Un)natural Bridges, (Un)safe Spaces.' In Anzaldúa and Keating (eds), pp. 1–5.

Anzaldúa, G. E. (ed.) (1990), *Making Face/Making Soul: Haciendo Caras: Creative and Critical Perspectives by Women of Color*, San Francisco: Aunt Lute.

Anzaldúa, G. E. and Keating, A. (eds) (2002), *this bridge we call home: radical visions for transformation*, New York: Routledge.

Badiou, A. (1994), 'Gilles Deleuze, *The Fold: Leibniz and the Baroque*.' Trans. Thelma Sowley. In *Gilles Deleuze and the Theater of Philosophy*, ed. C. V. Boundas and D. Olkowski, New York: Routledge, pp. 51–69.

Bergson, H. (1998), *Creative Evolution* (1907). Trans. Arthur Mitchell. 1911; rpt. Mineola: Dover.

Bersani, L. (1998), 'Is the Rectum a Grave?' In *AIDS: Cultural Analysis/Cultural Activism*, ed. D. Crimp, Cambridge: MIT Press, pp. 197–222.

Bersani, L. and Dutoit, U. (1993), *Arts of Impoverishment: Beckett, Rothko, Resnais*, Cambridge: Harvard University Press.

Bersani, L. and Dutoit, U. (1985), *The Forms of Violence: Narrative in Assyrian Art and Modern Culture*, New York: Schocken.

Bersani, L. and Dutoit, U. (1998), *Caravaggio's Secrets*, Cambridge: MIT Press.

Bhabha, H. K. (1994), *The Location of Culture*, New York: Routledge.

Boundas, C. V. (2005), 'Ontology.' In *The Deleuze Dictionary*, ed. A. Parr, New York: Columbia University Press, pp. 191–2.

Braidotti, R. (2005/2006), 'Affirming the Affirmative: On Nomadic Affectivity.' In *The Becoming-Deleuzoguattarian of Queer Studies*, ed. M. O'Rourke. A special issue of *Rhizomes* 11–12 (Fall/Spring), 8 November 2006. www.rhizomes.net/issue11/index.html.

Butler, J. (1990), *Gender Trouble: Feminism and the Subversion of Identity*, New York: Routledge.

Butler, J. (1999), *Subjects of Desire: Hegelian Reflections in Twentieth-Century France*. 1987; rpt. New York: Columbia University Press.

Carter, J. (1997), 'Normality, Whiteness, Authorship: Evolutionary Sexology and the Primitive Pervert.' In *Science and Homosexualities*, ed. V. A. Rosario. New York: Routledge, pp. 155–76.

Chesnutt, C. W. (1999), *Essays and Speeches*, ed. J. R. McElrath, Jr, R. C. Leitz III and J. S. Crisler, Stanford: Stanford University Press.

Cohen, C. J. (2005), 'Punks, Bulldaggers, and Welfare Queens: The Radical Potential of Queer Politics?' In *Black Queer Studies: A Critical Anthology*, ed. E. P. Johnson and M. G. Henderson, Durham: Duke University Press, pp. 21–51.

Deleuze, G. (1983), *Nietzsche and Philosophy* (1962), trans. Hugh Tomlinson, New York: Columbia University Press.

Deleuze, G. (1992), *Expressionism in Philosophy* (1968), trans. Martin Joughin, New York: Zone.

Deleuze, G. (1994), *Difference and Repetition* (1968), trans. Paul Patton, New York: Columbia University Press.

Deleuze, G. (1995), *Negotiations, 1972–1990* (1990), trans. Martin Joughin, New York: Columbia University Press.

Deleuze, G. (1999), *The Fold: Leibniz and the Baroque* (1988), trans. Tom Conley. 1993; rpt. Minneapolis: University of Minnesota Press.

Deleuze, G. and Guattari, F. (1987), *A Thousand Plateaus: Capitalism and Schizophrenia* (1980), trans. Brian Massumi, Minneapolis: University of Minnesota Press.

Deleuze, G. and Guattari, F. (1998), *Anti-Oedipus* (1972), trans. Robert Hurley, Mark Seem and Helen R. Lane. 1977; rpt. Minneapolis: University of Minnesota Press.

Dixon, M. (1987), *Ride Out the Wilderness: Geography and Identity in Afro-American Literature*, Urbana: University of Illinois Press.

Dixon, M. (2006), 'The Black Writer's Use of Memory' (1994). Rpt in *A Melvin Dixon Critical Reader*, ed. J. A. Joyce and D. A. McBride, Jackson: University Press of Mississippi, pp. 55–70.

Eng, D. L., Halberstam, J. and Muñoz, J. E. (eds) (2005), *What's Queer about Queer Studies Now?* A special issue of *Social Text* 84–85 23:3–4 (Fall–Winter).

Foucault, M. (1997), 'Friendship as a Way of Life' (1981), trans. John Johnston. In *Essential Works, Vol. 1: Ethics: Subjectivity and Truth*, ed. P. Rabinow, trans. Robert Hurley and others, New York: The New Press, pp. 136–40.

Gabilondo, J. (1997), 'Afterword to the 1997 Edition.' In Vasconcelos, pp. 99–117.

Garber, L. (2001), *Identity Poetics: Race, Class, and the Lesbian-Feminist Roots of Queer Theory*, New York: Columbia University Press.

Gilroy, P. (2000), *Against Race: Imagining Political Culture beyond the Color Line*, Cambridge: Harvard University Press.

Glissant, E. (2000), *Faulkner, Mississippi* (1996), trans. Barbara Lewis and Thomas C. Spear. 1999; rpt. Chicago: University of Chicago Press.

Grosz, E. (2001), *Architecture from the Outside: Essays on Virtual and Real Spaces*, Cambridge: MIT Press.

Grosz, E. (2004), *The Nick of Time: Politics, Evolution, and the Untimely*, Durham: Duke University Press.

Grosz, E. (2005), *Time Travels: Feminism, Nature, Power*, Durham: Duke University Press.

Grosz, E. (n.d.), 'Interview with Elizabeth Grosz.' Conducted by R. Ausch, R. Doane and L. Perez. *Found Object* 9. www.web.gc.cuny.edu/csctw/found_object/text/grosz.htm. East Carolina University, Joyner Library, 8 January 2007.

Hall, L. (1999), 'Writing Selves Home at the Crossroads: Anzaldúa and Chrystos (Re)Configure Lesbian Bodies', *Ariel: A Review of International English Literature* 30:2 (April) pp. 99–117.

Hallward, P. (2001), *Absolutely Postcolonial: Writing between the Singular and the Specific*, Manchester: Manchester University Press.

Hallward, P. (2006), *Out of This World: Deleuze and the Philosophy of Creation*, London: Verso.

Hames-Garcia, M. (2000), 'How to Tell a Mestizo from an Enchirito®: Colonialism and National Culture in the Borderlands', *Diacritics* 30:4 (Winter) pp. 102–22.

Haslanger, S. (2000), 'Feminism in Metaphysics: Negotiating the Natural.' In *The Cambridge Companion to Feminism in Philosophy*, ed. M. Fricker and J. Hornsby, Cambridge: Cambridge University Press, pp. 107–26.

Hicks, D. E. (1991), *Border Writing: The Multidimensional Text*, Minneapolis: University of Minnesota Press.

Hopkins, P. E. (1903), 'Echoes from the Annual Convention of Northeastern Federation of Colored Women's Clubs', *Colored American Magazine*, Oct., pp. 709–13.

Hopkins, P. E. (1905), *A Primer of Facts Pertaining to the Early Greatness of the African Race and the Possibility of Restoration by its Descendants – with Epilogue*, Cambridge: P. E. Hopkins.

Hopkins, P. E. (1988a), *Hagar's Daughter: A Story of Southern Caste Prejudice*. 1901/1902. Rpt in *The Magazine Novels*, pp. 1–284.

Hopkins, P. E. (1988b), *The Magazine Novels*, New York: Oxford University Press.

Hopkins, P. E. (1988c), *Of One Blood; or, The Hidden Self*. 1902/1903. Rpt in *The Magazine Novels*, pp. 439–621.

Jacobs, H. (Linda Brent) (1999), *Incidents in the Life of a Slave Girl*. 1861; rpt in *I Was Born a Slave: An Anthology of Classic Slave Narratives. Volume 2: 1849–1866*, ed. Y. Taylor, Chicago: Lawrence Hill, pp. 533–681.

Jaén, D. T. (1997), 'Introduction.' In Vasconcelos, pp. xi–xxxiii.

Jagose, A. (1994), *Lesbian Utopics*, New York: Routledge.

Jahn, J. (1961), *Muntu: An Outline of the New African Culture* (1958), trans. Marjorie Grene, New York: Grove.

Kaplan, C. (1990), 'Deterritorializations: The Rewriting of Home and Exile in Western Feminist Discourse.' In *The Nature and Context of Minority Discourse*, ed. Abdul R. JanMohamed and David Lloyd, Oxford: Oxford University Press, pp. 357–68.

Keating, A. (2002), 'Forging El Mundo Zurdo: Changing Ourselves, Changing the World.' In Anzaldúa and Keating (eds), pp. 519–30.

Keating, A. (2000), 'Risking the Personal: An Introduction.' In Anzaldúa, *Interviews/Entrevistas*, pp. 1–15.

Khanna, R. (2003), *Dark Continents: Psychoanalysis and Colonialism*, Durham: Duke University Press.

Lugones, M. (1992), 'On *Borderlands/La Frontera*: An Interpretative Essay', *Hypatia* 7:4 (Fall) pp. 31–7.

Mercer, K. (1994), *Welcome to the Jungle: New Positions in Black Cultural Studies*, New York: Routledge.

Moncef, S. el (2003), '*Übermenschen*, Mestizas, Nomads: The Ontology of Becoming and the Scene of Transnational Citizenship in Anzaldúa and Nietzsche', *Angelaki* 8:3 (December) pp. 41–57.

Moraga, C. and Anzaldúa, G. (eds) (1983), *This Bridge Called My Back: Writings by Radical Women of Color*, 2nd edn, New York: Kitchen Table.

Nelson, A. (ed.) (2002), *Afrofuturism*. A special issue of *Social Text* 71 20:2 (Summer).

Oksala, J. (2005), 'Feministinen filosofia nykyisyyden ontologiana.' In *Feministinen filosofia*, ed. J. Oksala and L. Werner, Helsinki: Gaudeamus, pp. 156–205.

Oliver Rotger, M. A. (2001), ' "Sangre Fértil"/Fertile Blood: Migratory Crossings, War and Healing in Gloria Anzaldúa's Borderlands/La Frontera.' In *Dressing Up for War: Transformations of Gender and Genre in the Discourse and Literature of War*, ed. A. Usandizaga and A. Monnickendam, Amsterdam: Rodopi, pp. 189–211.

Parr, C. S. (1981), 'José Vasconcelos: Thought and Ideology in the Chicano Literary Arts', *Denver Quarterly* 16:3 (Fall) pp. 52–60.

Perles Rochel, J. A. (2002), 'Revisiting the Borderlands: A Critical Reading of Gloria Anzaldúa's *Borderlands/La Frontera: Towards a New Mestiza* (*sic*).' In *Evolving Origins, Transplanting Cultures: Literary Legacies of the New Americans*, ed. L. P. Alonso Gallo and A. D. Miguela, Huelva, Spain: Universidad de Huelva, pp. 229–35.

Phelan, S. (1994), *Getting Specific: Postmodern Lesbian Politics*, Minneapolis: University of Minnesota Press.

Pratt, M. L. (1991), 'Arts of the Contact Zone', *Profession*, pp. 33–40.

Probyn, E. (2005), *Blush: Faces of Shame*, Minneapolis: University of Minnesota Press.

Raiskin, J. (1994), 'Inverts and Hybrids: Lesbian Rewritings of Sexual and Racial Identities.' In *The Lesbian Postmodern*, ed. L. Doan, New York: Columbia University Press, pp. 156–72.

Reid-Pharr, R. F. (1999), *Conjugal Union: The Body, the House, and the Black American*, New York: Oxford University Press.

Reid-Pharr, R. F. (2001), *Black Gay Man: Essays*, New York: New York University Press.

Roberts, T. T. (1998), *Contesting Spirit: Nietzsche, Affirmation, Religion*, Princeton: Princeton University Press.

Rohy, V. (2003), 'Time Lines: Pauline Hopkins' Literary History', *American Literary Realism* 35:3 (Spring) pp. 212–32.

Sedgwick, E. K. (1993), *Tendencies*, Durham: Duke University Press.

Senghor, L. S. (1991), 'Song of the Initiate.' In *The Collected Poetry*, trans. Melvin Dixon, Charlottesville: University Press of Virginia, pp. 136–9.

Smith Storey, O. (2004), 'Flying Words: Contests of Orality and Literacy in the Trope of the Flying Africans', *Journal of Colonialism and Colonial History* 5(3).

Sollors, W. (1999), *Neither Black nor White yet Both: Thematic Explorations of Interracial Literature*. 1997; rpt. Cambridge, MA: Harvard University Press.

Somerville, S. B. (2000), *Queering the Color Line: Race and the Invention of Homosexuality in American Culture*, Durham: Duke University Press.

Stepan, N. (1991), *The Hour of Eugenics: Race, Gender, and Nation in Latin America*, Ithaca: Cornell University Press.

Tuhkanen, M. (2006), 'Kuolema ja kirjallisen kokemus: Frederick Douglass orjuutta vastaan.' In F. Douglass, *Amerikkalaisen orjan omaelämäkerta* (1845), trans. Pekka Jääskeläinen, Helsinki: Like, pp. 167–83.

Tuhkanen, M. (2007), ' "Out of Joint": Passing, Haunting, and the Time of Slavery in *Hagar's Daughter*', *American Literature* 79:2 (June) pp. 335–61.

Vasconcelos, J. (1997), *The Cosmic Race/La raza cósmica* (1925), trans. Didier T. Jaén. 1979; rpt. Baltimore: Johns Hopkins University Press.

Violet, I. (2002), 'Linkages: A Personal-Political Journey with Feminist-of-Color Politics.' In Anzaldúa and Keating (eds), pp. 486–94.

Walters, W. W. (1997), ' "One of Dese Mornings, Bright and Fair/Take My Winds and Cleave de Air": The Legend of the Flying Africans and Diasporic Consciousness', *MELUS* 22:3 (Autumn) pp. 3–29.

Wilentz, G. (1989/1990), 'If You Surrender to the Air: Folk Legends of Flight and Resistance in African American Literature', *MELUS* 16:1 (Spring/Spring) pp. 21–32.

Young, R. J. C. (1996), *Colonial Desire: Hybridity in Theory, Culture and Race*. 1995; rpt. London: Routledge.

Notes

1. AnaLouise Keating has been most consistent in drawing our attention to this 'metaphysics of interconnectedness' in Anzaldúa's philosophy. See, for example, her introduction to Anzaldúa's *Interviews/Entrevistas* (Keating 2000) and the essay 'Forging El Mundo Zurdo' (Keating 2002).
2. For relevant discussions of Vasconcelos, see Gabilondo 1997: 106–7; Jaén 1997; Parr 1981; and Stepan 1991: 145–53. For Vasconcelos and Anzaldúa, see Raiskin 1994: 162–3.
3. For a more sustained consideration of Anzaldúa's philosophical allegiances, see Moncef's (2003) discussion of *Borderlands/La Frontera* and Nietzsche.
4. In addition to Anzaldúa, the only other contemporary queer thinker with a clear ontological bent is Bersani. Constantin Boundas has similarly pointed to Deleuze as one of only two ontologists – Immanuel Lévinas being the other one – in the field of poststructuralist philosophy (Boundas 2005: 191). I suggest very briefly some points of overlap between Anzaldúa and Bersani in the final section below.
5. The term 'contact zone' is Mary Louise Pratt's (1990).
6. In 1993, for example, she insists that 'to be human is to be in relationship; to be human is to be related to other people, to be interdependent with other people' (Anzaldúa 2000: 206). A few years later, she notes the shift in her thinking away from human-centredness: 'I now believe alliances entail interdependent relationships with the whole environment – with the plants, the earth, and the air as well as people' (Anzaldúa 2000: 195). In Deleuzian terms, such connectedness beyond the human – '[e]verything and everyone is in relationship with everything else' (Anzaldúa 2000: 242) – might be called rhizomatic relatedness.
7. In 'La Prieta' (Anzaldúa, 1983: 198) and her *Interviews* (Anzaldúa 2000: 19–20, 23, 78, 94, 169), Anzaldúa recalls being three months at the time of her first menstruation. In *Borderlands/La Frontera*, the narrator seems to suggest a later date for her bleeding: 'I was two or three years old the first time *Coatlicue* visited my psyche' (Anzaldúa 1987: 42).
8. Responding to Peter Hallward's important critique of Deleuze (see also Hallward 2006) and strands of post-colonial theory influenced by his philosophy is beyond the scope of this essay. The initial move in such a response might be to suggest the inassimilability of Deleuze's transcendental empiricism into Hallward's impressive but rather neat delineation of the field of post-colonial thinking into the categories of the specific and the singular.
9. On Hopkins, see Tuhkanen 2007.
10. Deleuze's reading crossbreeds Spinoza with Bergson, according to whom 'each of these elements (that compose "the most complex and the most harmonious organism") may itself be an organism in certain cases . . . An organism is composed of tissues, each of which lives for itself. The cells of which the tissues are made have also a certain independence' (Bergson 1998: 41).
11. See Carter 1997 and Somerville 2000: ch. 1 for discussions of the interlinked projects of nineteenth-century sexology and racial sciences.
12. Yet, the temporal vicissitudes of the *évolué*'s backward turn, proposed by negritude, require careful reassessment. For example, Janheinz Jahn's classic description of the African poetic tradition suggests that, like Anzaldúa's, the craft of négritude writers aimed at eliciting transformation: '[African p]oetry', Jahn writes, 'does not describe, but arranges series of images which alter reality in the direction of the future, which create, produce, invoke, and bring about the future. The present interpreted by the poetry is subordinated to the future.' For African poets, '[t]he present is material for transformation' (Jahn 1961: 149). Further, like Ranjanna Khanna in her careful reading of the mutual influence of

psychoanalysis and (anti-)colonialist thought, one needs to distinguish between different brands of négritude. See, for example, Khanna's distinction between the ideas of 'Africa' in the work of Suzanne and Aimé Césaire, Albert Memmi, Senghor and the French surrealists (Khanna 2003: 124–6, 132, 195).

13. For examples and discussion of varied ways to engage the concerns of post-colonial theories with those of queer studies, see Eng, Halberstam and Muñoz 2005.

14. Very briefly, I wish to point to Bersani's work as another potential resource for such reconfiguring or reorientation of queer thinking. The position of his work in queer theorising is similar to Anzaldúa's: both are frequently cited, yet the singularity of their approach remains little appreciated. Most often, Bersani is, not incorrectly, cited as a theorist of failure and violence: the failure of relationality in sexuality's solipsistic jouissance, the violently masochistic deracination of structured selves. Yet, like Anzaldúa, he affirms an ontological structure of the world, which he and Ulysse Dutoit find described and experimented on in the 'ontological laborator[ies]' of literature, art and film (Bersani and Dutoit 1998: 59, 63). In moments that echo Anzaldúa, Bersani and Dutoit depict '[an] essentially mysterious connectedness in the universe' (Bersani and Dutoit 1985: 46). The consistency of being is such that 'individuation' is conceptualised as 'a metaphysical error or crime. It violates the total relationality of being, which means, for example, that the human has affinities – of design, positioning, movement – with the nonhuman and that objects (including ourselves) are always being repeated and lost in other objects to which they correspond as forms' (Bersani and Dutoit 1993: 140). Such ontological interrelatedness – which, as in Anzaldúa's thinking, always exceeds the human realm – is variously called 'correspondence of forms', 'inaccurate replication' or 'homo-ness' in Bersani and Dutoit. Above all, what joins Bersani's project to Anzaldúa's and Deleuze's is his insistence on thinking about becoming such that the future is not rendered foreseeable in any anticipatory visions or conceptualisations. In Deleuze's terms, he thinks becoming not in terms of possibilities but virtualities.

15. 'The Future American' is the collective title that Charles Chesnutt gave to his trilogy of essays published in the autumn of 1900; see Chesnutt 1999: 121–36.

16. On afrofuturisms, see also Nelson 2002.

17. On Anzaldúa's ambivalence, see Hames-Garcia 2000.

18. On 'flying' in the African-American cultural tradition, see Dixon 1987: *passim*; Smith Storey 2004; Walters 1997; and Wilentz 1989/1990. While, in the French original, Deleuze's *fuite* does not refer to aviation, the connotations of 'flight' in the African-American tradition encompass escape and ascendance, theft and disappearance, all of which are registered in Deleuze's descriptions of the processes of deterritorialisation.

19. For some brief remarks on the instabilities of 'flight' and 'becoming' in slave narratives, especially Frederick Douglass's, see Tuhkanen 2006: 174–7.

Chapter 7

Prosthetic Performativity: Deleuzian Connections and Queer Corporealities

Margrit Shildrick

What could be more seductive – to a collectivity of binary breaking neo-materialist academics – than a book organised, to quote the editors, around minoritarian thinking/practices, a (con)text that promises to interpose DeleuzoGuattarian theory with queer becomings to enhance the productivity of both? Of course I shall join the project: I read and respect the work of my co-authors, regret missing the originating conference, and welcome the opportunity to explore my own emerging lines of flight. And yet . . . perhaps I have understood the proposal all the wrong way round. I do indeed work extensively in the field of minoritarian thinking/practices, more specifically in the field of Critical Disability Studies, where I am developing a Deleuzian approach, and yet there seems to be limited overlap between my material concerns and those of others whether they are Deleuzian scholars and theorists of disability. What *is* by now well established and growing, however, is a turn by many of the latter to the possibilities and insights of queer theory as an effective methodology for opening up understanding of the relation between bodies and of the constitution of corporeality in general. The binary of disabled and non-disabled undoubtedly lingers within that approach, but it is increasingly destabilised by the intimation that all forms of embodiment are subject to reconstruction, extension and transformation, regardless of the conventionally identified vectors of change and decay. And there is scope too for a further productive move: the strong take-up of queer theory within disability studies will lead, I suggest, to a reappraisal of the significance of notions like 'desiring-machine' 'assemblage' and 'body without organs', all terms that have the potential to radically disrupt the devaluation of the disabled body. It is not my claim, however, that either queer or Deleuzian theory will come to dominate critical disability studies, but rather that, vis-à-vis the academy, disability studies itself has a theoretical significance which, by working at the intersection of both, will be capable of taking on the role of critique that queer and Deleuzian theory now occupy.

In this chapter I want to take some initial steps in that direction by addressing the question of what it means to be an embodied subject, and more specifically a sexual subject, primarily as a matter of theory, but always keeping in mind the implications of that project for the material parameters that mark out which bodies are to matter.[1] Given that for any postmodernist analysis the complex issue of sexual subjectivity is always open to question and uncertainty, then to read the problematic, as I intend, through the field of disability, where sexuality has scarcely been theorised at all, is even more troubling. The widespread western uneasiness in acknowledging or even recognising erotic desire – an uneasiness that can be seen at play in the attempted effacement of childhood sexuality, or in the consignment of older people to a sexual limbo – is most clearly mobilised where the form of embodiment itself contests, either deliberatively or accidentally, the standards of normative corporeality. Whether the body in question has been intentionally transformed as in transsexual surgery or enhanced by body-building drug regimes, or has suffered severe trauma such as amputation or spinal injury, then the attributions of sexual desire and practice are likely to invoke discomfort and confusion. Even more disturbing, however, to the point of denial of any sexuality at all, are those modes of embodiment that are both radically anomalous *and* resistant – either projectively or retrospectively – to normative recuperation. The category of congenital or early onset disability is surely paradigmatic in that its exclusion from the very notion of sexual subjectivity is so underproblematised that it is taken almost as a natural fact. It is not necessary to re-essentialise sexuality, however, in order to contest the exclusionary violence of such a view. One option – which I shall go on to distort in a more productive Deleuzian manner – is to follow the phenomenological path taken by Michel Foucault and Judith Butler which makes clear that what is at stake lies in the performativity of sexuality, not as a potentially pleasurable bonus, but as a core element of self-becoming that infuses all aspects of the materiality of living in the world. As Merleau-Ponty (1963) suggests, sexuality is, quite simply, a modality of existence.

That this insight has profound implications for those who are differently embodied, for whom sexuality is both devalued and denied, is beyond question, for it suggests that to silence or strip sexuality of significance is to damage the very possibility of human becoming. What is at stake is an ethical matter[2] that devolves on the necessarily ambiguous nature of sameness and difference that cannot be encompassed by any facile appeal to equality, not least insofar as that concept is fatally compromised by its implicit reference to a system of values that is both reliant on and hostile to the non-normative. The issue, at heart, concerns the meanings and representations through which an embodied sexuality is constructed as a positive property of the normative subject, yet viewed as deviant, degraded or simply not acknowledged at all in the non-normative subject. Although my ultimate aim is to demonstrate the efficacy of a Deleuzian analysis in pursuit of an affirmative – indeed flourishing – account of disability and sexuality, we cannot yet quite forget Foucault. As with most major postconventional theorists, Foucault largely overlooked the significance of disability,[3] but it is necessary, nonetheless, to start with his work on uncovering the mechanisms in play in the construction and maintenance of the socio-cultural order. Despite some substantial signals of where 'bodies and pleasures' might subvert normative stability, Foucault is clearest in setting out the impressive array of disciplinary techniques that are aimed at the singular body in all its aspects, but above all in its sexual pleasures (Foucault 1979, 1980). As he shows, far from originating in an instinctual, biological ground, sexuality is always in a state of dynamic process that is neither predetermined nor fully open to intentional possibilities. Instead, sexuality is 'organized by power in its grip on bodies and their materiality, their forces, energies, sensations and pleasures' (Foucault 1979: 155). And, indeed, within Foucault's schema, those bodies themselves are equally constructed, and thus open to endless transformation, rather than given entities. Nonetheless his thinking of how those bodies materialise has some curious omissions.

What Foucault notoriously fails to address – as Butler's powerful setting out and take-up of the notion of performativity (1990) makes all too apparent – is the sense in which corporeality as sexed might be differentially constituted along the designated lines of male and female morphology. But that is only the most obvious omission. What, we might ask, of the enactment of other significant, and indeed intersectional, differences, not least that which constitutes the binary between able-bodied and disabled? It is not my suggestion that that particular division can ever be as clearly articulated as the one separating male from female – although both conventional distinctions call for a deconstructive analysis – but that there are similar urgent reasons to interrogate the initial occlusion that covers over difference. In short, and with due regard to the dangers of universalism, should we not conclude that the phenomenology of disability – with its potential absences, displacements and prosthetic additions to the body – generates its own specific sets of sexual possibilities that may both limit and extend the performativity of self-identity? If the normative standard against which the acceptability of sexual practice is judged is male-dominant, heterosexual intercourse between two adults ideally acting without overt external intervention, then in addition to an extensive range of familiar refusals mobilised by preference, or at least some form of subjective decision, there are also certain morphological constraints that quite simply preclude normative compliance. To have more or fewer limbs than the norm, to be unable to hear or see in the same way as the majority, to have a prostheticised body, or to be conjoined,[4] are all conditions that necessarily disrupt expectations of the 'proper' conduct of sexuality. It is not that any one of us – however we are embodied – can entirely fulfil normative demands, and yet some forms of non-compliance evoke not simply disapproval, but feelings of disgust, albeit a disgust that is threaded through with a certain fascination. Why is it that things of which the body is capable and incapable should generate such negative concern?

At least part of the reason emerges if the socio-cultural description of sexual normativity is underpinned by a more philosophical analysis. What confers value in the modernist western conception of the sexual subject are those familiar categories that constitute autonomy, that comprise notions of self-determination, separation and distinction, and corporeal wholeness. And those are precisely the categories both that will be contested by a Deleuzian approach, and in which the disabled body is deemed to be lacking. In contradistinction, then, to the example of homosexuality, which may offend against specific social mores around sexuality by failing primarily to perform appropriate models of masculinity or femininity, disability touches on a far more entrenched understanding of what it is to be a subject at all. Given that connotations of dependency and vulnerability – regardless of whether they are operative or not – are understood to be antithetical to the attribution of full subjectivity in general, then the anxieties provoked by those qualities are all the more acute when their embodiment appears in a context that is already beset by all manner of putative threats to the autonomous subject. What I mean is that most sexuality is inherently about intercorporeality, about a potential merging of bodies, wills and intentions, about a transmission of matter, and about an intrinsic vulnerability in which the embodied subject is not only open to the other in an abstract way, but is likely to be in a physical contact that is neither wholly predictable nor decidable. That the subject is never settled or simply present as a sovereign self, but intricately interwoven with the other in a dynamic process of self-becoming, is of course the basis of the phenomenological model of embodiment in a more general sense. But it is in the sexual relation, above all, that Merleau-Ponty's notion of the reversibility of touch (1968), with its implicit confusion of the boundaries between one body and another, and its potential for contamination, takes on a concrete materiality.[5] It is precisely because of the inherent risk of losing self-control and self-definition that the domain of sexuality is so highly disciplined and regulated, so saturated with performative constraints.[6] And where the body of the other is already uncertain and resistant to the demands of normative comportment and expression – as it is paradigmatically in disability – then touch figures a moment of real threat, a troubling of the subject's illusion of purity and self-sufficiency.

The implication is not that the corporeality of people with disabilities is uniquely unstable, vulnerable or interdependent, but rather that the nexus signals overtly what is more easily repressed in those whose embodiment satisfies the normative standards of western modernity. As Henri-Jacques Stiker puts it, disability is 'the tear in our being' (1999: 10), a corporeal mode that in the context of sexuality in particular reveals the incompletion and lack of cohesion of the embodied subject. But if the disabled body refuses recuperation to the project of selfsameness – not simply an-other, not like me, but deeply disruptive of the very parameters that constitute selfhood – then its fate is to be refused any recognition in terms of sexual subjectivity. The response is not so much punitive, as it is with so many forms of sexual otherness, but more typically takes the form of a silencing that intends a denial, and yet reveals precisely the complicity that it seeks to cover over. As Foucault notes:

> Silence itself – the things one declines to say or is forbidden to name . . . is less the absolute limit of discourse . . . than an element that functions alongside the things said . . . [silences] are an integral part of the strategies that underlie and permeate discourses. (1979: 27)

For Foucault, silence is an element of discursive power, but does it not suggest also a psychic dimension to performativity that he leaves aside? Despite their explanatory power, then, it seems to me that neither the wider phenomenological approach nor the model of exterior governmentality is adequate to the theorisation of sexuality. Although Foucault convincingly charts the operations of a transformatory power over and through the body – albeit one that is interiorised by each individual – he fails to take on the psychic significances of irreducible differences in embodiment. Similarly, despite developing elsewhere a sophisticated understanding of the unconscious processes at work in sexuality (Butler 1993), Butler's account of performativity per se, though non-volitional, remains a largely surface event.

My point is that if body image – and especially internalised body image – is never simply a material reality but a complex and fluid mix of corporeal, psychic and social components, then there is need for a more nuanced understanding, not simply of the *operation* of normative constructions of sexuality, but of the reasons for their emergence. In my attempts to theorise the question of disability and sexuality around such a problematic, I initially moved towards an analytic derived from psychoanalysis, particularly as deployed postconventionally. Despite its efficacy in uncovering the roots of the normative anxiety that grips that troubling conjunction, however, the paradigm seems to provide no way of unsettling a cultural imaginary that is closed to a more positive model of corporeally anomalous sexual relationality. In other words, psychoanalysis critiques but does not fully queer the parameters of what is to count and what is to be occluded. Like women's sexuality, or more specific categories like lesbian desire, that have suffered a certain erasure in which the unsaid indicates an unthinkable anxiety, the conjunction of disability and sexuality is referred back to an explanatory model that implicitly privileges active phallic desire and the illusory quest for the restoration of an originary corporeal unity. I am not claiming that either the psychic or performative operations of gender and disability are directly comparable, but that both pose the question of whether any model based on the normative performance of male-dominant forms of genital sexuality has the capacity to encompass its excluded others. Having explored the seductive lure of the psychoanalytic approach and its inherent shortcomings more fully elsewhere (2007), I will pass swiftly over that trajectory here and move on to open up an alternative that retains a sense of psychic underpinnings, but owes more to Deleuze and Guattari than to Freud or Lacan.

As I understand it, the psychoanalytic model, which offers an explanation of the mechanisms by which the emerging subject moves from infantile to adult sexuality and is recognised as a sexual being, gives no real consideration to what difference morphological diversity would make. Aside from the supposedly inescapable biological sex of male or female organised around the materiality of the penis, other differences play minimal part in the relevant theory. For both Freud and Lacan the acquisition and stabilisation of self-image is dependent on a certain corporeal introjection, not directly of the infant's own bodily boundaries and sensations, but of an ideal body image representing, as Elizabeth Grosz puts it, 'a map of the body's surface and a reflection of the image of the other's body' (1994: 38). In place of the maternal-infant dyad, the infant experiences a split which mobilises an endlessly substituted desire for that irrecoverable originary but undifferentiated wholeness. But if, as Lacan implies, the putative unity of the self relies on the reflective unity of the specular other – indeed on jubilantly casting aside the infant's actual 'motor incapacity and nursling dependency' (1977: 2) – then subsequently would not that new-found sense of self be radically shaken by any mark of dis-unity in the external image? The disabled body, then, could be read as both insufficient as an object of desire, and an unwelcome intimation of the *corps morcelé* that the emergent subject must disavow or abject. It is not that the disabled infant would fail to negotiate the mirror stage – for in the psychic register all self-identity is based on mis-recognition. Rather, in its apparent lack of wholeness, the infant becomes other, its self-positioning as a subject of desire – like that of women – denied recognition. In such an account, the potential of difference to queer the terms of reference is effectively closed down. To escape the Lacanian impasse, perhaps it is necessary to look elsewhere, and turn to a DeleuzoGuattarian alternative.

In decisively rejecting the Freudian/Lacanian model of desire as representative of, and mobilised by, lack, and by an implicit and impossible promise of completion and unity in a return to the mother, Deleuze and Guattari (1984, 1987) rewrite desire as productive, excessive to the embodied self, and unfixed. Rather than being goal-driven and singular, sexuality becomes, then, a network of flows, energies and capacities that are always open to transformation, and so cannot be determined in advance. Where for Lacan, the *corps morcélé* of early infancy – and arguably the persistence of that body as a figure of disability – is seen as that which must be covered over in order to bring into being the unified self who will become a sexed and gendered subject in the Symbolic, Deleuze and Guattari celebrate precisely corporeal dis-organisation. The fragmented body is reconceived as the body-without-organs, the body in a process of corporeal becoming, that mobilises desire as a fluid indeterminacy that has no fixed aim or object, and which could always be otherwise. Instead of figuring the conventional ideal of autonomous action, separation and distinction, Deleuzian embodiment persists *only* through the capacity to make connections, both organic and inorganic, and to enter into new assemblages – which in turn are disassembled. Clearly the meaning of the body-without-organs is not intended as a denial of corporeality as such, but is rather a way of rewriting it that avoids the Lacanian narrative of a move from fragmentation to – at very least the illusion of – a temporally and spatially stable unity that grounds the subject. It is, then, the normative organisation of the body that is at stake here, an organism and organisation that closes down and fixes its possibilities rather than operating as 'a body populated by multiplicities' (1984: 30). What Deleuze and Guattari want to promote is not a return to the staging of the pre-subjectival infant body, but a deconstruction, a queering, of *all* bodies that entails both 'taking apart egos and their presuppositions' and 'liberating the prepersonal singularities they enclose and repress' (1984: 362).

To think specifically of the disabled body in this context is not to single it out as different, still less as inadequate. Rather it is a material site of possibility where de-formations, 'missing' parts and prostheses are enablers of new channels of desiring production unconstrained by pre-determined – or at least normative – organisation. Although the risk of stalling around an assumption of lack is always present, as it is with any body, the anomalous nature of disability holds out the promise of an immanent desire that embraces the strange and opens up to new linkages and provisional incorporations. As Katherine Ott (2002) points out, the term 'prosthesis' has acquired rich abstract meaning in both psycho-analysis and cultural studies as a metaphor signalling some kind of medi-ation between an artificial device and the supposedly natural body, but it has also a complex material history mapping the literal interface between flesh and machine. I use the term in both senses, but want to stress the way in which people with disabilities may materialise some of the issues that underlie my concern with the performativity of the sexual self. On the one hand, prosthetic devices are intended to replace or enhance nor-mative function and appearance, figuring, in other words, a Foucauldian sense of the technological disciplining and regulation of the body, but on the other, their use may be radically subverted.[7] The intercorporeality – or rather the concorporeality – of the organic and inorganic, the assem-bly and disassembly of surprising connections, the capacity to innovate, and the productive troubling of intentionality are all experienced by dis-abled people who are prepared to explore the uncharted potential of prostheses. As with other minoritarian thought and practices, like the feminine, the breaking through of the expected limits and constraints of the resources to hand can both intensify the decomposition of binaries – body/machine; active/passive; biology/technology; interior/exterior – and multiply non-repressive forms of passionate vitality. As Deleuze and Guattari note: '[d]esire constantly couples continuous flows and partial objects that are by nature fragmentary and fragmented. Desire causes the current to flow' (1984: 5).

Interestingly, this freeing up of desire, both in its object and its aim, may remind us not of the Lacanian infant who after all greets its mirror stage escape from disorganisation with – as Lacan puts it – 'jubilation', but of the polymorphous perversity of the Freudian infant, who finds undifferentiated sexual pleasure not only in every aspect of its own body, but in a variety of external objects.[8] As Freud points out, such perversity in the trajectory of desire persists in adulthood even in such everyday practices as kissing (insofar as it has no genital aim), but for the most part, it must be abandoned – repressed that is – not for the sake of psychic health, but in the interests of socio-political organisation. Nonetheless, despite the potentially productive tension that is set up by Freud's recognition that the price of such repression is neurosis (1962: 104), his reluctant turn away from polymorphous perversity shuts down precisely the queer reading of desire that Deleuze and Guattari are to reopen. It is sometimes tempting to think of Freud as the first – albeit thwarted – queer theorist, but Elizabeth Grosz, in her own turn to a Deleuzian analytic, offers a less charitable view of polymorphous perversity. She warns against 'adopting the psychoanalytic position, which takes erotogenic zones as nostalgic reminiscences of a preoedipal, infantile bodily organization' or 'seeing the multiplicity of libidinal sites in terms of regression' (1995: 199). And it is precisely in the refusal to see alternative sexual pleasures as regressive that Foucault prefigures the queering of desire that is associated with Deleuze. Foucault's interest is both in what bodies can do, in how they are productive, rather than in how they respond to unconscious impulses, and in how the erotic can be redistributed to non-genital sites. In regard to S/M practice, for example, he is adamant that, '[t]hese practices are insisting that we can produce pleasure with very odd things, very strange parts of our bodies, in very unusual situations, and so on' (Halperin 1996: 320 quoting Foucault). People with disabilities who wish to assert an active sexuality might well find resonances in Foucault's words, not because they would necessarily identify with the celebration of fetishism as such, but because the dis-unified or prosthetic body demands a degree of innovation and inventiveness that most of us rarely experience. For Deleuze and Guattari, that sexual creativity is surely at the heart of their anti-Oedipal project.

The conventional psychoanalytic approach that supports the normative post-Enlightenment paradigm of a closed and invulnerable subject whose sexuality is organised around the presence or absence of the phallus, and whose sexual aim is to replace lack with plenitude, is supplanted, then, by a model whose potential positivity is unconstrained. In place of prohibition, repression and disavowal, Deleuzian desire is expansive, fluid and connective, grounding sexuality itself as highly plastic and as no longer reliant on the terms of any binary opposition such as those of male/female, active/passive or human/animal. And because the emphasis shifts from the integrity of the whole organism to focus instead on the material and momentary event of the coming together of disparate parts, bodies need no longer be thought of as either whole or broken, able-bodied or disabled, but simply in a process of becoming through the unmapped circulation of desire. At the same time, desire itself takes on a wider meaning that liberates it not simply from the bounds of genital sexuality per se, but more generally from the restricted parameters of what is usually defined as *sexual* relationality, whether that is accepting of, or challenging to, the conventions. Skin on skin in the bedroom is no more privileged than the sensation of fine sand running through my toes, or the sweet taste of a juicy peach on my tongue. In an essay that is explicitly concerned to rethink lesbian desire, but which might equally open up the arena to the erotics of disability, Elizabeth Grosz takes her cue from Deleuze and Guattari. She writes:

> there is not, as psychoanalysis suggests, a predesignated erotogenic zone, a site always ready and able to function as erotic: rather, the coming together of two surfaces produces a trading that imbues eros or libido to both of them, making bits of bodies, its parts or particular surfaces throb, intensify, for their own sake and not for the benefit of the entity or organism as a whole. They come to have a life of their own, functioning according to their own rhythms, intensities, pulsations, movements. Their value is always provisional and temporary, ephemeral and fleeting: they may fire the organism, infiltrate other zones and surfaces with their intensity but are unsustainable. (1995: 182)

Above all, what mobilises or stalls the rhizomatic proliferations of desire is the extent to which the connective nodules escape organised patterns of operation.

Desire is not an element of any singular subject; it is not pregiven; it is neither possessed nor controlled; it represents nothing; and nor does it flow directly from one individual to another. Instead it comes into being through what Deleuze and Guattari (1984) call 'desiring-machines', assemblages that cannot be said to exist outside of their linkages and interconnections, and which may encompass both the animate and inanimate, the organic and the inorganic. A desiring-machine expresses no necessary cohesion, continuity or unity, and nor do its part-objects seek a return to an originary wholeness, or find completion in an absent other.[9] What mobilises desire are not the endless substitutes for psychic loss, but the surface energies and intensities that move in and out of multiple conjunctions that belie categorical distinctions and hierarchical organisation. For Deleuze and Guattari, such conjunctions always engage the entire social and environmental field, centring not on the capacities of a unique individual, but on the scope and range of nomadic flows of energy – lines of flight – so that embodiment itself extends beyond the merely human. It is not that there is no distinction to be made between one corporeal element and the next, or indeed between the human and animal, or human and machine, but rather that becoming entails an inherent transgression of boundaries that turns the pleasures – sexual or otherwise – of the embodied person away from dominant notions of human subjectivity. As Tamsin Lorraine puts it: 'The self, rather than having a perspective upon and apart from the world of temporal becoming, is part of a process of dynamic differentiation' (2000: 185). This is not to deny that the interaction of bodies in time and space continues to produce subject effects, but it is only when those effects begin to coalesce and settle that the familiar sovereign individual of the post-Enlightenment could be said to appear. The performative repetition of particular patterns and modes of organisation serve to construct an illusion of stability and permanence which is, nevertheless, undermined not only by what Butler (1993) sees as the inherent slow-motion slippage of all reiterative processes, but by the unruliness of the leaky bodies whose fluidity, energies and contingencies are engaged in mutual transformations. These are bodies that come together – and break apart – in multifarious ways, always frustrating the anticipated outcome of performativity in consistent sexual identities. And where the stress is on the multiple possibilities of connection rather than on the putative dangers of contiguity and the risk of touch, then anomalous bodies are no longer a source of anxiety, but hold out the promise of productive new becomings.[10]

The stage is set, then, for a potential reclamation of disability and desire that is a very long way from the medium of an Oedipalised sexuality centred on the familial drama of 'mommy, daddy and me'. Like the female body, the corporeality of disability has widely figured in the western imaginary as disordered and uncontrollable, both seductive and repulsive, as threatening contamination of those who come too close, linked to disease, and so lacking in boundaries as to overwhelm normative subjectivity (Shildrick 2002). The link with sexuality is either disavowed or seen as overdetermined and abased, a matter of dangerous encounter that cannot but trouble the stability and self-presence of the unwary subject. That none of this reflects the reality of the lives of people with disabilities, or would be articulated as such, is of little consequence.

What matters is the power of the cultural imaginary to effectively exclude – in representative terms at least – a whole category of people from an important element in the socially normative process of self-identity. In contrast, what is offered by Deleuze and Guattari opens up a positive model of productive desire, the take-up of which is limited neither to those who already fulfil certain corporeal criteria, nor to the sedimentation of a characteristically modernist form of autonomous subjectivity. In place of the limits that the ideal of independence imposes on desire, the emphasis is on connectivity and linkage. It is not that people with disabilities are unique in relying on a profound interconnectivity, but that where for the normative majority such a need may be covered over in the interests of self-sovereignty, it has come to figure a deficiency that ostensibly devalues those unable to make such choices. The disabled woman who needs an assistant or carer to help her prepare for a sexual encounter – be it in terms of dressing appropriately, negotiating toilet facilities or requiring direct physical support to achieve a comfortable sexual position – is not different in kind from other women, but only engaged more overtly in just those networks that Deleuze and Guattari might characterise as desiring production. Similarly, a reliance on prosthetic devices – the linkages between human and machine – would figure not as limitations but as transformative possibilities of becoming other along multiple lines of flight.

We should caution, nonetheless, against taking an overly romanticised view of disability in which desire is always able to operate as an unchallenged positivity. There are clearly some constraints, some morphological differences and discontinuities, that continue to impede the flow of energies, particularly if that flow has been mapped in advance. But the model I propose here is not about unrestricted choice, or about a freedom that opens up all and every possibility. Like Butler's original exposition of performativity (1990), which was widely misunderstood to offer unbounded access to self-stylisation, the notion of desiring production must always be contextualised. The rewriting of performativity as intensely connective, and the slippage of reiteration as a more radical discontinuity, highlights precisely a lack of control that may exacerbate the frustration of intentionality for some people with disabilities. But rather than offering a route to sexual identity, the model proposes something rather different: a break with the putative emergence of a coherent sexual subject from the practices of embodiment, and a turn to the libidinal intensities which play not across unified and integrated bodies, but at points of connection between disparate surfaces or entities that may or may not be organic. The desire produced in and over the dis-organised body owes little to genital sexuality or the goal of self-completion in sexual satisfaction. As Elizabeth Grosz notes:

> desire is an actualisation, a series of practices, bringing things together or separating them, making machines, making reality. Desire does not take for itself a particular object whose attainment it requires; rather it aims at nothing above its own proliferation or self-expansion (1994: 165)

and elsewhere she characterises the appeal and power of such desire as 'its capacity to shake up, rearrange, reorganize the body's forms and sensations, to make the subject and body as such dissolve into something else' (1995: 204–5). It is not that Deleuze and Guattari allow no place for subject effects – 'you have to keep small rations of subjectivity . . . to enable you to respond to the dominant reality' (1987: 160) – but that they are unsustainable in fixed form, beyond the temporary or provisional. The molar politics of identity and subjectivity are never entirely dismissed, but are constantly confronted and displaced by the molecular politics of flows and intensities. What matters to Deleuze is the transformative potential of the process of becoming. In being excluded from full sexual subjectivity, then, those with disabilities have lost nothing of permanent value.

What this all indicates is that were the western privileging of autonomous individuality and integrated identity less rigid, the performativity of (sexual) subjectivity could be radically transformed. Despite its commitment to the productive instabilities of discursive construction, the notion of performativity remains focused on a form of individual agency that might be more radically queered by taking account of the emergence of the self precisely through an erotics of connection. Indeed, Deleuze himself goes further in his deconstruction of the relationship between a willing agent and desire: 'Far from pre-supposing a subject, desire cannot be attained except at the point where someone is deprived of their power to say "I"' (Deleuze and Parnet 1987: 89). As more and more theorists are beginning to acknowledge, the corporeality of disability is not that of an other fixed in a binary relation to the normatively embodied self, but is already queer in its contestation of the very separation of self and other.[11] The so-easily silenced whisper of a kinship that would be denied – for it unsettles the foundations of western subjectivity – is growing into a roar that marks a new understanding of embodiment which owes much to Deleuze. Having now entered 'the next century' of which Foucault (1977) claimed Deleuze as the philosopher, I should like to offer the equally bold speculation that the Deleuzian project will be realised at least in part through the medium of rethinking disability.[12] Once again, it is not that disability is a unique case, but only that its forms of embodiment, and its embrace of prosthetic enhancement, seem to overdetermine the fragility and instability of corporeality in general. The postmodernist acknowledgement that all bodies – normative and non-normative alike – are in a constant process of construction and transformation, brought about not least through interactions in the spatio-temporal dimensions of the social world, means that all are potentially hybrid, nomadic, machinic assemblages. Moreover, in the specific differences of its capacities – particularly with regard to its libidinal investments – the disabled body exposes the queerness of all sexuality.

That disability should be perceived as dangerous, and that its erotic capacities should be disavowed, speaks to the threat that it is able to unsettle the normative constraints that attempt to limit adult sexuality to a highly regulated set of impulses that cover over the rhizomatic operation of desiring-machines. For the most part, the libidinal possibilities of surprising, unpredictable, non-respectable, even dangerous conjunctions, which are in principle open to all of us, are kept in check by the rigid and repetitive structures of a normative sexuality that cannot easily countenance unauthorised variation or experimentation. To limit the erotic to the law of desire as it operates within the hegemony of the Symbolic is to assent to a system that can give no adequate account of corporeal difference nor of an alternative sexual imaginary, yet to be realised. It is to close down on fluidity, on connection and on intercorporeality, and to impose prohibition or denial on those who are assigned to positions of social marginality. For people outside the mainstream, then, those who are transgendered, HIV positive or people with disabilities, the choice may be between an apparent asexuality that comforts normative expectations in its very powerlessness to mount a challenge, or an expression of desire that will be necessarily exploratory and transformative. It is not of course that all disabled people are sexual radicals or have any urgent wish to liberate their desire from the constraints of normative thought and practice; as for all members of regulatory societies, it is impossible to stand outside the networks of disciplinary power/knowledge by any simple act of will. Nonetheless, as comparative outsiders, many such minoritarian figures are already engaged in a queer performativity that takes off from the innovative and intimate connections that are often a necessary part of life with a disability. I am thinking here both of the many forms of personal assistance that are available in the west, and which inevitably entail an embodied relationality that goes beyond normative encounters between putatively autonomous selves, and also of the enormous range of prosthetic devices that already may be incorporated into the experiential field of a person with a disability. For others, it is not so much a matter of describing present practice but of thinking otherwise about the promise of connectivity, and about what would follow from attending not to the being of a subject, but to the becoming and doing that constitutes a provisional and contingent subjectivity.

The substantive specificity of disabled bodies nonetheless poses something of a conundrum for those willing to deploy a Deleuzian rather than more generalised queer approach to the problematic of bodies that matter. Where queer theory explicitly intervenes in the parameters of social exclusion – and to an extent must always reiterate binary thinking in order to contest it – it readily lends itself to the critique of mainstream socio-cultural values and regulatory norms that people with disabilities engage with. The idea of assimilation is thoroughly rejected, and as Foucault recognised: 'It is the prospect that gays will create as yet unforeseen kinds of relationships that many people cannot tolerate' (1997: 153). As such the lure of identity politics lingers on, bolstered by queer theory's oppositional take on normativity that has broadened out to include differences in race, ethnicity and potentially embodiment, as well as sex and sexuality. The embrace of multiple and diverse minorities undoubtedly casts the dominant standards in an ambiguous light that troubles the centre, but it also appears to gesture towards the reappearance of a stable subject. In contrast, when Deleuze and Guattari refer to minoritarian practices, they are not ontologising any given category as an identity; instead 'all becoming is a becoming-minoritarian' (1987: 291). Moreover, their notions of becoming-woman, becoming-animal or becoming-minoritarian are not simply conceptually unattached to the groupings named and open to all, but refer to processes that operate only through the assemblages temporarily brought about by radically disparate machinic connections. Where, then, does this leave the substantive minorities, like people with disabilities? From a DeleuzoGuattarian perspective, they too must enter into the process of becoming, a process that entails both contesting the relations of power that structure every fixed subject position and leaving behind any existing modes of identification. It is risky and uncomfortable, but necessary insofar as the disabled body, however well adapted or accommodated, is – like the figure of 'woman' to whom Deleuze and Guattari consistently refer – always constituted by the repressive organisation of modernist principles.

So long as all fixed and unified identities rely on the performative exclusion of an abject domain of the unthinkable (Butler 1993), then certain bodies will never matter. If, on the other hand, our mutual and irreducible connectivity were recognised as quite simply a condition of becoming, and as the ground for the positivity and productive play of desire, then the notions of independent agency and self-containment that mark the normative subject might lose their exclusionary power. In place of the liberal demand for rights, choice and self-determination that presently shape the dominant discourse of disability activism, a more open and productive model that celebrates the qualities of those already living at the margins might be proposed. It is their very dis-organisation, and their necessarily overt contiguities with an array of others, that better enables such figures to breach the boundaries and explore what lies beyond the normative limits. An open-ended and ambiguous yet more positive Deleuzian mode of becoming has significant implications, not only for the hitherto disavowed conjunction of disability and sexuality but for everyone. The point is move away from the notion that desire represents or substitutes for an originary loss that codes all bodies in the same way; instead it maps the multiplicity of becoming. And once the plasticity of the erotic is acknowledged rather than repressed, then the circulation of desire and the partial satisfactions of pleasure would be a matter of differential exploration and experimentation, rather than the site of silence and shame. There are of course dangers – not all lines of flight will soar – but the possibilities of reconstruction and transformation, in sexuality as elsewhere, speak to the hope of personal and social flourishing. That term is deeply unfashionable within postconventional discourse, but it is precisely what I mean.

References

Butler, J. (1990), *Gender Trouble: Feminism and the Subversion of Identity*, London: Routledge.

Butler, J. (1993), *Bodies that Matter: On the Discursive Limits of 'Sex'*, London: Routledge.

Deleuze, G. (1994), 'Désir et plaisir', *Magazine Littéraire*, 325 (October) pp. 59–65.

Deleuze, G. and Guattari, F. (1984), *Anti-Oedipus: Capitalism and Schizophrenia*, trans. R. Hurley, London: Athlone Press.

Deleuze, G. and Guattari, F. (1987), *A Thousand Plateaus: Capitalism and Schizophrenia*, trans B. Massumi, Minneapolis: Minnesota University Press.

Deleuze, G. and Parnet, C. (1987), *Dialogues*, trans. H. Tomlinson and B. Habberjam, London: Athlone.

Diprose, R. (2002), *Corporeal Generosity: On Giving with Nietzsche, Merleau-Ponty and Levinas*, New York: SUNY Press.

Erickson, L. (2005), 'They call it struggle for a reason: a sex positive reflection on sites of shame as sites of resistance for people with disabilities.' Unpublished MA dissertation in Critical Disability Studies, York University, Toronto.

Foucault, M. (1977), 'Intellectuals and Power.' In D. F. Bouchard (ed.), *Michel Foucault: Language, Counter-Memory, Practice*, Ithaca, NY: Cornell University Press.

Foucault, M. (1979), *The History of Sexuality, Volume 1*, trans. Robert Hurley, London: Allen Lane.

Foucault, M. (1980), *Power/Knowledge*, ed. C. Gordon, London: Harvester Wheatsheaf.

Foucault, M. (1997), 'Sexual Choice, Sexual Act.' In Paul Rabinow (ed.), *Ethics, Subjectivity and Truth: The Essential Works of Michel Foucault*, New York: New Press.

Foucault, M. (2003), *Abnormal*, trans. G. Burchell, New York: Picador.

Freud, S. [1905] (1962), *Three Essays on the Theory of Sexuality*, trans. James Strachey, London: Basic Books.

Grosz, E. (1994), *Volatile Bodies: Towards a Corporeal Feminism*, Bloomington: Indiana University Press.

Grosz, E. (1995), *Space, Time, and Perversion: Essays on the Politics of Bodies*, London: Routledge.

Halperin, D. (1996), 'The Queer Politics of Michel Foucault.' In D. Morton (ed.), *The Material Queer*, Boulder: Westview Press.

Haraway, D. (1991), 'A Cyborg Manifesto: Science, Technology, and Socialist-Feminism in the Late Twentieth Century.' In *Simians, Cyborgs, and Women: The Reinvention of Nature*, London: Free Association Books.

Lacan, J. (1977), *Ecrits: A Selection*, trans. Alan Sheridan, New York: W. W. Norton.

Lorraine, T. (2000), 'Becoming-Imperceptible as a Mode of Self-Presentation: A Feminist Model Drawn from a Deleuzian Line of Flight.' In D. Olkowski (ed.), *Resistance, Flight, Creation: Feminist Enactments of French Philosophy*, Ithaca, NY: Cornell University Press.

McRuer, R. (2003), 'As Good As It Gets: Queer Theory and Critical Disability', *GLQ: A Journal of Lesbian and Gay Studies* 9.1–2.

McRuer, R. and Wilkerson, A. (2003), 'Cripping the (Queer) Nation', *GLQ: A Journal of Lesbian and Gay Studies* 9.1–2.

Merleau-Ponty, M. (1963), *The Primacy of Perception*, Evanston: Northwestern University Press.

Merleau-Ponty, M. (1968), *The Visible and the Invisible*, Evanston: Northwestern University Press.

Olkowski, D. (2002), 'Flesh to Desire: Merleau-Ponty, Bergson, Deleuze', *Strategies* 15(1) pp. 11–24.

Ott, K. (2002), 'The Sum of Its Parts.' In K. Ott, D. Serlin and S. Mihm (eds), *Artificial Parts, Practical Lives: Modern Histories of Prosthetics*, New York: New York University Press.

Parisi, L. (2004), *Abstract Sex: Philosophy, Bio-technology and the Mutations of Desire*, London: Continuum.

Paterson, J. (2007), 'Beyond clinical and heteronormative encounters between disability and sexuality: kinky agency and resistance'. Unpublished MA dissertation in Critical Disability Studies, York University, Toronto.

Shildrick, M. (2002), *Embodying the Monster: Encounters with the Vulnerable Self*, London: Sage.

Shildrick, M. (2004), 'Unreformed Bodies: Normative Anxiety and the Denial of Pleasure', *Women's Studies: An Interdisciplinary Journal*.

Shildrick, M. (2007), 'Dangerous Discourses: Disability, Anxiety and Desire', *Studies in Gender and Sexuality* 8(3).

Stiker, H.-J. (1999), *A History of Disability*, trans. William Sayers, Ann Arbor: University of Michigan Press.

Tremain, S. (2000), 'Queering Disabled Sexuality Studies', *Sexuality and Disability* 18 p. 4.

Warner, M. (ed.) (2003), *Fear of a Queer Planet: Queer Politics and Social Theory*, Minneapolis: University of Minnesota Press.

Notes

1. The material in this chapter is a reworked and expanded version of my article 'Queering Performativity: Disability after Deleuze' in the e-journal *SCAN: J. of the Media Arts* 2004, 1.3.
2. To speak of ethics in a postconventional sense is to move beyond the parameters of rights and duties or of harms and benefits in order to engage with the nature of encounter, and the relation between self and other.
3. His text *Abnormal* (Foucault 2003), which focuses on the monstrous, comes closest to exploring disability.
4. See Shildrick (2004) for an extended discussion of the sexed/sexuate performitivity of conjoined twins.
5. It is perhaps somewhat unusual to move towards a DeleuzoGuattarian perspective through phenomenology, but while Deleuze eschews phenomenology as such, he clearly takes up the notion of reversibility, and other aspects of Merleau-Ponty's work. As Dorothea Olkowski remarks: 'desire turns upon Deleuze's conception of the body, so that when the connections between flesh, feeling, and desire are examined in terms of the body, the relationship between Merleau-Ponty, Bergson and Deleuze begins to reveal itself to be as deep as it is broad (2002: 11).
6. Sexuality is the paradigmatic site in which it is clear that corporeal performitivity is inherently socially inscribed, always engaged with the other and never singular as Butler sometimes seems to imply. As Rosalyn Diprose (2002) points out, my meanings are never constituted personally.
7. I have been particularly impressed by the work of two Masters students at York University, Toronto. Loree Erickson (2005) has very effectively used photographic material to exhibit her own sexual inventiveness that highlights her bodily difference and long-term wheelchair use, while Jennifer Paterson (2007) has made a preliminary study of the participation of disabled people in the Toronto BDSM community.
8. It is unlikely, however, that even this polymorphous pleasure would fully appeal to Deleuze and Guattari. As Parisi explains, their understanding is that the economy of pleasure 'represses all divergent flows from the cycle of accumulation and discharge, the imperative of the climax: the channelling of all relations towards the aim of self-satisfaction' (2004: 198–9). See also Deleuze (1994) for his disagreements with Foucault over the concept of pleasure.
9. Deleuze and Guattari pose the question of 'how to think about fragments whose sole relationship is sheer difference . . . without having recourse to any sort of original totality . . . or to a subsequent totality that may not yet have come about' (1984: 42).
10. It is worth noting that where the ideas developed by Deleuze and Guattari with regard to the connectivity and implications of desiring-machines have struggled for understanding, the similar and almost contemporaneous – albeit partially ironic – imaginings of Donna Haraway in 'A Cyborg Manifesto' – originally a 1983 conference paper – have become, for feminist and queer theorists at least, seminal fare. Of the 'illegitimate fusions of animal and machine' she writes: 'These are the couplings which make Man and Woman so problematic, subverting the structure of desire, the force imagined to generate language and gender, and so subverting the structure and modes of reproduction of "Western"

identity, of nature and culture, of mirror and eye, slave and master, body and mind' (1991: 176).

11. Disability theorists have approached the notion of queer in both more and less radical ways, but most would concur with Michael Warner that queer is defined 'against the normal rather than the heterosexual' (1993: xxvi). See in particular work by Shelley Tremain (2000), Robert McRuer (2003), McRuer and Abby Wilkerson (2003), as well as several other articles focusing on the intersections between disability and queer in a recent issue of *GLQ: A Journal of Lesbian and Gay Studies* 9.1–2 (2003). Many of the papers from the seminal 2002 *Queer-Disability Conference* in San Francisco are available online at http://www.disabilityhistory.org/dwa/queer/paper_bell.html

12. Although to date I know of few other disability theorists working directly on and around Deleuzian insights, this is, I hope, no mere rhetoric. In critical disability studies at least, the limits of liberal notions of equity and justice have already mobilised a willingness to explore alternative paradigms, and specifically queer theory. Given the material concerns at stake, the step into a more fully committed Deleuzian approach seems inevitable. To make the move in the reverse direction, to recognise that the field of disability might serve as an exemplar of many of the key concepts – not only linked to desire but to the notion of becoming-minoritarian – may take longer, but I take it that it is as apposite to Deleuzian theory as gay sex once was to the emergence of queer theory.

Chapter 8

Unnatural Alliances

Patricia MacCormack

Gilles Deleuze and Félix Guattari use as a key example of becomings becoming-animal. Becoming-animal involves both a repudiation of the individual for the multiple and the human as the zenith of evolution for a traversal or involution across the speciesist plane of consistency. Deleuze and Guattari delineate the Oedipal animal, the pack animal and the demonic hybridisation of animal, human and imperceptible becomings. Various commentators have critiqued and celebrated Deleuze and Guattari's call to becoming-woman. In his taxonomy of living things Aristotle places women at the intersection of animal and human, so becoming-animal as interstices raises urgent feminist issues as well as addressing animal rights and alterity through becoming-animal. This chapter will invoke questions such as 'how do we negotiate becoming-animal beyond metaphor?', 'what risks and which ethics are fore-grounded that make becoming-animal an important political project?' and, most importantly, because becoming-animal is a queer trajectory of desire, 'how does the humanimal desire?'

> Anthropomorphism can go either up or down, humanising either the deity or animals, but if the vertical distance is closed in any way, i.e. between God and humans or humans and animals, many are disconcerted. (Adams 1995: 180)

> For on the one hand, the relationships between animals are the object not only of science but also of dreams, symbolism, art and poetry, practice and practical use. And on the other hand, the relationships between animals are bound up with the relations between man and animal, man and woman, man and child, man and elements, man and the physical and microphysical universe. (Deleuze and Guattari 1987: 235)

The above premise by Deleuze and Guattari invokes a paradigm which is resonant with many key concerns in poststructural philosophy. Jacques

Derrida's demarcation of isomorphism elucidates the phantasy of the binary or opposite as not a relation between two but as a subjugation of all others by a dominant one. Deleuze and Guattari critique taxonomy as not made up of a series of opposites but all alterity as fallen man. One could be tempted to say that this alone aligns the subjugated terms – animal, woman, children and so forth – as necessarily sympathetic to each others' conditions through various mechanisms of power, oppression and resistance. This concept has been suggested by many animal rights activists, feminists, children's rights activists and queer theorists. In other areas theories of the posthuman suggest that there is no longer a category of human, or, more precisely, the category of human was always the mythical zenith of an equally mythical arboreal structure which systematised human subjectivity through religious, metaphysical and evolutionary discourses. Instead of God making man, secular scientists now make their own possibility of dominance through discourses that demarcate the hu-Man as a hermeneutic and given 'natural' phenomenon. While many feminists, particularly Luce Irigaray, see the bifurcation between man and woman as the most obvious and deterministic binary, I would argue that that which divides man from animal encompasses a far wider colonisation of life through discourse. As feminists struggle with the conundrum of how to define ourselves without reifying or essentialising the female, all other entities drop away. Animal entities, more correctly non-human animals, in their almost infinite varieties, pose a far greater challenge to thought, be it through activism, philosophy or science. Closing the chasm between the human and the animal is like closing the gap between discourse and non-discourse, between thought and the unthinkable but nonetheless necessary, and between our own relationships with our human selves as what Guattari calls an ecosophy. Deleuze and Guattari emphasise that 'between the two there is threshold and fiber, symbiosis or passage between heterogeneities' (1987: 250), not relation but production. Despite the problems of unspeech or unthought in the face of pure alterity 'becoming can and should be qualified as becoming-animal even in the absence of a term that would be the animal become' (Deleuze and Guattari 1987: 238). While non-human animals cannot negotiate through human discourse, they each (not each species but each animal) emit powers, haeccities, singularities of force with which we and they can enter into a relation. How does this relate to queer theory? Deleuze is emphatic that

> desire circulates in this heterogeneous assemblage, in this kind of symbiosis . . . Of course this kind of desire will include power arrangement . . .

> Power arrangements would surface wherever re-territorializations, even abstract ones, would take place . . . Power arrangements would therefore be a component of assemblages and yet these assemblages would also include points of deterritorialization. In short, power arrangements would not assemble or constitute anything but rather assemblages of desire would disseminate power formations. (Deleuze 2000: 250–1)

Desire is inherent in all power formations, from the Church's desire for man's own self-realisation through God to science's desire for the power to naturalise self at the expense and explicitly through mechanisms of objectification and analysis of all others. The human is its own desire for itself. Desiring a relation with the power(s) of an irreducible other alters dominant power structures through desire, creating what Deleuze and Guattari call an 'unnatural alliance'. 'It is not sufficient to liberate ourselves from sexuality; it is also necessary to liberate ourselves from the notion of sexuality itself' (Foucault 2000: 245). Liberation from the notion of human liberates us from humanist transcendental metaphysics and the powers it expresses.

Memories of a Hybrid

Dualistically constructed society territorialises every system, every structure and every mode of existence. This sets up all entities as analogies of proportion or series – a is not b – and relations of proportionality or structure – as a is to b so c is to d. In hybrid theory as a queer theory the most important part of these analogous relations are not the terms but the gaps between the terms. Hybrids present an encounter of self as more-than-one. Hybrids frequently take the form of two entities involuted or collapsed into one form or event. Hybrids challenge the belief in unity, phyla and absolute differentiation of elements, species, things and subjects. Hybrids are not all alike, however. While the hybrid is more-than-one – usually a mix of two – the relation of two can vary greatly depending on its function, its spatio-temporal incarnation and its apprehension by its own self and others. The following section will explore some encounters between gender hybrids, animal hybrids and sexual hybrids as both evidence of reifying symbols of human culture and as potential becomings. Hybrids are frequently encountered as 'monsters'. Rosi Braidotti explains

> [monsters] represent the in between, the mixed, the ambivalent as implied in the ancient Greek root of the word monsters, *teras*, which means both horrible and wonderful, object of aberration and adoration. (Braidotti 1994: 77)

Thus beyond the monster as a hybrid entity, the response to and relation with the monster is hybrid. Monsters stereotypically are reviled as nature's mistakes, and physical deformity is frequently associated with mental or moral turpitude. The collapse of sexual perversion and animalised human hybrid offspring is seen everywhere from myth to modern popular apocrypha. The union between Leda and her swan lover resulted in the beautiful but destructive twins Clytaemnestra and Helen. Pasiphae's love for a bull produced Phaedra, whose incestuous desires resulted in the death of her stepson. The so-called 'elephant man' Joseph Merrick, wolf children and other victims of congenital deformities have the malformations which cause their bodies to deviate from the 'human' named after animals. The archetype animal is analogy rather than threshold encounter. As an arbitrary example, religious icons such as the Egyptian baboon who worships the sun or the knowledgeable Ibis whose beak reflects the arc of the moon, both incarnated as the god Thoth, represent wisdom. Of course, these early examples are hijacked and fetishised in modern culture; their original use and relation to society remain enigmatic. The strong eagle and the triumphant lion are some examples of recent and current nationalist symbols of superiority. Zoophiles are not becoming animal but are going steady with their Oedipal animal boyfriends and girlfriends. The Oedipal puppy baby no longer knows its own dogginess and is forced into a becoming-human. Similarly Donna Haraway warns against the Oedipalisation of dogs as surrogate children. However, in *The Companion Species Manifesto* she simultaneously claims the dog-human relation is a hybrid one, but nonetheless the dog term is a trained one, thus the dog is becoming-human. 'In reality the animal captured by man is deterritorialised by human force' (Deleuze and Guattari 1981: 100). In terms of animal rights 'the deterritorialized animal force in turn precipitates and intensifies the deterritorialization of the deterritorializing human force' (Deleuze and Guattari 1981: 100).

Speciesist language relies inherently on the use of animal euphemisms to explain uniquely human oppressive or offensive behaviour – behaving 'like' an animal, being a 'fat pig' or 'stupid cow' relegates those whose behaviour is seemingly monstrous to a hybrid state. All these examples of hybridity are symbolic, but the qualities the animals symbolise are entirely human creations established through rigidly human paradigms and perceptions, colonising animals not only with certain qualities but only allowing animals to exist within the single human system of reality and perception. Symbolic animal hybrids represent the animal as colonised by human phantasmatic investments of qualities and images.

The Minotaur is not half man-half bull and the stupid cow is not a human whose stupidity is 'like' a cow. These are what Deleuze and Guattari would call analogies of proportion. A cow here is a human's investment of a malignant human quality into a non-human entity to both reiterate human dominance and keep the human being as being human a flawless, refined and culturally self-authoring entity. Hybrids created through derogative language are usually made from the majoritarian with the female, homosexual or animal. Misogynist vernacular revels in the tasty thighs and breasts of women for sexual consumption. Insults as banal as 'girl', through the more extreme 'cunt', 'fag' and 'chicken', can only create hybrids if the insulted term is explicitly dominant. An insult is always a demand for rectification. It demands a turn away from the resonant intensity the majoritarian shares with the queer, female or animal. Just as 'queer' reclaims the insult to deny or reorient its derogatory power, an ethical becoming would reclaim derogatory insults of hybridity to launch majoritarian subjectivity on a line of flight toward other possibilities of power and desire.

Certain hybrids are celebrated in postmodernity that are not taken necessarily as aberrations, but as fetishisations of experimental sexuality, subjectivity and transgressive behaviours. Both Foucault and Deleuze have expressed disdain for the transgressive subject as a reactive rather than active or creative force. Transgressive subjectivity is an enunciation of identity. Announcing acts of transgression through descriptions of explicit sets of acts compels the repetition of those acts to maintain the transgression, even though all acts and all repetitions invoke different intensities. While transgressive hybridity has a place in concrete activations of power shifts, resistance comes from negotiations which are forced rather than fun (though they can be both). Becomings may also not be aware of the limits they access and challenge and these limits are usually only encountered accidentally. The purpose and function of becomings are also not known, so they neither structure their activation nor predict their effects, and of course becomings have no result. Transgressions risk subsuming their effects through speech – transgression is less important than to be seen to transgress or to articulate what and how one transgresses, a kind of inverse, reverse or perverse psychoanalysis. Transgression for its own sake lacks experimentation in its incarnations because it both relies on and reifies the limits it transgresses, not cutting a trajectory across or in-between binaries but challenging the one through various goading. Deleuze and Guattari's masochist is zero intensity, alone but not dividuated bodily signified self. Deleuze's masochist tends more toward a traumatised Oedipal entity seeking an impossible catharsis (1991). The too trendy switch-hitter bisexual has no becomings. While entering into different intensities with each gender, the 'each' affirms there are only two, and that desire is always dialectic, not between but as a structure of two. 'Bisexuality is no better a concept than the separateness of the sexes. It is as deplorable to miniaturize, internalize the binary machine as it is to exacerbate it; it does not extricate us from it' (Deleuze and Guattari 1987: 276). Queer refuses the binaries of heterosexual and homosexual and therefore male and female. Queer is the pure indeterminate of nothing or everything, but explicitly of the unspeakable and unrepresentable, not because queer is aberrant but because within majoritarian language there are no words. Like animal languages the language of queer does not translate syntactically and, most importantly, paradigmatically or epistemically. Similarly, dragging up, be it toward 'authenticity' or experimentally, maintains the symbols of each gender in order to draw attention to the transgression. Authenticity attempts to minimise signifiers of one gender, thus acknowledging and reiterating their symbolic importance, while intensifying the symbols of the other. The transvestite then is a mish-mash hybrid, teeming with symbols belonging to one or another, but not ambiguous enough to be constructed through the spaces between the symbols. The male-as-female or female-as-male is an established alliance at war, rather than an unnatural alliance. An over-symbolised body, even if the symbols jar with each other, is still an explicitly signified body and not the Body without Organs created from unnatural alliances and signified bodies. Dressing as a woman spatialises subjectivity, moving from one site to its opposite. Becoming-woman, like all becomings, puts an emphasis on movement not place, on force not form. Monique Wittig's famous 'lesbians are not women' (1992: 32) exploits the impossibility of two of the same being comprehensible as two in heterocentric society. In this instance one could argue transgressions of drag rectify the powers of refusing binaries by making two lesbians butch and femme. As the first step in becomings, through which Deleuze and Guattari argue women themselves must pass, is becoming-women, arguably lesbians are already moving toward becoming-otherwise. As they are not two they are always and already one and more than one, an unnatural alliance because two singularities together are not dialectic and yet not the same. They *are* the space in between. Becomings are proximities. Being in proximity with a same that is not the same (that is, a woman who is not a woman because 'she' is not opposed to a man as I am also not a woman but not the same as this not-woman) creates a particularly amorphic alliance. Indeed as before and beyond woman – the subjugated first binary term of the human – may mean lesbians are before and beyond the human. They are like animals in that all they are is what they are not – human. Lesbian 'identity' suggests inhuman identity, unable to be biunivocalised, thus lesbianism is a very unnatural alliance. Should all becomings pass through a becoming-lesbian? Or rather, through becoming the sound of lesbians?

> The musical problem of the machinery of the voice necessarily implies the abolition of the overall dualism machine, in other words, the molar formation assigning voices to the man or woman. Being a man or woman no longer exists in music. (Deleuze and Guattari 1987: 303–4)

Speech machines favour dualisms. Society fears packs that infect or recruit. Predatory lesbians, butch-animal and thus unnatural 'hairy-chested' feminists (an insult hurled at me personally!), animal rights activists are all on the prowl and on the howl because theirs is a speech of desire in a different language, imperceptible and incoherent to majoritarian ears. The lesbian language is perverse, the female language hysterical, the child's language undeveloped and the activist's language extreme and dangerous. Just as the wolf's howl is a call to desire through mating and to hunting, these minoritarian howls threaten through desire and hunting majoritarian language. Far from needing to be represented in society, the unrepresentability of the sound of lesbian desire is its power. I am not suggesting lesbians need not be recognised and acknowledged, but not recognised within male/female dualistic speech machines. Like animals, lesbians are a sonority, and like lesbians 'not only do animals have colours and sounds but they do not wait for the painter or musician to use those colours and sounds in a painting or music' (Deleuze and Guattari 1987: 305). Ethically it is the responsibility of the majoritarian to enter the designified and desubjectified sonorities and saturations of these terms, not to represent them within dualistic discursive machines. Becoming-animal is not colonising an animal with human perceptions of its nature, but finding an escape route from the human. 'You do not become a barking molar dog, but by barking, if it is done with enough feeling, with enough necessity and composition, you emit a molecular dog' (Deleuze and Guattari 1987: 275). Dog is intensity threshold, and barking a good example as it is difficult to signify as a language but is deeply corporeal and visceral if performed for long enough and with enough commitment to the bark and less to the self-barking. Experiments with the question 'what sound does a lesbian make?' could be the catalyst for an interesting becoming-project.

Another postmodern example of transgressive sexuality which creates non-becoming hybrids is animal sex.

Animals continue to haunt man's imagination, compel him to seek out their habits, preferences and cycles, and provide models and formulae by which he comes to represent [and make superior] his own desires, needs and excitements. (Grosz 1995: 187–8)

Furries, plushies, animal role-play, training and bestiality assimilate the animal toward the human rather than attempt entrance into other intensities. Man uses animals to express the most deplorable of desires which make his own sacred, and at turns uses animal desire to excuse certain human prejudices and urges as 'natural'. Fancying riding your lover with a horse tail in her anus, or a furry care-bear suit on, or having sex with your horse (beyond the deeply troubling ethical implications of raping animals) do not excite becomings but 'tame' them. The horse-boyfriend is part of the same family as the Oedipal dog.

The few examples above show that, while technically hybrids are defined by their inability to reproduce, certain hybrids are able to reproduce because they reproduce binary machines. They may attempt to redistribute the isomorphic intensity but end up with a continuous celebration, not of becomings, but of the variety of extensions and incarnations the human is capable of. The human becomes all through encroaching on the very intensities which threaten its sanctity. These hybrids exist within what Deleuze and Guattari, after Canetti, call enantiomorphosis:

> a regime that involves a hieratic and immutable Master who at every moment legislates by constants, prohibiting or strictly limiting metamorphoses, giving figures clear and stable contours, setting forms in opposition. (Deleuze and Guattari 1987: 107)

The desiring term is made invisible. The desiring master desires precisely through extricating the self from the object of desire, in animal hybrid sexuality, clearly the master of the animal or the subjugator of the cure fluffy, the parent of the Oedipal dog – hybridity as dissymmetry.

Monsters offer examples of unnatural participatory hybridity. Monsters are not metaphors but vibrate as bands or inflections of intensities. Deleuze and Guattari use the examples of vampires and werewolves. Werewolves elicit the becomings of others as themselves always and already hybrids, bitten and biting, transferring their becomings to others through desiring experiences. Enantiomorphosis collapses to effectuation. Werewolves come through two trajectories – the wolf as animal and the wolf as part of a pack. The wolf is not the form of a wolf, or the wolf as belonging to the taxonomy of the animal kingdom. Unnatural participations are interkingdom becomings, 'the wolf is not fundamentally a characteristic or a certain number of characteristics; it is a wolfing' (Deleuze and Guattari 1987: 239). The werewolf is part of a pack but is itself a pack as already contagion entity, infected, able to infect – molecular within and without. Simultaneously the werewolf is not a whole, neither man nor beast, but not referring

> in the least to an organism that would function phantasmatically as a lost unity or totality to come. Their dispersion has nothing to do with a lack, and constitutes their mode of presence in the multiplicity they form without unification or totalization. (Deleuze and Guattari 1996: 324)

As becomings never become, so one never becomes a vampire or werewolf but constantly oscillates between and within variable intensities created uniquely at the encounter. The vampire is a rare monster in that the victim's desire compels them toward a welcome and ecstatic death, an active victim open to infection. The vampire is seductive and dangerous, recruiting victims who desire differently into a pack. The sexual dialectic proliferates, against sexual structuration – hetero or homo – the vampire's victims victimise themselves, not desiring the vampire as a creature necessarily but desiring the infection or plague. The victim seeks the transformation and proliferation of the desiring self. The vampire infects the victim in order that the victim can deterritorialise their own molar sexuality toward molecular desires and pleasures. The spectre of the lesbian vampire in literature and film testifies to the horrors of a monster not being predatory but compelling, met less with terror than fascination. The lesbian vampire is not scary but sexy, usually requiring intervention by not heterosexuality but phallocentric discursive systems – religion and science – to cure the victim. Lesbian vampires conflate sexual aberration with biological disease. Desire for vampires and vampire desire celebrate or ignore the pain of the death of the organism, part of a genealogy or a kind, and births the hybrid which is unable to reproduce and thus neither belongs to one kingdom nor one sexual structure.

Vampires invoke queer as an inflection or dissipation of desiring self before and beyond act or object. Vampires are able to transform into animals. Obviously in many myths and novels the vampire becomes wolf, expressing Deleuze and Guattari's point that both are parts of bands that transform themselves and each other, a kind of monstrous or hybrid interkingdom beyond natural kingdoms, unnatural-unnatural participation, emphasising the infinity of interkingdom participations. The vampire becomes the bat, in Leviticus a forbidden and aberrant animal because of its interkingdom associations as both bird and mammal. Each example of a vampire and werewolf transformation creates a new hybrid – the colonisation through infection of each term by its animal and human qualities teems with new nodes and pulsations as various intensities cross each other for the first time, or the next time, where different molecules meet familiarly or as strange combinations. Werewolves and vampires are not monsters as spectacle forms but events. The wolf, essentially always part of a pack, infects through the bite. The mouth as site of consumption is deterritorialised, now the site of the bite, the animal kiss that expresses rather than incorporates. The mouth – more correctly the jaw or snout, fanged to infect, not to kill or eat – accesses the molecules of the 'victim'. The form is not eaten, killed or attacked, the mouth-snout creates a vacuum which mingles molecules, invoking becomings as the victim dissipates its cell-intensities to itself propagate as teeming pack of new formations, constantly mobile and thus constantly transforming. If nature anchors on reproduction, reifying genealogy and repetition as reiteration, the infective bite of the werewolf or vampire creates the hybrid that is 'sterile, born of a sexual union that will not reproduce itself but which begins over again every time' (Deleuze and Guattari 1987: 241). Deleuze and Guattari emphasise these 'animals' are not kinds but states (1987: 243). In myth and literature vampires also transform into fog. Fog is made of molecules, it is inapprehensible, breathed into lungs, obscuring sight, creating an in-between myopia or twilight perception, the time of vampire transformation in the evening and werewolf metamorphosis in the morning (traditionally 4 a.m. is the 'wolfing hour'). Fog seeps into animal, vegetable, mineral and ether. Ubiquitous fog invokes other kinds of hybrid monsters which begin as hyper-interkingdom animals and eventually other-universe and other-physics entities and collectives. Deleuze and Guattari use the work of H. P. Lovecraft to exemplify the interkingdom propagation beyond mammalian, animal, vegetable and carbon-based participations. 'Lovecraft applies the term "outsider" to this thing or entity, the Thing which arrives and passes at the edge . . . "teeming, seething, swelling, foaming, spreading like an infectious disease, this nameless horror"' (Deleuze and Guattari 1987: 245). Guattari emphasises that 'desire is always "outside"' (Guattari 1996: 59). Lovecraft's monster hybrid has gone beyond an unnatural participation to transform the entity as contagion itself. Walter Gilman in Lovecraft's *Dreams in the Witch house* is frightened by the human-demon-rat creature which scuttles around his house. Consequently this half-half hybrid is replaced by conical multi-armed entities and bubble-foaming entities which converge and diverge. And they live in his house with him, forming a very unnatural family indeed. The 'families' of Innsmouth in *The Shadow Over Innsmouth* have bred with the fish-frog creatures beneath the sea. The resulting flesh-fish-frog-humans are able to reproduce both with each other and with the fish-frogs, but each is unique – their reproduction results in entities but these offspring never resemble their genesis. Each citizen of Innsmouth is a unique and unrecognisable singularity. These are examples of queer production without reproduction. Gender, sexual union, genus and non-dividuation do not prevent offspring but do prevent reproduction as repetition. Lovecraft eventually offers imperceptible entities, including the becoming-imperceptible of human characters such as Randolph Carter in *The Statement of Randolph Carter*, whose great hybrid form is that of the simultaneously conscious and mindless – not present to himself. Here the hybrid is estranged from itself. Especially in Lovecraft, other demons and gods emerge (Cthulhu, Nyarlahotep and such), evoking transformation rather than the empty simulacrum reiterations enforced through religion, capitalism and other regimes of desire which encroach on bodies and desire.

Werewolves, vampires, flesh-fish-frog people, gender ambiguities and perverts are hybrid becomings. The focus here is on transformative potentialities or germinalities, interstices and qualities of each term and the unique vibrations produced as the specific intensities enter within each other. Contagion is movement, werewolves and vampires transform into melded thresholds, not symbolic half-and-halves. Deleuze and Guattari's threshold collapses the analogous proportion gap rather than splicing the terms into two demarcated halves stuck onto each other. The unnatural alliance closes the gap of proportionality, whereby strange relations are created that challenge the like-for-like sets of binaries that are often used covertly to give some minoritarians power as long as they continue to oppress others, thus maintaining majoritarian power. In phallologocentric society women get equality as long as they don't forget to stay women and don't become ambiguous; homosexuality is ok but don't let in the queers; 'we' treat animals better, enslaving them organically but eating them just the same. Traditional relations demand the minoritarian come up to the dominant. Unnatural alliances are molecular entrances into something else's politics, desires, alliances that traverse proportion and proportionality rather than swap it or change places within the maintained hierarchy. A line of flight cuts across, not up or down, and thus its trajectory is hybrid as it doesn't know the qualities of its journey. Transformation is not an act; the hybrid has no past, no birth born of a monstrous union or a collapse of two symbolic qualities. Female desire, implicit in becoming-woman, emphasises 'the fantasy of the non-human status of woman as android, vampire, or animal, the identification of female sexuality as voracious, insatiable, enigmatic, invisible and unknowable, cold, calculating, instrumental, castrator/decapitator of the male, dissimulatress or fake, predatory . . . ' (Grosz 1995: 203). The werewolf never starts or ends wolf or man but constantly unfolds and reorients its werewolfish aspects and force. The vampire is a femme-male seductive-monster queer (it doesn't have sex 'normally'), infecting (most often) women with lesbianism simultaneously with the disease of vampirism. Perhaps this example of lesbianism conceived as vampiristic contagion offers an entry for non-lesbians into the becoming-woman through which all women themselves must pass? The lesbian vampire has created a genre of monster all of her own. If lesbians are not women, perhaps lesbian vampires are not vampires, but yet another becoming-term toward which we can resonate. Lovecraft's Innsmouth folk and the non-Euclidian elder gods are monsters without genealogy or destiny and are to varying degrees imperceptible while nonetheless being present and affective. Perhaps I could suggest that these new gods which demand a forsaking of regimes transform sexuality to mystical desire: 'sexual liberation is a mystification . . . liberation will occur when sexuality becomes desire, and desire is the freedom to be sexual, that is, to be something else at the same time' (Guattari 1996: 56). This understanding of desire negotiates Foucault's disdain for the concept of desire, which for him suggests 'the medical and naturalist connotations that the notion of desire entails . . . tell me what you desire and I will tell you who you are' (Foucault 2000: 246). Hybrids are not nouns, but verbs. They are inherently unnatural and resist naturalisation because they cannot be placed within taxonomy – they move too fast and transform too quickly and, especially when they enter into imperceptible participations, cannot perceive themselves. 'We' as 'they' cannot speak a language that can be heard so we cannot tell, ergo cannot be. Because we are always singular instances we do not have a language of our own, only resonant sonorities with other entities. The medical and social study of aberrations – from congenital monsters to queers – could be resisted through a politics of hybridity, which requires the hybrid to be part of a pack that collects those who do not resemble each other.

Memories of Demonology

Deleuze and Guattari offer the following to exemplify pack as expansion: A Pack of wolfing-werewolf Wolves, a Swarm of cross genus non-mammalian Bees, a field of Anuses, a rhizomatic harvest deterritorialising the organised body. Collective nouns collect entities based not so much on their filiations but the desire to extricate them from forming unnatural participations with those belonging to different kingdoms. Collective nouns do not collect per se, their borders are infinite. Their instances are within rather than beyond. Collective nouns are created because collectives cannot be quarantined; they excavate the myth of purity of kingdoms and kinds. They are always within society, not alienated from it. A politics or ethics of hybridity requires a tentative individual volition toward a verbing not nouning, born of a need to mobilise majoritarian patterns, not be included within these patterns. Hybridity signs the pack pact, the tenets of which include willingness to repudiate the phantasy of purity of self, of sexuality as subjectivity, of biunivocal definition, of belonging to one kingdom. Hybridity is a permanent experiment that makes the self its own phylum, both always alone and also not known as self to self. Hybrids are made up of molecular intensities, many of which are unexpected, but some of which come from the initial desire toward becomings. These could be described as the political aspects of becomings. Entering into a hybridity involves losing the self in order to think through another trajectory in order to advocate political shifts in society without retaining the dialectic of advocate/victim (even if the advocate is the victim, which reifies the self as subject rather than as negotiating a condition of oppression). This is a key issue for Lyotard in his work on the differend, as he demands the turn from the individual and their capacity to speak for the victim or from their perspective on the victim – what Lyotard calls the 'silences'. Guattari elaborates:

> It is not only species that are becoming extinct [itself an Oedipal crisis which laments types rather than lives] but also words, phrases and gestures of human solidarity. A stifling cloak of silence has been thrown over the emancipatory struggle of women . . . this is not simply due to the complexity of the entities under consideration but more fundamentally to the fact that [ecosophies] are governed by a *different logic* to that of ordinary communication between speakers and listeners which has nothing to do with the intelligibility of discursive sets . . . it is a logic of intensities, of auto-referential existential assemblages engaging in irreversible durations . . . while the logic of discursive sets endeavours to completely delimit its object [both victim/other and advocate/desiring subject] the logic of intensities, or eco-logic, is concerned only with the movement and intensity of evolutive processes. (Guattari 2005: 44)

There is a head of the pack, a demon with which we make the pack pact. The demon head is a queer entity, in reference to gender and sexual activity, a monster who makes its partner a monster, a power of alliance inspiring illicit unions or abominable loves. This . . . tends to prevent procreation; since the demon does not himself [sic] have the ability to procreate, he must adopt indirect means (for example the female succubus of a man and then becoming the male incubus of a woman, to whom he transmits the male semen). (Deleuze and Guattari 1987: 246)

Making a pack with the demon lover abominates us. We become sorcerers, who invoke their lovers rather than being part of a structure which limits their selections. 'The sorcerer has a relation of alliance with the demon as the power of the anomalous' (Deleuze and Guattari 1987: 246). The head of the pack/pact can be a specific intensity between more than one or born of a volatility within the head, but the head can only exist through the necessary potentiality of the pack and its shifting numbers, directions, dissipations and other intensities. Guattari would suggest that while dialectic advocacy, desire or infection is a transference – from molar man to molar wolf, from traditional hetero to nomenclatured transgressive – an ecosophical creation of unnatural alliances are transversal – a mobile, teeming existential territory. A pack of wolves are all different and all the same at once. The monsters in Lovecraft cannot apprehend their own being as non-Euclidean physics is beyond traditional possibilities of perception. But they can apprehend the associations they have with their other-universe collectives. They have gods, which are demons with which they sign pacts that recruit them into the collective of those who have no common characteristics or filiations beyond what, politically, would be one intensity, not of shared quality but shared desire to decentre and dissipate aspects of systematics of desire. Like feminists, queers and political activists, these demonic assemblages think, speak and live according to different logics or negotiative practices. They are being, doing and relating differently, an abstract machine. Explicitly this is not metaphoric but thought as material and materiality as thought. Packs think but they never know. They do not know themselves as individuals within a pack or a pack within the world, but their different thinking, or logic, activates change. The head, which could be a moment, an encounter with the head or an infection according to Deleuze and Guattari, elicits fascination (1987: 239–40). Monsters are fascinating, and create fascinating unnatural alliances through the formation of a relation between the fascinated and the monster, collapsing the dialectic into a hybrid – no escape, no line of flight that can be retraced or reversed. Fascination is an irreversible making-queer-assemblage. 'This Real-Abstract is totally different from the fictitious abstraction of the supposedly pure machine of expression . . . Abstract machines thus have proper names (as well as dates), which of course designate not persons or subjects but matters and functions' (Deleuze and Guattari 1987: 142). Can we use fascination as a term to negotiate desire as a longing for an entity without the possibility of desire being satisfied through a dialectic coupling with the entity? As psychoanalytic desire is to satisfaction is queer hybridity fascination to pact packing?

The infective werewolf evokes both shared wolfing and irresolvable differences within the pack. The devil with which we make a pact/packed announces in the bible, and quoted by Deleuze and Guattari in *A Thousand Plateaus*, 'I am legion' (1987: 239). The enunciation continues 'for we are many'. Animal-vegetable-imperceptible becomings require nothing more than other-form otherworldly pack perception. Advocacy demands a territory shifting function without resolution. And the queer infects and recruits to shift planes of desire which (arguably) necessarily change dialectics, forms and subjects anchored by gender, sexuality, desire and the demarcation between desire as sexuality and 'everything else', between the sacred and profane, the sexual and the secular, the act/object and flows.

References

Adams, C. J. (1995), *Neither Man nor Beast: Feminism and the Defense of Animals*, New York: Continuum.
Braidotti, R. (1994), *Nomadic Subjects: Embodiment and Sexual Difference in Contemporary Feminist Theory*, New York: Columbia University Press.
Deleuze, G. and Guattari, F. (1981), *How to Make Yourself and Body Without Organs*, trans. Suzanne Guerlac. In S. Lotringer (ed.), *Semiotext(e): Polysexuality*, Vol. IV, No. 1, New York: Semiotext(e).
Deleuze, G. and Guattari, F. (1987), *A Thousand Plateaus: Capitalism and Schizophrenia 2*, trans. Brian Massumi, London: Athlone.
Deleuze, G. and Guattari, F. (1996), *Anti-Oedipus: Capitalism and Schizophrenia*, trans. Robert Hurley, Mark Seem and Helen R. Lane, Minneapolis: University of Minnesota Press.
Deleuze, G. (1991), *Masochism: Coldness and Cruelty*, New York: Zone Books.
Deleuze, G. (2000), 'Desire and Pleasure', trans. not cited. In S. Lotringer (ed.), *More and Less*, New York: Semiotext(e).
Foucault, M. (2000), 'Bodies and Pleasure', trans. not cited. In S. Lotringer (ed.), *More and Less*, New York: Semiotext(e).
Grosz, E. (1995), *Space, Time and Perversion: The Politics of Bodies*, Sydney: Allen & Union.
Guattari, F. (1996), *Soft Subversions*, trans. David L. Sweet and Chet Wiener, New York: Semiotext(e).
Guattari, F. (2005), *Three Ecologies*, trans. Ian Sander and Paul Sutton, London: Athlone.
Haraway, D. (2003), *The Companion Species Manifesto: Dogs, People and Significant Otherness*, Chicago: Prickly Paradigm.
Lovecraft, H. P. (1999), 'Dreams in the Witch house.' In *At The Mountains of Madness and Other Novels of Terror*, London: HarperCollins.

Lovecraft, H. P. (1999), 'The Shadow Over Innsmouth.' In *At The Mountains of Madness and Other Novels of Terror*, London: HarperCollins.

Lovecraft, H. P. (1999), 'The Statement of Randolph Carter.' In *At The Mountains of Madness and Other Novels of Terror*, London: HarperCollins.

Lyotard, J. F. (1988), *The Differend: Phrases in Dispute*, Manchester: Manchester University Press.

Wittig, M. (1992), *The Straight Mind*, Boston: Beacon Press.

Chapter 9

Schreber and the Penetrated Male

Jonathan Kemp

> Movement always happens behind the thinker's back
> Deleuze, *Dialogues*

Becoming-queer

The critical energy with which queer theory interrogates and refuses stable categories of being and knowledge finds its analogue in the resistance to totalitising notions of 'truth' and 'the human' to be found in all Deleuze's work. In this paper I aim to explore how Deleuze's critical energy and concepts can be marshalled into challenging the totalising notions of 'masculinity' and 'the body'. I will present a reading of the Schreber case as a DeleuzoGuattarian becoming-minoritarian/woman/queer which shatters the neat and stable confines of the concept 'man' – no longer a universal, unmarked and neutral monolith but a flux of radical jouissance, a surface shot through with holes into which and out of which sensations flow, deterritorialising masculine subjectivity and locating the penetrated/penetrable (male) body as a condition of territorialised male subjectivity. I am calling this move or phenomenon 'the behind', for reasons which will become clear as the discussion unfolds.

Following the logic of the neither/nor, this paper focuses on one aspect of embodiment so far ignored or misunderstood within critical theory: that of the penetrated male body. For too long the discussion on masculine embodiment has taken place within the confines of a binary understanding of gender subjectivity predicated on sexual positioning, with the consequence that the penetrated partner – regardless of gender – becomes understood as somehow 'female'. Only a culture characterised by high levels of anxiety concerning the visibility of the penetrated male body such as our own feels the need to rely on this feminine paradigm, because it is a culture that has always already hierarchised the so-called two genders. What still characterises most of our understanding of the male body is what Derrida calls phallocentrism and phallogocentrism (Derrida 1987: 191), by which masculinist discourse insists on a binaric logic that subsumes the second term to the first both in terms of value and of status.

At the heart of this problematic lies the taboo against the sensuous male body, a taboo the breaching of which is traditionally named 'feminine'. The development of the concept of the behind not only explores its links with a chain of equivalences that binds most representations of the penetrated male body to a culturally abjected 'feminine paradigm', however. The behind also – as both discursive 'blind spot' and erotic site of anxiety for many men – articulates a specifically modern 'poetics' – a poetics of instability, uncertainty and fluidity of meaning. This poetics is a way of re-stating a logic of the neither/nor as presented in Deleuze's work, both the single-authored texts and those co-authored with Félix Guattari.

As a vertiginously ongoing process of becoming, philosophy, according to Deleuze, is always already a queer practice, a question of taking past thinkers from behind, sharing, with Jean-François Lyotard, the dream of producing 'a philosophy of sodomites' (Lyotard 1993: 258). In *Dialogues* Deleuze describes his process of writing about other philosophers, such as Kant, Nietzsche and Bergson:

> the main way I coped with it at the time was to see the history of philosophy as a sort of buggery or (it comes to the same thing) immaculate conception. I saw myself as taking an author *from behind* and giving him a child that would be his own off-spring, yet monstrous. (Deleuze 1995: 6, emphasis added)

Leaving aside the notion that buggery and immaculate conception might amount to the same thing, if we assume that Deleuze isn't just being provocative here, and take seriously the claim that the history of philosophy can be viewed 'as a sort of buggery', then a profoundly erotic mode of engagement emerges at the heart of western thinking.[1] In ways that are unimaginable to the philosophical tradition that separates and hierarchises the mind from the body, conceptual thinking from corporeal being, such a move folds the body into the mind such that the verb 'to penetrate' is made to vibrate with the full valency of that move: to know becomes profoundly corporeal. Given that buggery isn't a one-way street, what are the consequences not only of taking an author from behind, but also of being taken from behind by an author? What kind of monstrous offspring would be born from that coupling?

I Must have a Body, it's a Moral Necessity, a 'Requirement'

I am trying to articulate a new way of thinking about bodies – specifically male bodies – that doesn't rely on the usual binary oppositions of gender as represented by the phallic economy. I want to suggest and explore alternative ways of thinking through and about the male body as a site of penetrability, not just physical but also, and importantly, psychical or existential.

Further, I want to suggest that all representation is the embodiment of erotic thought. By this I mean that what exists in terms of representation, far from being neutral or disinterested, or self-evident, or objective, is, rather, and importantly, an encoded response to being a body, having sensations, desires, which significantly contour our representations of the world in which those sensations, desires and bodies take place – even when, or especially when, those desires and sensations are being ignored, feared or denied. I want to suggest at the same time that there are protocols of representation that govern and direct what gets represented and how, and that these protocols, as much as what form representation takes, are expressions of sensation, of being a particular body in a particular culture at a particular time. As such, I am arguing for a radical *continuity* between mind and body, against the traditional separation or discontinuity of those two terms, a separation that has been attributed to Descartes, and is known – for better or for worse – as the Cartesian split. That separation is itself a consequence of representation and not a given, *a priori* 'reality'. Subjectivity is not so neatly packaged, and objectivity does not parade towards us in pairs like animals entering the ark. Further, that separation into binary opposites violently hierarchises the two terms, and in the case of the mind/body opposition, that structuration is gendered such that it is the repression or denial or conceptual feminisation of the body that seeps into and shapes the representations of 'mind', 'culture', 'reason', etc.

I want to challenge the standard approaches to masculine embodiment that explain it as a form of denial or absence: instead, I would like to suggest that the male body – in its always already penetrated state – is a presence, an excess; one that I will name the 'behind' in order to suggest that penetration is a condition of modern masculine subjectivity. I maintain that the submission by which 'masculinity' conforms to the protocols of representation, or, to put it another way, registers within the socio-symbolic order, is effected by a process of penetration that remainders the male body, marking it as 'waste' and associating it with a pejorative femininity. Through the traditional cultural associations that exist between the concept 'body' and the concept 'woman', the name 'feminine' is given to any breach of the taboo against penetrating the male body.

In this sense, the 'behind' as I am using it attempts to name the non-conceptual, and such non-conceptuality is brought to bear on the concept of the male 'body'. In other words, the 'behind' registers both as discursive aporia and corporeal liminality. Modern male subjectivity, as such, is revealed as a highly unstable process. Penetrability becomes a condition of the emergence of modern male subjectivity within the rubric of its own logic. One major consequence of such conditionality is that thought must be seen as in a very real sense 'embodied', and that this process of embodying thought is predicated upon an eroticism that is subsequently denied. The 'behind' names that denial. But it also names the process by which that denial is itself denied, and the openness and penetrability of the male body explored and affirmed. As such, the penetrated male body appears not as the radical other of traditional western masculinity, but rather as what David Savran calls its 'pathologized double' (Savran 1998: 27); as that which lurks *behind* it like a shadow.

Central to this endeavour – and to the reading of Schreber presented here – is the notion of a boundary, both physical and psychological/existential, and, following this, a concern with the openings of the male body. Why are the body's openings so disturbing to the concept of unified subjectivity? And why is their penetration considered so dangerous? Is the closed body a result of the foreclosing of language, or is language modelled on the ideality of a safely closed body enclosing a safely closed subject? Can opening one open the other, like Chinese boxes? Can the movements and flows of an opened body be represented, or does representation itself only function upon a foreclosure of such nomadic flesh?

In this way, the term 'behind' tries to make a clear link between the so-called crisis of masculinity and the so-called crisis of reason. To characterise a certain anxiety that is common to both corporeal and intellectual uncertainty, the full erotic charge of the term *behind* – as a homograph that binds together a physical as well as an epistemological location – must be allowed to fluctuate between those two significations and vibrate with the movement thus described. As Deleuze writes in *The Fold*: 'fluctuation of the norm replaces the permanence of a law' (Deleuze 1993: 19). Indeed, writing the behind is so inherently fraught with the dangers of this *double entendre* that the foundations of masculine discourse themselves are revealed as anything but secure. The male behind and its attendant cultural anxieties are linked here to the 'behind' of discourse, to what lurks behind, and thus, by extension, to analysis itself, that intellectual process of exposing what is hidden, of penetrating the unknown.[2]

Too Little Importance has been Attached to the Use of this Word 'Multiplicity'

In *Anti-Oedipus*, Deleuze and Guattari famously corrupt the concept of 'subjectivity', fragmenting our understanding of what it means to be an individual in order to explore other ways of being a subject, ways not predicated on separation and loss in the post-Freudian manner, but more on a becoming without ontology or *telos*, or rather a becoming *as* ontology *and telos*. To quote Claire Colebrook, with this move 'they challenged the idea that there was anything like a "psyche" at all' (Colebrook 2002: 5). Deleuze and Guattari develop a theory of subjectivity which posits the subject as a residue of the processes of coding and overcoding by which the flows and multiplicities of the social body are mapped and restrained, or, as they say, territorialised. The chaotic unravelling of these restraints – as in cases of psychosis, such as Schreber's – they call decoding. They argue that in advanced societies such as ours decoding and coding are almost indistinguishable processes. That is, the high levels of complexity found in modern life necessitate an understanding of the subject as always already fractured, or what they call 'schizzo'. In short, fragmentation at the level of the ego is the inevitable outcome of modern overcoding. Because of this, their form of 'schizo-analysis' regards the so-called psychotic as having something fundamentally profound to say about the nature of the processes of overcoding by which the body is repressed. Furthermore, they link these processes to the original privatisation of the anus – the first erogenous zone that the infant learns to repudiate, by repressing its possibilities for pleasure. They adopt the Freudian notion of the anus as 'the symbol of everything that is to be repudiated and excluded from life' (Freud 1977: 104n). It is a process, however, which – due in part to the close proximity of the anus to the genitals – remains profoundly contradictory and unstable. For Freud, anal eroticism is never fully repressed.

Deleuze and Guattari argue that the anus was 'the first organ to suffer privatization, removal from the social field' (Deleuze and Guattari 1983: 143); as a consequence 'the entire history of primitive coding, of despotic overcoding, and of the decoding of private man' is founded on 'the model and memory of the disgraced anus' (Deleuze and Guattari 1983: 211). They argue that the process of language acquisition is not only governed by the primacy of the phallus as the master signifier, as Lacan proposes, but also that the acts of separation and rejection characteristic of defecation prefigure the differentiation techniques of signification. In other words, language is not only acquired through the removal of the anus from any social function, but also through the displacement of the processes of shitting onto the systematic use and application of language structures. This process of psycho-corporeal separation and differentiation sets up a strategy mirrored in the process of making sense of words, establishing an inherent link between the scatological and the lexical that can be found in Schreber's *Memoirs*.

Kristeva makes a similar claim in *Revolution in Poetic Language*, when she writes that

> Language acquisition implies the suppression of anality; in other words, it represents the acquisition of a capacity for symbolization through the definitive detachment of the rejected object, through its repression under the sign. (Kristeva 1984: 152)

For Kristeva, poetic language continues to retain and express a certain aspect of anality, a certain jouissance associated with the anal. Similarly, Deleuze and Guattari argue that the privatisation or overcoding by which the public self is consolidated and its desires held in check takes as its model the sublimation of anality. According to this, learning when to shit and when not to shit are coterminous with learning what to say and what not to say. Both are a form of discipline. Bodily regulation of flows and discursive decorum go hand in hand. Entry into the symbolic order would seem to foreclose the possibility of certain, more open (and therefore dangerous) experiences of desire, except perhaps in the realm of the imaginary, a realm whose co-ordinates become structured by the very unspeakability in which desire is held. For this reason, Deleuze and Guattari – like Kristeva – insist that the flow of desire in its least restrained and most chaotic form is inherently revolutionary. Through the experience and articulation of what is in excess of the overcoding's strictures the inherent fallability of those strictures is exposed. This complex relationship between language and the body plays itself out in interesting and informative ways in the text I wish to turn to now, *Memoirs of My Nervous Illness* by Daniel Paul Schreber. Here, the appearance of the penetrated male body disrupts not only the psychic map of the self, but also the plateau of language, displacing, like a root bursting through paving stones, the neat patterns of language and meaning; the anus becomes not only a metaphor for some kind of psychosis but also a metonym for the male body itself: 'the behind' both appears and disappears at the same time; seems furthest when closest to hand.

Life in its Estranged Form

Daniel Paul Schreber (1842–1911) suffered two serious mental break-downs during his adult life, for which he was institutionalised both times. He worked in the German courts and was successful enough to be appointed *Senatpräsident* or presiding judge of the third chamber of the Supreme Court of Appeals at the age of fifty-one, the youngest man ever to be appointed to that position. The first breakdown in 1884 followed his failure to be elected for the National Liberal Party, and his primary symptom was hypochondria. He spent six months in a clinic run by Dr Paul Flechsig, the same doctor to whom he turned eight years later when his second breakdown occurred, which was also the outcome of a certain failure of his civic role. A month after taking up his new prestigious post of *Senatpräsident*, Schreber's anxiety over his ability to perform this task was such that hospitalisation was required again, this time for a period of nine years. This time, however, his main symptoms were delusional and paranoid. His delirium was grounded in the belief that, in the words of the medical expert's report:

> he is called to redeem the world and to bring back to mankind the lost state of Blessedness. He maintains he has been given this task by direct divine inspiration. [. . .] The most essential part of his mission of redemption is that it is necessary for him first of all to be transformed into a woman. (cited Schreber 1988: 272)

Schreber's transformation into a woman was to be achieved by an act of divine penetration, to keep it within what Schreber called the Order of the World. The fact that beyond his own 'mad cosmology' such transformation was *not* within the order of things, but the sign of a radical psychosis, tells us as much about that order – its limits, its laws and strictures – as it does about Schreber's 'madness'.

Upon his release in 1902, Schreber began writing *Memoirs of My Nervous Illness*, based on the notes he had been keeping since 1897. It was published in 1903, and the text was given to Freud sometime in the summer of 1910 by Jung. Freud published his own interpretation of the Schreber case in 1911, the year of Schreber's death.[3] The two men never met.

Several months before the onslaught of his psychosis, Schreber recalls having the following experience:

> One morning while still in bed (whether still half asleep or already awake I cannot remember), I had a feeling which, thinking about it later when fully awake, struck me as highly peculiar. It was the idea that it really must be rather pleasant to be a woman succumbing to intercourse. (Schreber 1988: 63)

This lazy, hazy, half-dream of sexual submission occurs within and establishes a limit: a border zone or fold, between the unconscious state of sleep and the conscious state of wakefulness. While submission is clearly aligned with 'becoming-woman', its contemplation provokes ambiguity, instability, forgetfulness ('whether still half asleep or already awake I cannot remember'). An idea considered 'highly peculiar' when revisited in the cold light of day was, within the relative safety of a dream-like state, thought 'rather pleasant'. This zone or fold, this 'dream', has been isolated by Freud as the cause and origin of the *Senatpräsident*'s mental breakdown, and is interpreted by him as a simple homosexual wish-fulfilment, which he derives from Schreber's delusional belief in his becoming a woman.

Unlike Freud, Deleuze and Guattari want to know what Schreber can teach us, rather than seeing him simply as 'mad'; they see his position outside of 'normality' as lending his story critical weight; heuristics rather than hermeneutics, schizoanalysis rather than interpretation. They refuse to locate Schreber's breakdown within the framework of the triadic Oedipal unit,[4] even in the broader form of Freud's formulation offered by Lacan in the shape of the symbolic order. Deleuze and Guattari prefer to locate Schreber's psychosis within a politico-cultural context which interprets his witnessing as a reaction to, and movement against, the totalising forces of capitalist and psychoanalytic normativity. And they associate his experiences with the privatisation of the body by discourse, its colonisation by language. Furthermore, they place Schreber's anus at the centre of his psychosis, as the primary point of his miraculous body, a zone of intensity as productive as it is destructive: 'Doubtless the former paranoiac machine continues to exist in the form of mocking voices that attempt to "de-miraculate" the organs, the Judge's anus in particular' (Deleuze and Guattari 1983: 11).

They use the anus and its status as the original taboo in order to propose a less structured theory of desire, one which may account for the bodily flows so feared by identity thinking in general. Deterritorialisation of the body threatens subjective coherence, but this tension produces something that can be expressed in language. They write:

> Judge Schreber has sunbeams in his ass. *A solar anus.*[5] And rest assured that it works: Judge Schreber feels something, produces something, and is capable of explaining the process theoretically. (Deleuze and Guattari 1983: 2)

Schreber's behind is certainly the source of both great anxiety and great pleasure throughout the *Memoirs*. He refers to a process of 'picturing . . . female buttocks on my body . . . whenever I bend down'

(Schreber 1988: 181) – as if his body were a *tabula rasa* – anticipating God's penetration, anticipating, even inviting, an 'intimacy with the gods without seeing their faces' (Lyotard 1993: 15). He demonstrates an enthusiastic preoccupation with the scatological (a word which, literally, means the science, the logic, of shit). 'Like everything else in my body', writes Schreber, 'the need to empty myself is also called forth by miracles' (Schreber 1988: 177). Therefore, his struggle to hold onto his shit is a struggle for supremacy against Divine omnipotence, a classic Freudian characteristic of the infant's anal phase (Freud 1977: 205–15). However, this act of rebellion is used against him, and he is made to feel too stupid to shit, making the act itself a defiant one (Schreber 1988: 178). Stupidity leads to God's withdrawal, and God's withdrawal results in pain being inflicted on Schreber. Therefore, he is caught between holding onto his faeces in order to retain his sense of reason, and the urge to empty his bowels because doing so always results in 'a very strong development of soul-voluptuousness' (Schreber 1988: 178) and soul-voluptuousness attracts God, who then re-enters him. In short, like Freud's infant, Schreber enjoys defecating. Already, we can see the confused yet productive tension generated by these two contradictory states and the lack of any form of reconciliation. The fact that the divine miracle rays induce in Schreber the need to defecate 'every day at least several dozen times' (Schreber 1988: 177) indicates a highly charged – indeed, vertiginous – anal eroticism. 'The President's arse will pass into solar incandescence', as Lyotard comments (Lyotard 1993: 59).

All Becoming is a Becoming-Minoritarian

Much has been made of Schreber's *Grundsprache*, or basic language – the language in which God addresses him. For Freud, it is the language of the unconscious, containing residues of the symbolic relations as found in dream analysis (Freud 1974: 201). One thing is clearly certain, and that is that the basic language Schreber talks about is inherently ambivalent about the meaning of words, rendering meaning unstable. Schreber writes that it is 'especially characterised by its great wealth of euphemisms' (Schreber 1988: 13). This 'ground-speak' proves vertiginously ungrounded, or groundless. While it constitutes a system – what Schreber calls the 'writing-down-system' – it remains nevertheless

> extraordinarily difficult to explain to other people even vaguely. That it exists is overwhelmingly proved to me day after day; yet it belongs even for

me to the realm of the unfathomable because the objective it pursues must be recognised by all who know human nature as something in itself unattainable. It is obviously a stop-gap measure and it is difficult to decide whether it arises from a wrong (that is contrary to the Order of the World) intent or from faulty reasoning. (Schreber 1988: 119)

Wrong intent or faulty reasoning – these are the proposed origins of Schreber's basic language. As a consequence, Schreber claims that whatever is said in this basic language, the reverse meaning is intended. For example, Schreber tells us that 'souls which had not yet undergone the process of purification were not, as one would expect, called 'non-tested souls', but the exact reverse, namely 'tested souls' (Schreber 1988: 50). Such a reversal of meaning indicates not only a violent breach between signifier and signified, but also an about-face, which, for Jean-François Rabain, constitutes a sodomising of language, language flipped over onto its belly and taken from behind. Rabain renders *Grundsprache* in the French (*langue fondamentale*) to make explicit its anality, its connection to the fundament (see also Niederland 1984: 43).

Such reversibility places the ambiguous quality of language close to the sexual ambiguity acting itself out on Schreber's body (Rabain 1988: 63, 65). 'The basic language', writes Jean-François Rabain, 'questions the value of the sign, its annulment, and its function of reversibility by allowing the free play of ambivalence and *the transformation into the contrary*' (Rabain 1988: 68, emphasis added). Schreber's transformation into a woman is coterminous, then, with a breakdown in meaning, his equivocal flesh mirroring his equivocal language, and vice versa. As Lecercle points out, for Schreber,

> language is directly connected with the body; nerve speech, as its name indicates, is language embodied [. . .] as it is also the cause of voluptuous sensations, there is a concordance between grammar and physical pleasure [. . .] the persecution of which he is a victim takes the form of a dereliction of grammar. (Lecercle 1985: 126)

Not only did Schreber believe that the 'basic-language' used by the rays came from outside, but the 'writing-down-system' by which Schreber's experiences are recorded is equally a phenomenon of exteriority: 'I cannot say with certainty who does the writing down', he confesses (Schreber 1988: 119). The sovereignty of the unified, identifiable subject is replaced here by a multiple personality. These multiple personas which inhabit Schreber – and which include 'an Alsatian girl who had defended her honour against a victorious French officer', and a 'Hyperborian woman' (Schreber 1988: 93) – all aid in the writing-down-system. As such, they undermine the position of author(ity): there is no 'I' from which the text springs, only a collaborative plague of voices. As Derrida writes, 'we must be several in order to write' (Derrida 1987: 226); and as Lecercle notes, such 'proliferation is always a threat to order' (Lecercle 1985: 95).

This proliferation reaches a point for Schreber at which 'the writing-down-material has increased to such an extent that it now includes almost all the words used in the human language' (Schreber 1988: 222). Stretched across the supposedly stable language structure of reason, Schreber places, like a veil, a parallel language, the meaning of which is, word for word, the exact opposite of its corresponding homonym. All language, for Schreber, is homonymic, each word harbouring its chaotic twin, its opposite meaning, within its seemingly self-evident appearance.

Schreber's becoming-woman/becoming-queer is exemplary of the ways in which the penetrated male body registers within discourse. It is a becoming-minoritarian not simply in the physical sense of the body and its sensations (which register and are read within a feminine paradigm), but also in the linguistic sense: loss of communication, a reversal of language's meaning, attend its appearance. The process results in the production of a kind of assemblage that unsettles stable meanings and readings as it unsettles the question of the body. 'Our sexual body is initially a Harlequin's cloak' (Deleuze 1990: 197).

In his study of Foucault, Deleuze usefully identifies the process of 'visual assemblage' by which 'Panopticism' operates, highlighting not only the role played by surveillance and discipline in the registering of the body, but also the fragmented and multiple nature of the body that results from this registration: its status as an assemblage (Deleuze 1986: 32). For Deleuze, the assemblage is 'the minimum real unit' (Deleuze and Parnet 1987: 51). Because it suggests something other than a totalised unity it functions to render all meaning inherently and immediately multiple. Through what Deleuze terms a 'sympathy' or symbiosis, the assemblage allows for 'the penetration of bodies' (Deleuze and Parnet 1987: 52) within fields of force that generate representation. Within an assemblage 'bodies interpenetrate, mix together, transmit affects to one another' (Deleuze and Parnet 1987: 70). This fundamental gap, then, which Foucault and Deleuze have identified as the thing which makes possible the multiplicity and fragmentation of bodies and texts, is that through which such (inter)penetration occurs. The gap or hole – what I am calling the behind – is therefore primary in that it contours the field of representation while remaining stubbornly resistant to representation.

Each Intensity is Itself a Difference

The assemblage is a close relation or an alter ego/doppelganger of the rhizome, that other DeleuzoGuattarian concept which also lays claim to a radical and non-reducible multiplicity. In *A Thousand Plateaus*, the second volume of Deleuze and Guattari's two-volume work on *Capitalism and Schizophrenia*, they develop a theory of the rhizome as an analytic process predicated on multiplicities rather than binarisms, series of difference rather than discreet identities in mutual opposition. In its botanical sense a rhizome is an underground tuber that ramifies and diversifies, producing new shoots, extensions into new territory. Deleuze and Guattari oppose it to what they call arboric systems of knowledge – based on the model of a tree – which solidify in visible and immovable forms (Deleuze and Guattari 1992: 5). The rhizome as they propose it is therefore both occluded and motional, a network of connections across which things flow and disperse. In this sense, it is a mapping, an in-between, a becoming, and as such is always minoritarian. The rhizome oscillates between the lines established by the arboric systems, and as such is 'fuzzy' rather than aggregated (Deleuze and Guattari 1992: 505–6). Like the Body without Organs it disrupts the idea of a unified totality by gesturing to an 'elsewhere' that is both incapable of being represented and constitutive of representation.

The kind of subjectivity suggested by the rhizome, then, is not singular but multiple, inhabited by a radically constitutive and productive otherness. Furthermore, this rhizomatic subject is in a state of multiplicity contingent upon a shifting body, suggesting a constant rearrangement of the self which exceeds the ideality of a stable and unified 'identity'. Having no centre, no structure, no unity, the rhizome exists in an intense (and intensely productive) state of disarray, or becoming, which makes generalisation through any act of representation impossible. The rhizome is therefore in a very real sense non-representable, and thinkable only through a concept of multiplicity that shatters the unity of the subject and the fixed meanings of logic. Rhizomorphosis is a radical state of fragmentation such as cannot be accounted for within existing protocols of representation, such as language, but which nevertheless exists as a kind of chaos or chaosmosis suppurating underneath any representation.

This means that if language is to be used to represent the material body, then it must confront those aspects of the body deemed 'unfit' for discursive representation, such as sexuality or scatology. More, it must present the material body as something not reducible to enforced social categorisations based on anything so crass as mere anatomical sexual difference. As such, 'the rhizome . . . is a liberation of sexuality not only from reproduction but also from genitality' (Deleuze and Guattari 1992: 18). For what would be the 'opposite' sex for a man who experienced himself as somehow embodying both male and female?

Becoming-woman/queer/minoritarian is precisely the process of unmanning as described by Schreber, which

> consisted in the (external) male genitals (penis and scrotum) being retracted into the body and the internal sexual organs being at the same time transformed into the corresponding female sexual organs. (Schreber 1988: 73)

It is a process he claims to have experienced himself. He writes: 'several times (particularly in bed) there were marked indications of an actual retraction of the male organ' (Schreber 1988: 132). As the signifier of his social status recedes, his penetrability increases. It is also a process Schreber was clearly unhappy not only with experiencing but with recounting. 'In order not to lose through such a confession the respect of other people whose opinion I value', writes Schreber, he must endeavour to *justify* the importance of talking about such things. He must *make sense* of his exposure to and experience of penetration. To this end he explains:

> Few people have been brought up according to such strict moral principles as I, and have throughout life practised such moderation especially in matters of sex, as I venture to claim for myself. Mere low sensuousness can therefore not be considered a motive in my case; were satisfaction of my manly pride still possible, I would naturally much prefer it; nor would I ever betray any sexual lust in contact with other people. But as soon as I am alone with God, if I may so express myself, I must continually or at least at certain times, strive to give divine rays the impression of a woman in the height of sexual delight, to achieve this I have to employ all possible means, and have to strain all my intellectual powers and foremost my imagination. (Schreber 1988: 208)

It thus becomes Schreber's moral duty to 'imagine myself as man and woman in one person having intercourse with myself, or somehow have to achieve with myself a certain sexual excitement etc. – which perhaps under other circumstances might be considered immoral' (Schreber 1988: 208). To conform to God's wishes, he strives to make 'absolute passivity [his] duty' (Schreber 1988: 145). There is thus not simply a reversal of gender in Schreber's new world, but a reversal of morality – indeed, gender and morality become almost interchangeable terms, such that gender itself becomes a form of morality: there are 'good' genders and 'bad' genders. With this reversal, what Schreber knows to be unacceptable or immoral behaviour according to his strict moral upbringing, that is, 'mere low sensuousness', becomes not simply acceptable but obligatory. What had hitherto been the sign of 'moral decay ("voluptuous excesses")' (Schreber 1988: 72) becomes instead the sign of moral duty. As Eric Santner argues, 'Schreber discovers that power not only prohibits, moderates, says "no", but may also work to intensify and amplify the body and its sensations' (Santner 1996: 32). But in order to do so, Schreber must become-(a)woman.

Within the late nineteenth-century discourse on sexuality and gender, Schreber's experience of his body as 'female' could only be subsumed by and occasion madness, because within its mutually exclusive terms *having* a (male) body was always contingent on *losing* one's mind. Excessive sensual pleasure in either men or women is often considered socially unacceptable but in women it is less often deemed 'abnormal' because 'woman' is always already 'man's' Other, always already 'body', 'unconscious', 'nature', 'sexuality'. In men, however, excessive physical pleasure tends to carry with it the danger of placing the body above the mind, and such sexualisation, being, at heart, a 'feminization', inevitably cancels out reason – the one thing that supposedly gives men their superiority over nature/woman/body.

A rhizomatic body thus surpasses and eludes any simple taxonomic move that would confine it to one of two gender groups based on genitalia. By its very nature, its recognition can only serve to disrupt such taxonomic logic. Endlessly productive, 'a rhizome may be broken, shattered at a given spot, but it will start up again on one of its old lines, or on *new lines*' (Deleuze and Guattari 1992: 9, emphasis added). And these new lines, these experimental, code-breaking nomadic metamorphoses of words, are capable of folding bodies within the very discourse out of which they have been excised. In short: language brings us closer to the material body when it stops making sense, or when it constantly undermines the sense that is being made. Or, rather, the sense that is made is more rooted in sensation, in sense as an experience, a feeling, a limit, rather than – as it is commonly interpreted – as 'meaning'. Put yet another way, language brings us closer to the material body when it makes us feel rather than think, when it is a becoming rather than a being. As Deleuze and Guattari state: 'becomings are minoritarian; all becoming is becoming-minoritarian'. Thus, lurking 'behind President Schreber's paranoid secret all along' was 'a becoming-feminine, a becoming-woman' because 'only a minority is capable of serving as the active medium of becoming' (Deleuze and Guattari 1992: 289, 291). Given the body's minor (and thus minatory) status within discourse, one could add to the list of becomings *becoming-body*; and *becoming-body* is always becoming-body-without-organs, always a becoming-*dis*organised, depraved.

Desire Can Only be Understood as a Category of 'Production'

Schreber's acceptance of his role as 'God's whore', though, is by no means immediate. His initial response is one of resistance; he battles against this unmanning by which he is to be robbed not only of his masculinity but of his reason: 'my whole sense of manliness and manly honour, my entire moral being, rose up against it', he writes (Schreber 1988: 76). For Schreber, to become unmanned – to become a woman – is coterminous with losing one's Reason (Schreber 1988: 78–9, 99). Schreber's unmanning is intimately connected to – and signified by – an extreme bodily jouissance, or what Schreber himself calls 'voluptuousness', a feeling of intense pleasure he tells us is usually only attainable after death, when a 'state of blessedness' is bestowed upon the disembodied soul (Schreber 1988: 50–2). Voluptuousness, in turn, is connected to the nerve language through which God's rays speak to Schreber by penetrating him and causing his body to be experienced as the site of sensuality. Important here is the sexual difference Schreber ascribes to these nerves of voluptuousness, for, Schreber argues, while they occupy the *whole* of a woman's body, in a man's body they remain solely in the genitals. He writes:

> my whole body is filled with nerves of voluptuousness from the top of my head to the soles of my feet, such as is the case only in the adult female body, whereas in the case of a man, as far as I know, nerves of voluptuous-ness are only found in and immediately around the sexual organs. (Schreber 1988: 204)

At the heart of Schreber's psychosis, then, is a certain pleasure or jouissance he considers to be specific to female flesh, a becoming-woman which is also, always, a becoming-minoritarian, a becoming-queer.

Deleuze and Guattari use Schreber's *Memoirs* to demonstrate the productivity of the desiring-machine and the impossible multiplicity of the body without organs – a patchwork of fragments, a multiplicity that is residual within discourse and characteristic of everything that discourse articulates: in short, an assemblage, or a becoming. If desire can 'only be understood as a category of "production"' (Deleuze 2004: 232), then what it produces is a surface, a body without organs. In the *Memoirs*, Schreber receives instructions from God's rays such as 'do not think about certain parts of your body' (Schreber 1988: 141). Schreber is the *Ur*-body without organs. Consider this extract from the medical officer's report:

> He maintains that in the earlier years of his illness he suffered destruction of individual organs of his body, of a kind which would have brought death to every other human being, that he lived for a long time without stomach, without intestines, bladder, almost without lungs, with smashed ribs, torn gullet, that he had at times eaten part of his own larynx with his food, etc. (Schreber 1988: 272)

Thus the BwO constitutes a different organisation of the body, a *disor-ganisation*, consisting of several strata, and 'behind each stratum, encased in it, there is always another stratum' (Deleuze and Guattari 1992: 159) – the BwO is a multiplicity. It thus constitutes a challenge to the conformity to which bodies are exposed, the command that 'You will be organized, you will be an organism, you will articulate your body – otherwise you're just depraved' (Deleuze and Guattari 1992: 159). It is an erotic depravity that dissolves organisation of the body's intensities, that loses control of its mastery over sensations. It is also a resistance to individuation. It is not a question of having a Body without Organs, but of existing upon it – 'it' being nothing more, though nothing less, than 'connection of desires, conjunction of flows, continuum of intensities'. There isn't one BwO, but infinite numbers, according to how one experiments, but at the same time all BwO are the same experience of disorganisation. It is an impossible multiplicity – impossible not because it cannot exist, but because it cannot be thought: 'the body without organs is closed on a full depth without limits and without exteriority' (Deleuze 1990: 198).

It is a concept that re-imagines the lineaments of desire, a concept that disorganises the body, a concept of such primary nomadism that it refuses to be grasped definitively. A concept that slips the noose of definition not by remaining hopelessly abstract but by insisting on such radical concreteness that it remains not only impossible to represent but impossible to think. It is a concept of difference that extends into an infinity that is not merely virtual but all too breathtakingly real: the infinity of being, the event of consciousness itself.

Becoming-Deleuze

In the concluding pages of her book on Deleuze, Claire Colebrook comments that 'the consequences for Deleuze and literary studies have yet to be spelled out with the degree of intensity that characterizes film, political and feminist theory', and she ends by stressing that 'above all . . . the challenge of "Deleuzism" is not to repeat what Deleuze *said* but to look at literature as productive of new ways of saying and seeing'. In other words, it's not a question of taking a Deleuzian theory or model and applying it to a given text, but of using literature to disrupt commonplaces of literary theory, or just of theory: to follow Deleuze's example rather than his method; to find in literature a way of saying something else, a way of imagining, or creating new concepts, concepts which will serve the purpose of challenging accepted ways of thinking. One might say, it is a question of becoming-Deleuze, which is always already a question of becoming-queer. Through this reading of Schreber's *Memoirs* and the development of the concept of the behind I have attempted such a becoming, in the interest of formulating a new way of considering the (penetrated) male body and the discursive regimens through which it appears.

References

Colebrook, C. (2002), *Gilles Deleuze*, London and New York: Routledge.

Deleuze, G. (1983), *Nietzsche and Philosophy*, trans. Hugh Tomlinson, London: Athlone Press.

Deleuze, G. (1986), *Foucault*, trans. Sean Hand, Minneapolis and London: University of Minnesota Press.

Deleuze, G. (1990), *The Logic of Sense*, trans. Mark Lester, London: Continuum.

Deleuze, G. (1991), *Coldness and Cruelty*, trans. Jean McNeil, ed. C. V. Boundas, New York: Zone Books.

Deleuze, G. (1993), *The Fold: Leibniz and the Baroque*, trans. Tom Conley, Minneapolis: University of Minnesota Press.

Deleuze, G. (1995), *Negotiations 1972–1990*, trans. Martin Joughin, New York: Columbia University Press.

Deleuze, G. (2000), *Cinema 2: The Time-Image*, trans. Hugh Tomlinson and Robert Galeta, London: Athlone Press.

Deleuze, G. (2004), *Desert Islands and other texts*, trans. M. Taormina, ed. D. Lapoujade, Los Angeles and New York: Semiotext(e).

Deleuze, G. and Guattari, F. (1983), *Anti-Oedipus: Capitalism and Schizophrenia*, trans. Robert Hurley, Mark Seem and Helen R. Lane, Minneapolis: University of Minnesota Press.

Deleuze, G. and Guattari, F. (1992), *A Thousand Plateaus: Capitalism and Schizophrenia*, trans. Brian Massumi, London: The Athlone Press.

Deleuze, G. and Parnet, C. (1987), *Dialogues*, trans. Hugh Tomlinson and Barbara Habberjam, London: Athlone Press.

Derrida, J. (1987), *The Post Card: From Socrates to Freud and Beyond*, trans. Alan Bass, Chicago: Chicago University Press.

Edelman, L. (1994), *Homographesis: Essays in Gay Literary and Cultural Theory*, London and New York: Routledge.

Foucault, M. (2000), *Essential Works 1954–1984 Volume 2: Aesthetics*, Harmondsworth: Penguin.

Freud, S. (1971), 'Psycho-Analytic Notes on an Autobiographical Account of a Case of Paranoia (Dementia Paranoides)' in *Standard Edition*, trans. James Strachey, Vol. XII, London: Hogarth Press.

Freud, S. (1974), *Introductory Lectures on Psychoanalysis* in *Pelican Freud Library*, trans. James Strachey, ed. J. Strachey and Angela Richards, Harmondsworth: Penguin.

Freud, S. (1977), 'Three Essays on the Theory of Sexuality' in *Pelican Freud Library*, trans. James Strachey, ed. Angela Richards, Vol. 7, Harmondsworth: Penguin.

Halperin, D. M. (1995), *Saint Foucault: Towards a Gay Hagiography*, New York and Oxford: Oxford University Press.

Kristeva, J. (1984), *Revolution in Poetic Language*, trans. Leon S. Roudiez, New York: Columbia University Press.

Lecercle, J.-J. (1985), *Philosophy Through the Looking-glass: Language, nonsense, desire*, La Salle, IL: Open Court.

Lyotard, J.-F. (1993), *Libidinal Economy*, trans. Iain Hamilton Grant, London: Athlone Press.

Niederland, W. G. (1984), *The Schreber Case: Psychoanalytic Profile of a Paranoid Personality*, New Jersey: The Analytic Press.

Rabain, J.-F. (1988), 'Figures of Delusion.' In Allison, de Oliveira, Roberts and Weiss (eds), *Psychosis and Sexual Identity: Towards a Post-Analytic View of the Schreber Case*, Albany: State University of New York Press.

Santner, E. L. (1996), *My Own Private Germany: Daniel Paul Schreber's Secret History of Modernity*, Princeton, NJ: Princeton University Press.

Savran, D. (1998), *Taking It Like a Man: White Masculinity, Masochism and Contemporary American Culture*, Princeton, NJ: Princeton University Press.

Schreber, D. P. (1988), *Memoirs of My Nervous Illness*, trans. MacAlpine and Hunter, Cambridge and London: Harvard University Press.

Notes

1. Interestingly, Derrida makes a similar move in *The Post Card: From Socrates to Freud and Beyond*, trans. Alan Bass, Chicago: Chicago University Press (1987). See pp. 18–44. See also Lee Edelman, *Homographesis: Essays in Gay Literary and Cultural Theory*, London and New York: Routledge, 1994, pp. 185–7.

2. For isn't to turn one's back, as Derrida remarks, both 'a very amorous position' *and* 'the analytic position' (Derrida 1987: 178)?

3. Freud, *Case Histories II: 'Rat Man', Schreber, 'Wolf Man', Female Homosexuality, Pelican Freud Library*, Vol. 9, trans. J. Strachey, ed. A. Richards, Harmondsworth: Penguin, 1984, pp. 138–223.

4. For Schreber's early life, see Morton Schatzman, *Soul Murder: Persecution in the Family* (Harmondsworth: Penguin, 1976) and W. G. Niederland, *Schreber: Father and Son* (1959, *Psychoanalytic Quarterly*, 28 pp. 151–69).

5. See Bataille, 'The Solar Anus' in *Visions of Excess: Selected Writings 1927–1939*, Minneapolis: University of Minnesota Press, 1985, pp. 5–9.

Chapter 10

Butterfly Kiss: The Contagious Kiss of Becoming-Lesbian

Chrysanthi Nigianni

> Art is never an end in itself. It is only an instrument for tracing lines of lives, that is to say, all these real becomings that are not simply produced in art, all these active flights that do not consist in fleeing into art . . . but rather sweep it away with them toward the realms of the asignifying, the asubjective . . . (Deleuze and Guattari 2003: 187)

This essay will attempt to conduct a twofold experiment: on the one hand, it will attempt to make the shift from a psychoanalytic thinking about lesbianism as identity corresponding to a certain psycho-social mode of 'being a lesbian', to a schizoanalytic thinking that conceives of it as a becoming-lesbian, a schizophrenic process that constitutes 'a rupture, an eruption, a break-through which smashes the continuity of personality and takes it on a kind of trip through "more reality"'' (Deleuze 2006: 27). The essay will thus argue for a 'schizophrenic' lesbian desire not in its clinical but in its critical meaning: an 'anoedipal, schizoid, included, and inclusive' desire whose excess (rather than lack) violates strict definitions and exceeds linguistic meaning and signifiers; a desire whose 'meaning' can be nothing else than its forces and effects.

Deleuze's use of medical terms in philosophy resonates with his belief that philosophy, art and science, although distinct and autonomous, necessarily enter into relations of mutual resonance and exchange.[1] Thus, Deleuze and Guattari depart from a clinical concept so as to open it up and reveal intensities of becomings that lurk underneath 'normal' bodies and 'healthy' subjectivities, to shed light on migrations that are under way on an affective rather than perceptive or cognitive level; in other words, to trace lines of becomings:

> *I feel* that I am becoming woman, *I feel* that I am becoming God, that I am becoming clairvoyant, that I am becoming pure matter . . . (Deleuze 2006: 22)

Rather than restricting schizophrenia to narrowly defined psychological characteristics and medical symptoms, Deleuze and Guattari conceive of it in broader social, cultural, libidinal and material terms. More precisely, schizophrenia constitutes a dynamic both produced and repressed by capitalism: a revolutionary code-breaking force, a process of constant erasure of stable meanings and beliefs, an intensification which leads to an a-logical explosion of signs that in turn end up losing their (common) sense or meaning. In other words, schizophrenia as a process disrupts the static structures of signification, by initiating a frenzied process of endless re-signification; a process which ends up producing 'a properly schizophrenic non-sense' (Deleuze 2006: 22).

Thus, schizophrenia for Deleuze and Guattari is a form of 'unlimited semiosis', both psychical and social, which the system has to control and constrain for its own survival through the promotion of a counter-dynamic, what they call 'paranoia' (with the schizophrenic as a medical case being produced by the repression caused by paranoia):

> Whereas schizophrenia designates the affirmation of the signifying process itself without stable codes or familiar meaning, in paranoia not only is everything coded and meaningful, but it all means the same thing – whatever the terrifying god or despot says it means. (Deleuze and Guattari 2004: 192–4)

Hence, while schizophrenia is related to a free, immanent, (a-)signifying process of auto-creation that produces new meanings, which overturn established truths, paranoia is a process of submission under one dominant, transcendent signifier; hence, a controlled production of equivalences that supports and enhances the established order of things. Consequently, for Deleuze, any description of schizophrenia in negative terms like those of 'dissociation', 'autism' and 'loss of reality' is convenient and politically useful for those who wish to silence schizophrenics and deprive them of their 'ability' to disrupt the political economy of capitalism; an economy developed upon acts of axiomatisation, capture and appropriation, which in turn engender a reality of static molarities, frozen categories and suffocating identities, all subsuming to a superior signifier (to name but a few, the phallus, the-name-of-the-Father, logos, the capital, discourse, etc.). Hence, what is threatening about the schizophrenic is his/her inherent instability, his/her stubborn resistance against any form of identity, his/her allergic reaction to processes of coding and overcoding, his/her 'incapacity' to conform to any category of 'being', even that of the self. And it is precisely these 'incapacities' that provide the schizophrenic with a revolutionary force, with active lines of flight that escape the 'normality' of a system based on codification and subjectification:

> Unlike the paranoid whose delirium consists of restoring codes and reinventing territories, the schizophrenic never ceases to go one more step in a movement of self-decoding and self-deterritorialisation (this is the schizophrenic break-through, the voyage or trip, the process). The schizophrenic is like the limit of our society but an abhorred, always suppressed, always cast out. (Deleuze 2006: 28)

Thus, by turning the focus on schizophrenia as a positive and revolutionary breakthrough (and not a breakdown), 'not only [as] a human fact but also a possibility for thought' (Deleuze 2004: 185), Deleuze and Guattari develop a counter to the psychoanalytic form of analysis which is non-transferential, non-interpretative but instead inventive (Guattari 1995): schizoanalysis, which aims at a reconceptualisation of both desire and body in non-psychoanalytic terms. More precisely, schizoanalysis argues for a desire which is anoedipal, spontaneous, free from social coding (what they call 'desiring machines' conceived of as 'endless connections, nonexclusive disjunctions, non-specific conjunctions, partial objects and flows' (Deleuze and Guattari 2004: 61)) while it re-posits the body in terms of the concept of the 'Body without Organs'; that is, the body seen primarily as a potentiality, free from the restraints of the organism and the hierarchical organisation of (signified) organs.

Consequently, approaching lesbianism through a schizoanalytic framework means a de-oedipalization of lesbian desire: a desire free from fixed subjectivity and complete-object representations, which is positive and productive (rather than reproductive) by producing 'anarchic multiplicities',[2] myriad partial-object connections, unnatural relations of an 'estranged sameness'[3] that defy dialectic alterity; a desire that is not constituted by lack and negation (for example, the trauma of castration) but by positivity and affirmation. No longer an issue of an either/or identification, an either/or object-choice or orientation, lesbian desire is no longer considered to be springing from an originary loss (the maternal body) or lack (the phallus), but constitutes instead one among other expressions of the desire to become-woman-other that leads to a process of serial differentiations: a differentiation emerging from productive (non-)sameness, from a monstrous auto-affection. In other words, it leads to the multiplication of the potentialities of the female body: a body in which the sexual investments of specific organs and erotogenic zones (that is, signified differences that are produced by a devaluing process of othering) give way to zones of intensity, affective lines that sketch out the

Body without Organs (BwO).[4] A body in absolute nakedness (disinvested from fantasies, social significations and cultural codes), an intensive raw materiality, an organless body inhabited by impersonal and de-facialised organs[5] of an infinite nature that lack nothing: 'a' breast, 'a' mouth, 'a' hand, whose connections eschew interpretations and thus become a-signifying. Connections between 'a' mouth and 'a' breast, 'a' nose and 'a' rose, 'a' finger and 'a' cunt, which produce new intensities and unknown sensations, and enhance a desire that desires only its own expansion and proliferation. Within this new economy, organs acquire new meanings intrinsically tied to the temporality and the singularity of the machinic connection they are part of, so that:

> the fingers become flowers, become silver become torture instruments . . . these bodily relations are not anonymous, quick encounters, but rather a relation to a singularity or particularity, always specific never generalisable. Neither anonymous nor yet entirely personal, they are still an intimacy of encounter, a pleasure/unpleasure always of and for themselves. (Grosz 1995: 182–3)

It is through this molecular revolution, through the eruption of 'new' organs produced by micro-affections, that the virtual body is born: no longer a 'possible' body that is realised in pre-determined choices of 'straightness', 'gayness', 'lesbianism', but the 'unknown' body of a becoming(-lesbian) as the overcoming of closure and permanence in bodily connections and desiring encounters, as the loss of faith in dominant signifiers and the structures of signification. Hence, becoming-lesbian constitutes the woman's becoming-woman process; that is, the experiencing and exploration of the creative and experimental potentialities of a minoritarian nature, which lead to the opening and expansion of the economy of the Woman, the Subject, the Human. As a result, *a* lesbian body emerges – conceived of as a desiring surface of an unlimited semiosis that overturns stable, fixed patterns of connections – which enables an anarchic 'erotics of connection' (Shildrick 2004) and effectuates ontological transformations into the field of sex acts.

However, the concepts of the schizophrenic lesbian desire and body, in order to be conceived, require a new image of thought, or better, a thinking-image that is able to move beyond the semiotic perspective, since the latter blocks schizophrenia's expressivity by restricting thinking to processes of analogy, comparison, resemblance and identity (Grosz 1994). Such a new thinking-image is to be found (though not exclusively) in the Deleuzian concept of the cinematic 'time-image'.[6] According to Deleuze, time-image signals the passage from the image of resemblance and the possible to the image of the simulacrum and the virtual; an image that no longer depicts, reflects, represents but becomes-other-in-time, producing thus a schizophrenic narrative. This new thinking-image will be sought in the cinematic event of 'Butterfly Kiss' (1995) directed by Michael Winterbottom; a film which, in my opinion, manages to incarnate (rather than merely present) in a rather explicit and violent way the links between madness, sexuality, identity, selfhood, desire, and thus constitutes a journey of schizophrenisation as the process of going through more reality; a process, which provokes an earthquake in the ontological grounds of our reality and our sense of 'being'.

Hence, the second experimental move of this paper is related to the field that is generally known as film analysis, and consists of its distancing from established and dominant linguistic/semiological paradigmatic frameworks of reading/analysing films (the Saussurian, Althusserian or Lacanian approach). More specifically, it will attempt the shift from 'cine-psychoanalysis' to 'cine-schizoanalysis',[7] so as to draw a new cartography of lesbian subjectivity, by highlighting the traces a butterfly's kiss leaves behind: a contagious kiss that spreads and takes us over, forcing our thinking to move from the 'paranoia of being' to the 'schizophrenia of becoming-lesbian'.

More specifically, the turn from cine-psychoanalysis to cine-schizoanalysis requires the replacement of an 'interpretation of texts' with the 'mapping of territories'. A shift that in turn requires a parallel shift in language: apart from the traditional analytic discourse, a poetic writing should be included as well, that will be able to 'sketch the diagrams'[8] of the schizophrenic body and desire; or even more radically, it will be able to actually produce the schizophrenic body and desire (rather than simply depict or sketch them, since the schizo cannot be represented, only continually produced). This is mainly due to poetic language's intrinsic capacity to bring form and matter together.

In addition, thinking cinema through schizoanalysis requires the forgetting of the grand theatre of the Oedipal drama, so as to connect with a virtual heterogeneity that cannot fit into the narrative of Oedipus. It thus signals the move from the figure of subjectivity as a molar, oedipal entity, a representation of some wholeness endowed with a subjective articulation, to the figuration of a 'machinic'[9] character as the carrier of a collective enunciation. Or even better, the move towards what I call the 'cinematic persona' as the 'intercessor'[10] between thinking and feeling, perception and the percept, affection and the affect: a shady existence of undecidability, which rather than following and doubling its actual body (the filmic character), complements and expands it through contradictions and deviations produced by the act of dialoguing. A dialogue consisting of asymptomatic monologues that set adrift schizophrenia's unlimited semiosis and thus enable a thought of the multiple to be reached. Hence, the produced schizophrenic dialogical delirium[11] will not consist of clearly distinguished interlocutors (how could it be in any case?). On the contrary, the individual voices will often be confused by a third term – the intervention of an indirect discourse – that will set off the transition from 'a personal expression [of the filmic character] to a demonic possession [of the cinematic persona]' (Massumi 1992: 28, parentheses added); the move from a personal voice to the howling of the pack that articulates a 'properly schizophrenic nonsense' of an unconscious agency. A nonsense which,

> Rather than look(ing) at schizophrenics as people who are paralysed inside their own body and need tutelage, [. . .] seeks to map (and not interpret) how they function in the social domain in which they struggle, and what are the transversal, diagrammatic questions they address to us. (Guattari 1984: 172)

Thus, the collective, heterogeneous voice of the cinematic persona produces new utterances and thus introduces another kind of movement into image; a movement in thought that gives rise to new pre-signified concepts and a-subjective affects and percepts. Concepts that do not require interpretation but are linked to a limit-experience, producing thus a stammering effect in language and the structures of signification.

A schizoanalytic experimentation with films will thus aim at revealing the voices of abstract figurations; an abstraction that denotes the figure's de-facialisation and impersonalisation, so as to achieve the distancing from organising structures of subjectification, enabling thus a polyphony to be heard. Rather than aiming at a supposed purification of ideas and concepts, the abstraction of the figurative aspires to magnify the character's speeds and affects, its intensities, giving voice to the mute delirium of becoming-schizophrenic-minoritarian within one's own language, thus allowing the orgasmic sound of the becoming-lesbian (trapped within the organism) to come out.

'I' for Invisibility

Repeating 'Butterfly Kiss' differently

'U'[12] for Good Victory

Look at us.
It's me.
Here I am![13]

An 'I' that moves constantly and desperately, in an attempt to find its place, to be self-defined, located and positioned, determined by being spatialised, solidified and stabilised: an 'I' that insists on moving to a 'here and now' position (to an 'am'), on lines of becoming-actual, becoming visible.

> Look at us – it's me.
> Here I am.
> Look at us!
> Look at us!
> It's me.
> Here I am!

The call for a gaze that will take her out of her invisibility, that will make her an 'I' by pushing her forward from a 'she' to an 'I' position, by reducing the distance from the self to the Other. The desire for a gaze of the invisible that will reflect back an 'us', a multiplicity, a pack, by inducing and embracing the non-visible, the imperceptible, the imageless: the other-within-herself. A cry for the other, a cry against the other that occupies her place, substitutes her, forgets her, and condemns her to invisibility.

> You don't see enough of me.
> I was trying to kill her – but she still wouldn't look at me.

> Look at us – it's me.
> It's me!

A visible invisibility, a mute delirium, a soundless musicality, a failed declaration of localities, an unsuccessful statement of missing 'I's: a performativity that fell short of the rules, that forgot its lines, that missed the gestures, appearing thus discordant within a harmonious whole. No it's not a failed mimicry, a sad parody, a playful imitation of the 'I', of U-the-other. It's just my incapacity to find the way, to reach 'being', to read maps, to reach ends.

> I always get lost. And I always end up in the wood.
> Déjà vu.
> Over and over again.

An orphan faith, a stray desire, a nomadic movement, a roaming body, a wild howling:

> They've forgotten,
> God has forgotten me.
> God's forgotten me.
> God's forgotten me.

Is it vain? Shall 'I' insist on believing without God, existing without her, living without home, being without U? Can 'I' endure her absence? Keep on searching? Keep on moving? Where are You? 'I' the enemy, 'U' the good victory. Vanity becomes stubbornness, rage, persistence, despair . . . loss becomes fulfilment, absence becomes affirmation: 'I' has to keep moving. Looking for her is a life goal, not finding her the impossibility of my reaching a point of stillness, the condition of my becoming.

> I've looked all these roads.
> Looked for what?
> I don't know someone to love me I suppose.

Lines of a lost highway: molar lines, molecular lines, lines of life and death, abstract lines, cracking lines, composing lines, lines of love . . . they all intermingle. Lines that meet, collide, connect, disconnect changing the map, transforming the landscape, getting me lost. Where am I? 'I': one line among others, one movement among movements, a different speed along speeds. 'I' becomes you, she, it, they. 'I' becomes anything, everything. Falling short of the 'superior race' of humanity, of the majoritarian subject, 'I' becomes the world.

> I am everyone and anyone.

And this is hard, painful, it hurts. You have to become a stranger to the self, stranger to perception and (re)cognition . . . 'I' has become a stranger to my inner feeling, alienated from interiority, an outsider to exteriority: an un-recognisable, imperceptible (non)being. 'I' becomes the world by losing the face, taking off the skin and thus destroying the affective bridges between 'I' and 'not-I'; bridges that bring I and U together in their distance. I am thus becoming-indiscernible, -imperceptible, invisible. I am

> no longer anything more than an abstract line,
> or a piece in a puzzle
> that is itself abstract.
> (Deleuze and Guattari 2003: 280)

No, she can't search for her inside . . . where is my soul? Nor outside . . . where is the world? Neither up . . . where is God? Nor down . . . where are U? Everything becomes her, she becomes *with* everything, she becomes *with* the world. Her journey seems motionless – am I moving at all? Yet it feels shaky, overwhelming, devastating.

> I'm a human bomb today.

The goal is different now: to miss goals, orientations, end points . . . to move around, to draw new maps, to make diagrams, to expand not to develop, to fly not to make steps, to create not to predetermine, to forget not to remember. They say forgetting is wrong, immoral, a sin, a violation: forgetting is the violation of what is forgotten.

I know the song . . . but I cannot remember how it's called.

It's a love song . . . it goes tatatatatatata . . .
it's not really a love song;
it's a song *about* love.

Is forgetting it a violation of love?

'Cause people when nobody loves them,
They end up killing someone . . .
Even if it's only themselves.

I must find it. I need to remember it. But it's there in me . . . I'm sure. Its music echoes inside me, expands my life-lines, detonates my body. What I cannot remember is how to name it, to articulate it, to put it in words. Does it have a name? No, it can't have a name. Every time a name appears, the music vanishes. Naming destroys everything, kills hope, reaffirms vanity, confirms absence. Only love songs have names; songs about love have feelings, affects: a fleeting existence below and above cognition, beyond naming.

'*Don't take away my power to love* . . .'
(Deleuze and Guattari 2003: 187)

I must find it, find her. I must find love,
I must find Judith.

You're not Judith!
. . .
You've got to find somebody to love You.
. . . they end up killing someone
even if it's only themselves.
. . . when nobody loves them . . .
You're not Judith.
Are you Judith?
What's your name then?

Judith will not come.
She is not here.
She doesn't see me.
Where are U?

Look at me!
. . .
You've got to find somebody to love you.

> People, they end up killing someone . . .
> . . . somebody to love you
> Haven't you?
> Now I have to do it again.
> I kill people
> And nothing happens.
> Look at me!
> Now I have to do it again.
> Where everyone could see.
> . . .
> . . . somebody to love You.

Love is a war machine . . . life becomes death becomes life. Production becomes destruction becomes production. Being becomes becoming, becomes imperceptible, becomes non-being . . . a circular game of sameness, a vicious circle of differentiation(s). No assurance for the outcome . . . the war is still on: either incompatible, broken lines, unable to connect, or else creative lines, lines of love: lines of reconstitution, composition; lines of writing, musicality, pictorialism through which 'I' become(s)-animal-demon, U becomes-child, -woman, Us becomes-imperceptible.

'Us' as uncoupling, the escape of conjugality; 'us' as the doubling of sameness, the differentiation of doubles, the non-reflective mirrorings, the production of serial differences, auto-affection's monstrous child.

> Either 'I' or 'U' . . . or . . . or . . .

We're no longer one, two, three . . . numbers fail us. We have always been more: a band, a pack, a peopling that 'mates' through contagion rather than reproduction: the spread of migrations, the explosion of dangerous nomadic desires, the burst of lethal diseases, the unnatural eclectic coming together of multiplicities.

> 'I' the enemy, 'U' the good victory.

How does 'I' love U? How does 'I' come closer to U? 'I' the periphery, the Loner, the Demon. U the centre, the heart of the pack. I must become lines, veins to reach U by keeping the distance, by running the distance, by experiencing it. 'Cause I still have to come back here, be on the sidelines to protect the pact, be at the front to lead the pact: I am the skin of this new landscape. I am the holes. I am the entries and the exits.

Take off the face and kiss you perhaps? That's what keeps us lonely, isolated, individual: the face.

> *The face, what a horror . . .*
> (Deleuze and Guattari 2003: 190)

How do I take off the face? Do I have to forget the face?
They say forgetting is violation . . . is violation the means to forget then?
A process towards oblivion?

> We must forget in order to remain present,
> forget in order not to die,
> forget in order to remain 'faithful'.
> (Augé 2004: xii)

My body is in chains. My body is in pain, my body desires pain, my body
hurts. My body wants to be forgotten. Violating the body is the desire to
forget it; leave the organism behind, put organs into oblivion, so as to let
them be born anew and find a new body to inhabit. A violated body that
wishes to become a body without organs, without face, without memory;
an amnesiac body which dares to ask:

> Why not walk on your head, sing with your sinuses,
> see through your skin, breathe with your belly?
> (Deleuze and Guattari 2003: 149–50)

My body screams:

> They've made me an organism!
> They've wrongfully folded me!
> They've stolen my body!
> (Deleuze and Guattari 2003: 159)

> That's what I really want: someone to kill me.

I'm looking for someone to get me rid of my body, render my organs
orphans, kill me so that I become-other, release me from my self, from my
sex, so that a sexless 'I' encounters the organs for the first time. Look at
them! You are not Me any more; you are not mine and I am not yours.
Who are you? Are you my breast? Are you her eye? Are you her hand? Are
you my mouth? How do we connect now? How can 'I' kiss 'U'? I forgot
how to kiss . . . is it with the lips? Why not with the hands or the eyes?

> . . . no longer to look at or into the eyes but to swim through them . . .
> (Deleuze and Guattari 2003: 187)

A faceless, non-human kiss . . . an animal kiss perhaps? Almost like a
butterfly kiss: another touch, a strange sensation spreading through the
body. 'I' swims through the eyes; 'I' leaves the body and swims through
U to an unknown landscape, an unknown sea . . . 'I' becomes fluid, runs
inside you, becomes with you.

I have to forget the organism so that 'I' becomes; that's the battle. I the enemy, U the Good Victory.

Tell me what you forget, and I'll tell you who you are, who you are not, what you become, what you will never be.

> I will be a victim,
> A sacrificial victim,
> A present to God.

But God does not see me. He does not see me. Neither does he see U.

> God's forgotten me.
> God's forgotten me.
> He doesn't see me.

> I kill people
> And nothing happens.

> Look at us!
> It's me.
> Here I am!

He doesn't listen. He can't hear.

> The face is a veritable megaphone.
> (Deleuze and Guattari 2003: 179)

Without the face I am mute. I am invisible. He doesn't see me. Do I have to be Christianised, facialised again? Do I have to be like Him? Like the White Man face, the face of the Christ?

> Jesus died at the cross for you.
> He died at the cross for me.
> He died so the whole wide world
> could see that only his love is true.

Does he love me though? Does he love U? Why do I feel alone then?

> Look at us!
> . . . *only* his love is true
> only *his* love is true . . .

Is my love to U true? Am I capable of love? I'm evil . . .
. . . because since you do it then it's done.
'I' killed him.

My desire for U killed him. 'I' fell short of the face, short of the standard, short of the norm. 'I' lost the face by taking it off, and then

> It's done. You are finished.
> You can't go back and undone it.
> Nobody will forgive it.

I killed him to save me from the face of Christ, from the Universal Man face . . . or did he kill Me first? 'I' the Evil, U the Good. U told me once:

> I'll do it for you. To save you.

'U' has always been like me: evil.
'Us' has always been beyond God.

> All my selves have reached this stage
> because as far as I am concerned
> I'm not listening to you.
> (Artaud 1995: 75)

I am not listening to you! I am not listening to Him. I can do what I like.

Where is my face? Where is my body?
'I' for Impossibility. U for hope.
Incapable of loving a Face, capable of loving *without* a face.
That's my love.
It's not *his* love anymore.
It's *my* love, *a* love *to* U.[14]

> I have become capable of loving
> by abandoning love and self
> (Deleuze and Guattari 2003: 199)

'I' is the gift to U. 'I' is a victim of forgetfulness, the sacrifice of memory, the killing of the enemy. 'I' has become

> Defenceless
> Helpless
> Sinless

> I deserve to be hurt.

Becoming-organless, faceless, subjectless, living in pieces. That's my present to U: pieces of my self, fragments of my realities, breaks of my ego.

That's my victory: I am crossed by U, traversed by U.
I feel that I am becoming with You,
'I' becoming-U,
The becoming-U of the non-I.
I have always been You after all.
'I' has always been 'U'.

> *I feel* that I am becoming woman,
> *I feel* that I am becoming God,

that I am becoming clairvoyant,
that I am becoming pure matter . . .
(Deleuze 2006: 22)

I feel that I am becoming-lesbian.
That's my victory.

References

Artaud, A. (1995), *Watchfiends & Rack Screams*, ed. and trans. C. Eshleman with Bernard Bador, Boston: Exact Change (E).
Augé, M. (2004), *Oblivion*, Minneapolis: University of Minnesota Press.
Braidotti, R. (2006), 'Affirming the Affirmative: On Nomadic Affectivity', *Rhizomes* 11/12, http://www.rhizomes.net/issue11/braidotti.html [Retrieved 9 January 2007]
Deleuze, G. (1991), 'Coldness and Cruelty', in *Masochism*, New York: Zone Books.
Deleuze, G. (1995), *Negotiations – 1972–1990*, New York: Columbia University Press.
Deleuze, G. (2004), *Difference and Repetition*, London and New York: Continuum.
Deleuze, G. (2006), *Two Regimes of Madness*, New York and Los Angeles: Semiotext(e).
Deleuze, G. and Guattari, F. (2003), *A Thousand Plateaus – Capitalism and Schizophrenia*, London and New York: Continuum.
Deleuze, G. and Guattari, F. (2004), *Anti-Oedipus*, London and New York: Continuum.
Girard, R. (2001), 'Delirium as a system' in *Deleuze and Guattari: critical assessments of leading philosophers*, ed. Gary Genosko, Vol. 2, Guattari, London: Routledge.
Grosz, E. (1994), *Volatile Bodies*, Bloomington and Indianapolis: Indiana University Press.
Grosz, E. (1995), *Space, Time and Perversion*, London and New York: Routledge.
Guattari, F. (1984), *The Molecular Revolution*, London: Penguin Books.
Guattari, F. (1995), *Chaosmosis*, Bloomington and Indianapolis: Indiana University Press.
Irigaray, L. (1996), *I Love to You*, New York and London: Routledge.
Irigaray, L. (2004), *Everyday prayers*, University of Nottingham and Paris: Maisonneuve and Larose.
MacCormack, P. (2007), 'Unnatural Alliances.' In *Deleuze and Queer Theory*, Chrysanthi Nigianni and Merl Storr (eds), Edinburgh: Edinburgh University Press.
Massumi, B. (1992), *A User's Guide to Capitalism and Schizophrenia, Deviations from Deleuze and Guattari*, Cambridge, MA: The MIT Press.
Rodowick, D. N. (1997), *Gilles Deleuze's Time Machine*, Durham and London: Duke University Press.
Shildrick, M. (2004), 'Queering Performativity: Disability after Deleuze', *SCAN: Journal of Media Arts* 1.3 www.scan.net.au/scan/journal

Notes

1. 'The critical (in the literary sense) and the clinical (in the medical sense) may be destined to enter into a new relationship of mutual learning' (Deleuze 1991: 14).

2. 'A pure and dispersed anarchic multiplicity, without unity or totality, whose elements are welded and pasted together by the real distinction or the very absence of a link' (Deleuze and Guattari 2004: 324).

3. 'As they [lesbians] are not two they are always and already one and more than one, an unnatural alliance because two singularities together are not dialectic and yet not the same' (MacCormack, this volume).

4. 'The BwO is what remains when you take everything away. What you take away is precisely the fantasy, the significances, and the subjectifications as a whole. Psychoanalysis does the opposite: it translates everything into phantasies, it converts everything into phantasy, it retains the phantasy' (Deleuze and Guattari 2003: 150).

5. 'Hand, breast, stomach, penis and vagina, thigh, leg and foot, all come to be facialized . . . It is not a question at all of taking a part of the body and making it resemble a face . . . Facialization operates not by resemblance but by an order of reasons . . . in which the role of the face is not as a model or an image, but as an overcoding of all the decoded parts' (Deleuze and Guattari 2003: 170).

6. Time-image could be described as a prolific serialisation of images that aim at their own limit and not at the constitution of a closed narrative; by giving time an ontological priority, time-image produces provisional truths which falsify established truths: 'time as becoming questions every formal model of truth' (Deleuze, cited in Rodowick 1997: 15).

7. It is only through the schizoanalytic lenses of the unlimited semiosis that time-image, as an a-signifying narrativity of singular creation, brings out the fullest of its potentialities. Any other (post-)structuralist analysis drains image from its temporal, transformative movement.

8. 'In writing poems, I sketch diagrams, I find the words which will allow a new stage in my thinking' (Irigaray 2004: 29).

9. 'The machinic for Deleuze is yet another figuration that expresses the non-unitary, radically materialist and dynamic structure of subjectivity. It expresses the subject's capacity for multiple, non-linear and outward-bound inter-connections with a number of external forces and others' (Braidotti 2006).

10. 'Whether real or imaginary, animate or inanimate, you have to form your intercessors. It's a series. If you're not in some series, you're lost. I need my intercessors to express myself, and they'd never express themselves without me: you're always working in a group, even when you seem to be on your own' (Deleuze 1995: 125).

11. 'Delirium can serve as a weapon against analytic formalism' (René Girard, 'Delirium as a system', trans. Paisley N. Livingston and Tobin Siebers).

12. The letter 'U' here is used in its written representation so as to denote three things simultaneously: the meaning of the word 'you', the sound U as the shortening of the name Eunice that is the main character's name (a biblical name that also means 'good victory'), as well as the shape of the womb, given by the iconic representation of the letter 'U'. Hence, it is a play of doubles between the 'I' and the 'You' which forms the same person: Eunice. A war of opposites that leads to the 'good victory', a relation of sameness-in-difference, the coming together of singularities through the mediation of a
She-the-body, she-the-affect, she-the-Other, she-the-lover.

13. All the written parts put in the middle of the page are quotes from the actual film, though playful repetitions and rearrangements of the order of words and phrases are added by me.

14. 'I love to you means I maintain a relation of indirection to you. I do not subjugate you or consume you. I respect you (as irreducible)' (Irigaray 1996: 109).

Notes on Contributors

Claire Colebrook

Claire Colebrook is Professor of Modern Literary Theory at the University of Edinburgh. She is the author of *New Literary Histories* (1997), *Ethics and Representation* (1999), *Gilles Deleuze* (2002), *Understanding Deleuze* (2003), *Irony in the Work of Philosophy* (2003), *Irony: The New Critical Idiom* (2004) and *Gender* (2004).

Verena Andermatt Conley

Verena Andermatt Conley is a visiting Professor of Romance Language and Literature at the University of Harvard. Some of her publications are: *Littérature, Politique et communisme: Lire 'Les Lettres françaises,' 1942–1972* (Lang, 2004), *Ecopolitics: The Environment In Poststructuralist Thought* (Routledge, 1997), *Rethinking Technologies*, edited book (Minnesota, 1993) and *Writing the Feminine: Hélène Cixous* (Nebraska, 1984).

Anna Hickey-Moody

Anna Hickey-Moody is a Postdoctoral Fellow in the Faculty of Education at Monash University, Victoria, Australia. She has co-edited a collection of works on applied Deleuzian ethics titled *Deleuzian Encounters: Studies in Contemporary Social Issues* (Palgrave, 2007). Anna is also co-author of *Masculinity Beyond the Metropolis* (Palgrave, 2006). Her ongoing research interests include gender, youth arts and aesthetics, affect, disability, the work of Gilles Deleuze and Félix Guattari, and corporeality. Anna is planning further research into Deleuzian spatialities, the aesthetics of affect and youth.

Jonathan Kemp

Jonathan Kemp gained his doctorate from the University of Greenwich in 2003. He teaches creative writing and literary theory at Birkbeck College, as well as Visual Culture and Comparative Literature at Goldsmiths, London. He is also a fiction writer and his first novel, *He Whore*, is currently being considered for publication.

Patricia MacCormack

Patricia MacCormack is senior lecturer in Communication and Film at Anglia Polytechnic University, Cambridge. Her PhD was awarded the Mollie Holman doctorate medal for best thesis. She has published on perversion, continental philosophy, feminism and Italian horror film. Her most recent work is on Cinesexuality, masochism, necrophilia and Becoming-Monster in *Alternative Europe*, *Women: A Cultural Review*, *Thirdspace*, *Rhizomes* and *Theory Culture and Society*. She is currently writing on Blanchot, Bataille and Cinecstasy.

Chrysanthi Nigianni

Chrysanthi Nigianni has recently joined the thinking-machine of a neo-materialist feminism. Educated in social sciences – she holds a sociology degree from Panteion University (Athens) and an MSc in Sociology from LSE – she then took the turn to philosophy and feminism with the focus being on queer theory, theories of sexuality and continental philosophy. She is a PhD candidate at the University of East London. She is co-editor of the *New Formations* issue on 'Deleuze and Politics'.

Dorothea Olkowski

Dorothea Olkowski is Professor and Chair of Philosophy, and former Director of Women's Studies at the University of Colorado at Colorado Springs. She has recently completed three books: *The Universal (In the Realm of the Sensible)*, a co-publication of Edinburgh University Press and Columbia University Press (2007); *Feminist Interpretations of Maurice Merleau-Ponty*, co-edited with Gail Weiss (Penn State University Press, 2006); and *The Other – Feminist Reflections in Ethics*, Helen Fielding, Gabrielle Hiltman, Dorothea Olkowski, Anne Reichold, eds (Palgrave, 2007). She is also the author of *Gilles Deleuze and The Ruin of Representation* (University of California Press, 1999), edited

Resistance, Flight, Creation, Feminist Enactments of French Philosophy (Cornell University Press, 2000) and co-edited *Re-Reading Merleau-Ponty, Essays Beyond the Continental-Analytic Divide* (with Lawrence Hass) (Humanity Books, 2000), *Merleau-Ponty, Interiority and Exteriority, Psychic Life and the World* (with James Morley) (SUNY Press, 1999) and *Gilles Deleuze and the Theater of Philosophy* (with Constantin V. Boundas) (Routledge, 1994). She is currently working on a book, *In Search of Lost Selves*, for Columbia and Edinburgh University Presses.

Luciana Parisi

Dr Luciana Parisi is Lecturer in Interactive Media and is best known for her research on nonlinear or endosymbiotic dynamics of evolution in information transmission. She has worked extensively on cybernetic thinking as a way to understand the transformations of contemporary media culture with the Cybernetic Culture Research Unit. She has published various articles in *Tekhnema, Parallax, Ctheory, Social Text, Mute, TCS, Sexualities, Culture Machine* concerning the relation between science (molecular biology, chaos and complexity theories, quantum physics, endosymbiosis, Darwinism and neo-Darwinism), technology (digital technologies and biotechnologies) and the ontogenetic dimensions of evolution in nature and capitalism. Her research has also focused on the impact of biotechnologies on the notions of the body, sex, femininity and desire. In 2004 she published *Abstract Sex: Philosophy, Biotechnology and the Mutations of Desire* (Continuum Press). Her interest in interactive media technologies has also led her to research the relation between image and sound, synaesthesia, affect and sensation, and the generative simulation of perceptive space. Currently she is working on the bionic transformation of the architectural sensorium of the body.

Mary Lou Rasmussen

Mary Lou Rasmussen is a Senior Lecturer in the Faculty of Education at Monash University, Victoria, Australia. In 2004 she published an edited collection entitled *Youth and Sexualities: Pleasure, Subversion and Insubordination* (with Susan Talburt and Eric Rofes). In 2006 a monograph entitled *Becoming Subjects: Sexualities and Secondary Schooling* was published by Routledge. Mary Lou is currently undertaking research related to young people, subjective change and creative spaces.

Margrit Shildrick

Margrit Shildrick is Reader in Gender Studies at Queen's University Belfast, and Adjunct Professor of Critical Disability Studies at York University, Toronto. Her research interests lie in postmodern feminist and cultural theory, bioethics, body theory and critical disability studies. She is the author of *Embodying the Monster* (Sage, 2002), and *Leaky Bodies and Boundaries* (Routledge, 1997), and joint editor of *Ethics of the Body* (MIT Press, 2005) with Roxanne Mykitiuk; and *Feminist Theory and the Body* (Edinburgh University Press, 1999) and *Vital Signs* (Edinburgh University Press, 1998) both with Janet Price. Recent articles include work on Derrida, Foucault, Lacan and Deleuze in relation to disability.

Mikko Tuhkanen

Assistant Professor of English and African Studies at Texas A&M University, Mikko Tuhkanen has published essays in *diacritics*, *American Literature*, *Modern Fiction Studies*, *African American Review*, *GLQ*, and elsewhere.

Index